LAUGHING MATTERS

LAUGHING MATTERS

ON WRITING *M*A*S*H*, *TOOTSIE, OH, GOD!*, AND A FEW OTHER FUNNY THINGS

LARRY GELBART

RANDOM HOUSE

NEW YORK

Linc.

Portions of this work were originally published in the following publications: *Emmy* magazine, *Harper's Bazaar, Live!* magazine, *The New York Times, Punch,* and *TV Guide.* In addition, portions appeared in *City of Angels* (New York: Applause Theatre Books, 1991), *Standup* (New York: Museum of Radio and Television), and on WGABBS (the Writers Guild of America electronic bulletin board) and PAGEBBS (the Professional Authors Group Enterprise electronic bulletin board system).

Grateful acknowledgment is made to Ernest Lehman for permission to reprint an excerpt from *Screening Sickness & Other Tales of Hollywood,* by Ernest Lehman '(New York: Perigee Books, 1982). Copyright © 1982 by Chenault Productions, Inc. Reprinted by permission of Ernest Lehman.

ISBN 0-679-42945-X

Random House website address: www.randomhouse.com

Printed in the United States of America on acid-free paper

24689753

First Edition

Book design by J. K. Lambert

To Pat:

for always being in my corner—
sometimes in all four at the same time

To write comedy is to report on life as viewed through a special lens, one that shows us and reminds us of all that we share in common, and all that we refuse to admit we do.

The ultimate reward of illuminating those truths, dreads, and denials in surprising and entertaining ways is laughter—the outward expression of a nerve well struck.   —L.G.

PREFACE BY ALAN ALDA

As you bite into a Larry Gelbart sandwich of irony, satire, protest, wit, hate, longing, and lust, crammed between two slices of wry compassion, you may *think* that you appreciate his work as much as anyone can.

But I'm sorry to tell you that you'll always be a piker at appreciating Larry—unless you've sat at the table at nine o'clock in the morning, waiting to read his script for the first time, wondering what he's come up with during the night.

And often we *would* be seeing it for the first time and he *would* have come up with it during the night because there were many weeks writing *M*A*S*H* when Larry would let the pot simmer until the last minute, and then in a midnight burst of bravado and inspiration he would write the whole thing, finishing at dawn, handing us copies at nine, and watching pleasantly as we'd slide off our chairs in clinical convulsions.

Our admiration wasn't just for the high-wire of it. Or even the brilliance of it. It was also that someone who could do this, someone who could go into the void and steal a whole finished script and get out before the gods knew it was gone, a script that would probably still be funny fifty years from now—that this person with the nerves of a Jesse James could at the same time be so *affable* was extremely annoying. Who could match it?

Everyone wanted to be the one sitting next to Larry. He wasn't just funny, he made you feel as if *you* were funny.

You also wanted to be next to him because with one deft word he could hilariously devastate someone who wasn't there. You didn't want to be the one who wasn't there.

But mostly you were sure that the talent that oozed from his pores would probably run down his arm and spill all over you.

And everyone would wonder how you got so affably clever when only yesterday you were just pleasantly dull.

But it wasn't just talent. Larry never quit.

If something in the script didn't seem to work, he'd ride over to the stage from his office on a bicycle. He'd listen to the problem, and then he would do this strange thing. He'd stand with his face against the wall and in about thirty seconds a piece of dialogue would come to him. He claimed there was a little old man who actually wrote his stuff and this was how he communicated with him.

After Larry left, we missed him. Especially those of us who wrote for the show. But the fact is, no matter how long you stand facing the wall, the little old man prefers talking to Larry.

CONTENTS

EDITOR'S INTRODUCTION

This book affords a glimpse into the creative life of one of America's premier humorists.

The usual listings of our outstanding funny writers would include, deservedly, such names as Dave Barry, Christopher Buckley, Roy Blount, Jr., Fran Lebowitz, Calvin Trillin, Bailey White, et al. A less usual list, such as that anthologized by Gene Shalit in his wonderfully generous book *Laughing Matters: A Celebration of American Humor,** goes further and brings in the work of cartoonists like Jules Feiffer, Garry Trudeau, Gary Larson, and Charles Schulz, as well as wits like Mel Brooks and Woody Allen.

The latter two, Brooks and Allen, remind us of a "hidden" group whose members too often elude inclusion as humorists, the writers-turned-performers, and vice versa. Thus, one would have to include, among others, Elaine May, Carl Reiner, Fannie Flagg, Garrison Keillor, and, increasingly, Steve Martin.

The name and work of Larry Gelbart remind us of another, frequently neglected category in any attempt at such listings, that of the playwright–screenwriter–TV script writer (many of whom are concealed behind the title "Producer"). Nora Ephron might make

---

*Doubleday & Co., Inc., 1987; Ballantine Books, 1989. That two such durable funny men (Shalit is the longest-running feature performer on the *Today* show—he began as a writer) should have come up independently with the same title for their books, discovered just as this one was going to press, might seem to demonstrate great minds thinking alike. But the real embarrassment is the undersigned, a mind not thinking. I was the publisher of Shalit's book and the editor of this one.

Let us hope that they will be sufficiently separated by the distinction of their authors and the distinction between their subtitles.—Ed.

this list, but many such honor rolls might miss Julius Epstein, A. R. Gurney, Billy Wilder, I.A.L. Diamond, Wendy Wasserstein, and the writers Gelbart deals with in this book.

Of course if one were to classify living American humorists by what they are paid (a sort of income taxonomy), writers who work in media other than print would rise to the top of the list.

To be sure, much of the work produced for TV shows and movies is ephemera, but now and then a classic slips through and Gelbart has been behind too many to consider them coincidence. As the *Los Angeles Times* said on January 1, 1997, "One of the finest comic voices of our time, Gelbart has a sharp, precise wit that can be both lethal and astonishingly lovely." The reasons why he stands so tall are several.

For one thing, he is a writer in love with language. He is drawn irresistibly to the pun, the multiple entendre, the linguistic accident, the aside, the parenthetical remark, the penetrating on-the-mark or off-the-wall observation. He likes words that jostle and bump and overlap each other redundantly. There is no cliché whose tail cannot be twisted.

He obviously adores the great color, texture, and suppleness of English, the sense and especially nonsense that can be made of it. Reviewing the first production of *Mastergate* at Harvard's American Repertory Theatre for *The New York Times* on February 14, 1980, Frank Rich pronounced the show "the most penetrating, and . . . surely the funniest, exegesis of the [Iran-Contra hearings] fiasco to date." The play's "priceless doublespeak," Rich added, "is more reminiscent of *Catch-22* than of *M*A*S*H*." None of the characters is warm and fuzzy but most are fuzziness itself.

Mastergate is almost as much a protest against the abuses of language and perversion of meaning by both witnesses and elected officials as it is a thrust against such hearings as a perversion of the "political process."

A few pages on in this book, Mr. Gelbart reveals that English was not his first language. This puts him, nicely, in the company of other writers—Conrad, Nabokov, William F. Buckley, Jr., and others—who are virtuosi of the language, although the suggestion would embarrass him. But, as with many Chinese Americans, or English-speaking Africans and Indians of the subcontinent whose diction is a marvel of clarity, more precise than that of those of us who were born to it, there is reason to suspect that coming to English a little late is less a handicap than an asset.

Indeed, as the author said to an interviewer: "I became word-conscious very early. I didn't speak English until I was five. Never read books . . . wasn't that good at school. But I listen to good writing almost as if it's a second language. . . ."

He also was dazzled by theater, at a time when a first-run feature movie in Chicago was followed by "a big show of live entertainment." And especially he remembers the comics, can still quote a routine he first heard at seven. "Of course there were the movies themselves," Gelbart recalls, "and all the famous brothers—Marx, Ritz, and the Stooges."

His sensitivity to language and routines and to stories told all around him is linked to an original sense of form. His unusual architecture makes form part of the fun: *Movie Movie* (a movie within a movie), *City of Angels* (a movie within a play), *M*A*S*H* (some episodes were documentary in nature and at least one was improvisational television), *Mastergate* (a TV newscast of a congressional hearing done as theater). He is always, as the current phrase has it, pushing the envelope, and form is one of the reasons why, when an award-giver asks for "the envelope, please," the name inside has so frequently been Gelbart's.

Thus, when working with his publishers, he devised a new form—part memoir, part primer, part sampler. Invited by Random House to allow some of his writings to be collected, he responded by saying he'd rather write a new text. "Given the choice," as Gelbart once put it, "I would always rather be going about the business of writing what I'm writing about than whatever it is I wrote." Asked for an indication of what shape this might take, he said, "A book in three acts, and a couple of intermissions."

Another reason for Gelbart's string of successes is that he collaborates well. He was reluctant to offer here, as his own, comedy material that he had created with others. Still, once convinced that we wanted to see and show what it was he had written, as well as his writing about the writing, he entered enthusiastically into the collecting process.

At one point, when I wrote him and referred in passing to the need for at least some of the material to follow a chronological, autobiographical order, he faxed back, asking wistfully, "Am I writing an autobiography?"

Assured that he wasn't, not in any formal sense, he asked only that I assemble the "scenes," etc., and write headnotes.

If Gelbart is, in the best sense, a collaborationist, it is because he works in collaborative media and because he works well with those he respects. He even collaborates gratefully with the dead as well as the living, as witness his affectionate regard herein for Plautus and for Raymond Chandler. He has ended up with friends everywhere. This is not to say that Gelbart hasn't been tested and found testy. He is on the cutting edge of language and form, but also of opinions, and his verdicts on the uninformed, uniformed men in suits who are happy to help out by the wholesale rewriting of scripts pervade this volume.

Then, too, his commentary on such "players," living as well as dead, as Bob Fosse, John Belushi, David Merrick, Jerome Robbins, and Dustin Hoffman shows that he does not bury or harbor ill will. He just lets it rip.

Critics have pointed to his dark side. Like most great wits, he yearns to be taken seriously and one has a hunch he hums *Pagliacci* while writing. He sometimes refuses to wear the lampshade at a party, and he's perfectly prepared to rain on any parade that deserves it. Listen in on his remarks when invited to present the awards for screenwriting at the Oscar ceremonies in 1986:

At the risk of throwing a pall over the celebratory nature of these proceedings, the time has come to reveal the possible peril to our planet . . . caused by the destruction of so many forests to provide the paper for countless screenplays, the conversion of Sequoias into sequels that are taken home every weekend and read by motion picture executives with such intensity that they are often left with lips that are cracked and bleeding.

The writer is, of course, a vital participant in the filmmaking process, as vital as a virgin at an Aztec sacrifice. The only one of God's creatures that can self-conceive, a young writer begins by trying to prove himself worthy of a place at the grown-ups' conference table, and ends up an oldster pitching ideas to a fetus in a three-piece suit.

The successful screenwriter—one who is the author of more than a clever set of license plates—is a poet-pragmatist, ready to change the script so that the part of Mother Teresa can be played by Goldie, or Dusty—or Whoopi. And if the writer is ready and willing, but considered unable—perhaps a matter of water on the brain, water that the director has no trouble walking across—the writer is either rewritten, or partnered with one or more collaborators, often unknown to each other until their hands meet over the same award.

Here are this year's triumphant survivors of a system that would have made the Marquis de Sade cry "Uncle!"

Gelbart is that paradox, a man skeptical and openly critical of the "system," and yet he flourishes within it, refusing in the end to play for sympathy, capping one achievement with another, a master of many media. Not merely well liked but much respected, a favorite eulogist as well as testimonial maker for the living, he'll always be able to eat lunch in this or any other of his towns (those profiled in his "Location Shots," as well as New York, London, Paris, etc.).

As such, he is always being asked, lately on the Internet, questions of craft, technique, experience, and advice, and he almost always answers. For example, in response to certain inquiries by John W. Lowell of *Music International Theatre* magazine, he said, in part:

1. I write for the theater because I enjoy collaborating with audiences.

2. I write for television because it lets you serve your work while it's hot.

3. I write for the movies because there is no finer form of masochism.

4. I write to find out what it is I really feel strongly about.

5. While I did not create the character of *M*A*S*H*'s Hawkeye Pierce, by writing him, year in and year out in the television series, eventually I was able to make him a surrogate for me.

6. The Roman playwright Plautus has been the greatest influence on my work. I'm in good company. He also influenced Shakespeare, Jonson, Molière, and anyone else who has written comedy for the last two thousand years.

7. I've had the good fortune to have worked with every actor I ever had my heart set on. In some cases, good fortune's not all it's cracked up to be.

8. My family is no distraction to my work. They are more like fuel for the creative engine.

9. To what I said about hoping that if Hitler is still alive, he's out of town with a musical, I'd add: if he's still alive, I hope he's in previews with one in New York.

10. My five favorite words? *Act One* and *The Curtain Falls*.

May the curtain never fall, ten or twelve minutes too early (to get laughs), on our Mr. Gelbart.

—Sam Vaughan

CREDITS

Danny Thomas (Maxwell House Coffee Time)
Duffy's Tavern
Command Performance (Armed Forces Radio Service)
The Eddie Cantor Show
The Jack Paar Show
The Joan Davis Show
The Jack Carson Show
The Bob Hope Show

The Bob Hope Show
The Red Buttons Show
Honestly, Celeste! (The Celeste Holm Show)
Caesar's Hour
The Patrice Munsel Show
The Pat Boone Show
The Art Carney Specials
The Danny Kaye Show (developed and consulted, first season)
The Marty Feldman Comedy Machine (writer/producer)
M*A*S*H (developed for TV, principal writer, sometime director and coproducer, first four seasons)
Roll Out! (writer/coproducer)
Karen (writer/coproducer)
United States (created)
AfterMASH (developed)
1985 Academy of Motion Picture Arts and Sciences Award Show (writer/coproducer)

1986 Academy of Motion Picture Arts and Sciences Award Show (writer)
Mastergate (Showtime, 1992)

MOTION PICTURES

The Notorious Landlady (Columbia, 1962)
The Thrill of It All (Universal, 1963)
The Wrong Box (Columbia, 1966; also associate producer)
Not with My Wife, You Don't! (Warner Bros., 1966)
Oh, God! (Warner Bros., 1977)
Movie Movie (Warner Bros., 1978)
Neighbors (Columbia, 1981)
Tootsie (Columbia, 1982)
Blame It on Rio (Twentieth Century–Fox, 1984; also executive producer)
Barbarians at the Gate (HBO, 1993)
Weapons of Mass Distraction (HBO, 1997)

STAGE

My L.A. (revue)
The Conquering Hero (musical)
A Funny Thing Happened on the Way to the Forum (musical)
Jump! (play)
Sly Fox (play)
Mastergate (play)
City of Angels (musical)
Power Failure (play)
Peter and the Wolf (American Ballet Theatre)

RECORDINGS

Peter and the Wolf (revised narration)
Gulliver (narration adapted from *Gulliver's Travels*)

OTHER

Contributing editor, *Harper's Bazaar*

DIRECTED

Several episodes of *M*A*S*H*

A Funny Thing Happened on the Way to the Forum (Chichester Festival Theatre, England, 1986)

AFFILIATIONS

Writers Guild of America, West

Dramatists Guild

Authors League

Motion Picture Academy of Arts and Sciences (two-term board member)

PEN International

ASCAP

Directors Guild of America

Northwestern University (artist-in-residence, 1984–85)

National Constitution Center

Kennedy Center Honors Committee

AWARDS

Antoinette Perry Award (Tony) for coauthoring *A Funny Thing Happened on the Way to the Forum*
Antoinette Perry Award for Best Book, *City of Angels*
Antoinette Perry Award for Best Musical, *City of Angels*

Academy nomination for *Oh, God!* screenplay
Academy nomination for *Tootsie* screenplay

Emmy Award for *M*A*S*H* (with coproducer Gene Reynolds)
Emmy Award for *Very Important People* (Best Humor Program)
Emmy Award for *Barbarians at the Gate* (Outstanding Made-for-Television Movie)

Oh, God!
Movie Movie
Tootsie
M*A*S*H (three episodes)
Barbarians at the Gate
Various other nominations by the Writers Guild of America for other works
Laurel Award for Television Writing Achievement (1981)

OTHER

Humanitas Award for *M*A*S*H*

Peabody Awards for *M*A*S*H, The Danny Kaye Show*

Christopher Award for *Movie Movie*

Sylvania Award for the Art Carney Specials

Edgar Allan Poe Award for *Oh, God!*

Edgar Allan Poe Award for Best Mystery Play, *City of Angels* (1990)

Los Angeles Film Critics' Award for Best Screenplay, *Tootsie*

New York Film Critics' Award for Best Screenplay, *Tootsie*

National Society of Film Critics Award for Best Screenplay, *Tootsie*

Nomination for British Academy for Best Screenplay, *Tootsie*

Golden Rose, Montreux, Switzerland, TV Festival, for writing/producing *The Marty Feldman Comedy Machine*

Doctor of Letters, Honorary Degree, Union College (1986)

Pacific Broadcasting Pioneers Award for Creativity and Achievement in Radio and Television (1987)

Lee Strasberg Award for Lifetime Achievement in the Arts and Sciences (1990)

Outer Critics Circle Award for Contribution to Comedy, *Mastergate* and *City of Angels* (1990)

Outer Critics Circle Award for Outstanding Broadway Musical, *City of Angels* (1990)

Drama Desk Award, Best Achievement, Book for a Musical, *City of Angels* (1990)

New York Drama Critics Circle, Best New Musical, *City of Angels* (1990)

Spotlight Award, Beverly Hills Theater Guild (1991)

Honorable Mention, San Francisco International Film Festival, *Mastergate* (1993)

Program of the Year, Television Critics Association, *Barbarians at the Gate* (1993)

Best Made for Television Motion Picture, American Television Awards, *Barbarians at the Gate* (1993)

CableAce Award, Best Movie, *Barbarians at the Gate* (1993)

Golden Globe Award, Miniseries or Telefilm, *Barbarians at the Gate* (1993)

London Evening Standard, Best Musical, *City of Angels* (1993)

London Critics' Drama Award, Best New Musical, *City of Angels* (1993)

Olivier Award (England), Best Musical, *City of Angels* (1994)

LAUGHING MATTERS

At the outset, it is appropriate to reproduce what Mr. Gelbart wrote, at the invitation of the editors of *The New York Times Book Review,* in 1993. They—and he—were remarkably prescient. Said the *Times:* "On Wednesday, Bill Clinton will be inaugurated as President of the United States. On Thursday, news outlets will analyze, at length, his inaugural address. On Friday, nobody will remember a word of it—only that it was long. . . .

"*The New York Times* cannot command the services of such a skilled and durable speech writer as Abraham Lincoln; but what it can do, it does." It asked five "wise, distinguished, politically au courant writers" to do "short, pithy, memorable inaugural addresses" for the new president, adding that "if Mr. Clinton's address cannot live in memory, perhaps infamy will do."

Mr. Gelbart was the first writer, and we include his draft here to be . . . well, inclusive. —Ed.

SUMMIT
UPON SUMMIT

Because of the importance of the following passage in his inaugural address, President-elect Clinton has asked that Hillary Rodham Clinton deliver it, should he lose his voice due to an allergic reaction to Chief Justice Rehnquist.

Based on the success of my recent economic conference, a gathering composed of a wide diversity of the rich, which proved conclusively that 330 heads are better than one, and because of my experience at Renaissance Weekend in South Carolina, a yearly gathering designed to solicit the ideas of only the best and the famous, I will, as president, initiate a series of consensus-seeking summits, subjecting the nation's most vital problems to short bursts of concentration in search of long-term solutions.

First, in line with my amply demonstrated opposition to the notion that a woman's place is in the kitchen cabinet, I am establishing the creation of a Feminist Conference, where women of every persuasion may speak to the issue of gender equality. To demonstrate bipartisanship, Senator Alan Simpson has volunteered to participate by making token and frequent male interruptions. (This meeting will be followed by a Summit of Women Who've Been Harassed by Senator Packwood, providing we can find a hall big enough.)

I am equally keenly interested in the children of this country. I wrestled for some time with the idea of appointing a child to my Cabinet, deciding against it only because I couldn't bear to see any one of them abused by the press.

Accordingly, I have arranged for a Children's Conference, which will entertain ideas of empowering our youth, ranging from lowering the voting age to five to penalizing thoughtless adults by limiting their voting rights to only two terms.

Anxious to learn from mistakes of the past, I have invited a number of men who have made many of the most memorable ones to convene for an Ex-Presidents' Retreat. Former Presidents Nixon, Ford, Carter, Reagan, and Bush have graciously agreed to attend and give us all the benefit of whatever is left of their wisdom. I am especially pleased that for this occasion, President Ford is graciously waiving his customary fee for a handshake. Special thanks, too, to President Nixon, who will participate in a second event, a Conference of Distinguished Americans Who Have Had the Honor of Receiving Presidential Pardons. Following discussions on ways to strengthen the Fifth Amendment, as well as presidential privilege, these patriotic lawbreakers will conclude with an All-Pardonees' Softball Game, umpired by a Presidential Pardon Hall of Famer, George Steinbrenner.

These events are only the beginning. Throughout the next four years, I intend to assemble countless conferences, confabs, summits, seminars, parlays, panels, teach-ins, write-ins, call-ins, discussions, dialogues, and debates. The Clinton-Gore administration needs to know all that it can before we can swing into the kind of action that will bring about the changes we promised you.

Which brings me to the subject of 1996. . . .

Which brings us to, approximately, 1942. (See Act One.) —Ed.

RADIO AND
TELEVISION DAYS

HARRY AND FRIEDA

Probably the least surprised by my improbable career as a writer were the authors of my life: my father, Harry, a barber since his half of a childhood in Latvia, and his bride, the former Frieda Sturner, pretty enough to be a deb, if anyone had ever heard of such a thing in the farming village of Dumbrova, Poland. Sharp, perceptive, with a good eye and a sharp tongue, my mother's chief form of defense was humor. She was an immigrant youngster transported to two new and altogether strange roles: as a seamstress in the state of Illinois and as a wife in the state of marriage.

Harry and Frieda and the newborn me lived with my mother's parents, where nary a word of English was spoken, and not much more understood. I spoke only Yiddish until I was four. Though my father was a consummate storyteller, my mother could be funny, too. If some of my work is needlelike, cauterizing as it pierces—that was my mother's influence. Many of my attitudes were her attitudes toward life. Not much—maybe 90 percent.

Wed as teenagers in Chicago, my parents' connubial collaboration had a second result: me and, seven years after my birth, a spectacularly beautiful sequel, my sister, Marcia. Their chief goal became seeing if their two kids couldn't get a better shake in life than they'd been handed. Maybe even fame, celebrity, "becoming somebody." Accordingly, at age seven, I was given weekly tap dance lessons, in the hope that I might become the next Fred Astaire. It took only one year for me to become the ex–next Fred Astaire; twelve precious months of my youth were wasted trying to get my right foot to stop acting as a second left foot. Since I had danced my way to the bottom, a clarinet was placed in my mouth in the hope that I would not turn out to have two left hands as well. Actually, I was very good, studying for the next ten years under a masterly teacher named Duke Rehl, who had taught the instrument to a boy named Goodman years before at Chicago's Hull House. Skilled as I was to become, Benny Goodman was to remain the next-and-only Benny Goodman forever.

In the summer of '42, my father packed his scissors and razors and took his act and his family on the road. California was the destination, a second America for my parents, a better place for their kids to get that better shake they felt they owed us. In Chicago, my father's clientele had consisted of other personal service people, bookies, sports figures, and characters who spent most of their time on the shady side of life. In Los Angeles, these would soon be replaced by actors, agents, and a goodly number of equally pale characters.

And in a barbershop, jokes are the currency.

SCENE 2

BECOMING SOMEBODY

DINGLE   *How could you humiliate me like this? Disgrace me? Insult me? How could you make me feel so rotten?*

JELLICOE   (offended) *I said* I was sorry!

> (This is the first joke of mine ever aired on radio. An exchange between Danny Thomas and the actor Bobby Jellicoe, it was performed sometime in the spring of 1944.)

One of my father's earliest clients from the entertainment world was the comedian Danny Thomas. Having made a reputation for himself in a Chicago nightclub called the 400 Club, Thomas landed a spot on a half-hour national radio show, *Maxwell House Coffee Time,* which starred the legendary comedienne Fanny Brice and was broadcast every Sunday from the CBS studios in Hollywood. With Brice playing her stock bratty little girl character, Baby Snooks, Thomas had a six- or seven-minute segment of his own every week, cast as a Walter Mitty type called Jerry Dingle, the Mailman. Dingle would begin his segment by delivering a letter to the Snooks household, where he would always find himself slighted by someone, usually someone with a better job than he, Dingle, had.

Dingle/Thomas would walk away (actually, he stood perfectly still—the sound effects man walked in place to create the illusion) muttering all of the quick responses he *should* have come up with, the put-downs he *should* have fired off to the character who had offended him, then envisioning himself as that character—anything from a brain surgeon to a test pilot.

My father used to shave Thomas's thick, quick-growing, dark beard before each of his radio appearances in the comedian's CBS dressing room. Before too many Sundays passed, my father began talking about this very clever son he had who had a gift for writing comedy. This claim came from my father's imagination, his ambitions for me and no doubt for himself as well. (My father knew more jokes per square haircut than anyone else in the business.) It was nothing we ever discussed. I didn't encourage it, and I was quite surprised to learn from him that he had done it. At sixteen, I had never aspired to be a writer. My only real "gift" was for showing off, doing imitations, putting together sketches, speeches, monologues at Fairfax High School. That was my total writing experience.

Thomas's response was "Have the kid write something and let's see just how good he is." I picked an obvious premise: I had Danny, as Jerry Dingle, envision himself as a barber and wrote a sequence that conformed to the show's formula. Thomas showed it to the head writer on the show, a man named Mac Benoff. Mac liked it enough to say, "Why don't you sit with me and work with me on a couple more sketches?" More than half a century later, some part of my brain is still reeling in reaction to that invitation.

〜〜〜

What followed was a very loose arrangement. After a day at school, I would join Mac in his home study (I had to be driven there) and "pitch," as we say, several jokes that, I hoped, would make their way onto the air. To my amazement, a number of them did. That fact alone sustained me whenever the CBS ushers would make me leave the backstage area at CBS, thinking I was a fan hanging around trolling for autographs. At the end of two or three weeks, at the end of my mini-contract, Mac gave me my first earnings as a "writer." It was a check for forty dollars. "Buy a sport jacket with it," he said. I wish I'd framed it. That *and* the sport jacket. I would give considerably more to still be able to fit into it.

SCENE 3

DANNY

Danny Thomas was considered the best comic storyteller in the business.

His initial goal was to become a dramatic actor, but he had a simple, compelling motive for switching to comedy: he didn't want his family to starve. After kicking around as a radio performer in the Midwest in the forties, doing everything from character parts to sound effects, Thomas began working as an emcee in nightclubs—basic-training grounds for comedians and the toughest place for anyone to work a crowd alone other than in a bullring. (And think how much ruder and more dangerous a bull would be with a few drinks under his belt.) It was soon clear that Thomas had no use for standard stand-up fare, the string of one-liners, the quickies. None of that "A panhandler came up to me and said he hadn't had a bite in a week, so I bit him" stuff.

Thomas would take that sort of throwaway joke and apply a mosaic of minutiae to it. He would describe with great care and even greater detail how the panhandler became a panhandler. He would infuse the man with blood and cover him in flesh. We would learn how life had cruelly deprived the pitiful creature of family and fortune, how a once-proud merchant prince was reduced to begging in the street. By the time Thomas finished, you were so filled with sympathy, you wanted to find the man and give him a dollar. Once he'd worked his audience into that frame of mind, "so I bit him" became much more than just a punch line. The cruel payoff would blow away all the cheap sentimentality Thomas had so artfully constructed and stirred in you. You would laugh not only at the story. For having been suckered into believing such a maudlin tale, you would be laughing at yourself. Now, *that's* identification.

Like all gifted comedians, Thomas was expert at editing his material, knowing instinctively what it took to make a particular joke or routine unmistakably his own. I saw at close hand the way he exercised his craft by building one particular, simple joke into a piece of classic storytelling.

My father, that inveterate joke teller (not too hard to get laughs when you're wielding a straight razor), told Thomas about a man who takes his parrot, one that happens to be a brilliant linguist, to synagogue with him on Rosh Hashanah and wagers with members of the congregation that the bird can conduct the High Holiday service better than the temple's cantor. When the big moment comes, the parrot remains silent. Later, about to be punished by his outraged owner for the costly silence, the only thing that saves the bird's life is when he opens his beak and snaps: "Schmuck. Think of the odds we'll get on Yom Kippur!" A simple enough joke, not all that taxing. Listening time, probably less than a minute.

For some time, Thomas had been looking for a replacement for his famous jack story, the tale of the hapless motorist who gets a flat on a lonely country road and sets out to find a car jack.* Although the routine was a favorite with his audiences, after a couple of decades Thomas had grown awfully weary of it. He wanted something fresh.

---

*Trudging through the dark, rainy night, he works himself to an emotional frazzle imagining what some garage is going to charge him for the sale of a jack, how outrageously he is going to be exploited. When miles later, soaked, freezing, and at the height of his paranoia, he arrives at a gas station, he tells an innocent, incredulous mechanic exactly where he can stick his jack. (Being a comic and a gentleman of the old school, Thomas never completely finished the phrase.)

While the parrot story was hardly new (a new joke, no matter how ancient it may be, is one you've never heard before), Thomas immediately saw its potential. He began using it in his act, gradually inventing new particulars, improvising dialogue, embroidering the situation endlessly, lovingly. To make a long story short, he made a short story long. He took a mundane barbershop gag and turned it into a ten-minute mini-movie.

Thomas's pre-TV work in the forties and fifties says as much about the audiences of those days as it does about Thomas himself. While he had the skill to tell them extended stories at a leisurely pace, they had the patience to listen. That was a time when babies played with rattles instead of remote control channel changers. Audiences had yet to be exposed to uncountable half hours of sitcoms or to the population explosion among stand-up comics. They had yet to grow callous, hearing sick material about assassinated heroes or monologues about serial killers or jokes about minority groups (the latter told in locker rooms, yes; on the air, never) or watching comedians do impersonations of blind men such as Ray Charles or Stevie Wonder. They had yet to experience *Laugh-In*, the MTV of comedy, which taught a nation to get a joke in nanoseconds.

Thomas, in the tradition of Jack Benny and George Burns, could and did take all the time he needed, knowing the audience would not grow restless, that they were just where they wanted to be, watching just whom they wanted to watch; that they would, in a sense, work with him. And like most of his peers, Thomas worked clean. He knew all the other words. Who doesn't? Each generation discovers smut for itself. Modern audiences are the first, however, to have so much of it hurled at them from every direction: from the stage, the screen, on their TV sets, in rock and rap lyrics that double as sex manuals. Thomas was not a prude; he just got his laughs the hard way. He sought to involve his audiences in the lives of those who populated his stories. He complained for them, he ranted and raved for them. He was an ombudsman in search of belly laughs. To enhance the timeless, tribal tradition of the storyteller, Thomas often echoed the rage of the Old Testament.

Of all of Thomas's tales, the one that surprised and impressed me most was how he determined what became the story of my own life. He sent it in a direction as improbable as it remains unreal to me. Giving me my first professional writing job, thanks to my combination Mama Rose and Sweeney Todd of a father, he generously handed a career and a sense of purpose and direction in life to the son of his barber.

As we said at home, not only a great storyteller, Danny Thomas was also a fabulous tipper.

SCENE 4

DUFFY'S TAVERN

(sound: phone rings)

ARCHIE   (answering phone) *Hello, Duffy's Tavern, where the elite meet to eat, Archie, the manager, speakin', Duffy ain't here right now . . . Oh, hello, Duffy . . . Business? It's S.R.O. . . . . Right. Schultz, Reagan, and O'Brien.*

The house now belongs to mouse mogul Michael Eisner, but what doesn't these days? In 1945, when I went there for the first time to report for work, the owner of the gracious Bel-Air spread was Ed Gardner, star of a popular NBC radio show of the period, *Duffy's Tavern.* Gardner, a former New York ad man, created *Duffy's* in collaboration with comedy writer and budding legend Abe Burrows. (Burrows's son, Jimmy, is now the undisputed king of TV comedy directors—see *Taxi,* see *Cheers,* see *Frasier.* Must have been something funny in the water in that house.) Unable to find a suitable actor to play Archie, the tavern's malappropriate manager (Duffy, the owner, never made an appearance), Gardner took on the role and the show became a broadcasting classic.

Owner of the program, able to hire and fire, Ed Gardner did a good deal of both. He was most mercurial, to say the least, in his selection of writers. When under the influence, which is where he spent eighty to ninety proof of his time, he went from mercurial to maniacal, creating a virtual revolving door through which writers went after he paid each as near to a pittance as he could manage. When his brother wrote asking him to contribute a couple hundred bucks toward the purchase of a headstone for their father's grave, Gardner, constantly on the prowl for material for his weekly show, agreed, but for that kind of money, he told his brother, he expected him to write a few jokes for the program as well. I don't know what made Gardner unhappier—the fact that his father had been plowed under or the poor jokes that his brother sent.

The man responsible for my getting on Gardner's writing staff was George Gruskin, Danny Thomas's agent at the William Morris Agency. While agents are always fair game for ribbing (e.g., agent's secretary bidding her boss good-bye, as he leaves the office on Tuesday night: "Have a nice weekend"), George Gruskin was a caring and creative man. His trademark cigarette a-dangle in his lips, he took me into a backstage corner at CBS one Sunday to say that, despite my youth, he would like to represent me for future work as a radio writer. My instantaneous "Yes" ended the meeting, cutting off the secondary smoke he was sending my way and the secondary acne I was sending his.

A few months after I signed with Morris (actually, my father signed the contract; I was still a minor), Gruskin sold Ed Gardner on the idea of hiring me and my real education in comedy writing began.

~~~

There were many funny radio shows in those days, but two of the greatest quality were *Duffy's Tavern* and *The Fred Allen Show*. They had a different approach, a higher script standard than most of the others. To be connected with either show was as much a compliment as it was a challenge. Hiring a seventeen-year-old high school student must have appealed to Gardner's whimsy. At fifty dollars a week (one half of my dream of making a hundred dollars), I was an inexpensive enough novelty, a writing toy, he must have felt, one that put very little strain on the show's writing budget. To his surprise, I was able to pull my weight. I caught on quickly to the way the show was done, what was required. I loved playing with words, and that show was mostly wordplay. As with all the best comedians, Gardner was a wonderful editor. To observe his choice was to learn how to make your own. *Duffy's* served, in a sense, as my higher education, because I never went on to college. I felt that though I was losing something by not attending school, I was gaining tremendous practical experience.

My first day of work on *Duffy's* coincided with Abe Burrows's last. I was obviously not there to replace him. Because I was young and not making much, I didn't represent a threat to anybody. Or maybe it was just the gentler nature of the times, but people were genuinely helpful, and I wasn't competition for anyone.

Abe's replacement as head writer was a young man named Bill Manhoff. Bill went on to write *The Owl and the Pussycat* and a great deal of early television. He replaced Gardner as my day-to-day mentor.

Bill would explain what a certain kind of joke was called. His vocabulary may have applied exclusively to *Duffy's Tavern,* I don't know. He'd say, for example, "We need a bull here." A "bull" was a joke whereby someone talks about himself in what he thinks is a positive manner, when in fact he's insulting himself, e.g., "I don't need any help being stupid." There were many more categories of joke lines. Bill would say that we should look for a certain kind of line here, another there. The lexicon has changed. We used to call the comedy end of a scene "the payoff." Now it's called "the blow." We weren't allowed to even *think* that word back then.

What I learned, mainly on *Duffy's,* is that there are an infinite number of comic variations in any single word. That lesson has stayed with me. If you turned the picture off on *M*A*S*H* episodes and simply listened, I think they would make fairly good radio shows. I found that I could apply that lesson constantly once I started using a word processor. By seeing the physical shape of a word on the monitor, I see the "company" in which the word is traveling and quickly discern some anagrammatic or spooneristic possibilities. But you must deal with the language without violating the idea. Sometimes you can be too clever by half. You can't dazzle your audience to the point of losing whatever it is you're saying. "Murder your darlings," Oscar Wilde is reputed to have said (although to practice what he preached would have made him a serial killer).

I wouldn't say I was writing at this point in my life. What I was doing was exercising a particular knack that some people have for making up funny lines. I didn't get to really writing for a long time. On *Duffy's* we would create story lines, loose situations to hook the show's continuing cast of characters together for the half hour, and that was instructive. Mostly what you learned was the art of coming up with a script every week and completing it on time (usually in four to five days).

Duffy's, as was the case with all comedy shows of the period, was on the air once a week, thirty-nine weeks of the year. That was followed by a thirteen-week hiatus and then the show returned for the next cycle of thirty-nine. It was a daunting schedule with no margin for failure in meeting the relentless deadlines. We wrote to the minute. We would finish one show and then start right in on the next. It was wonderful training for what was to be a lifetime of deadlines.

On *Duffy's* I learned to tailor material for the program's ensemble: Archie, the bartender; Eddie, the bartender; Miss Duffy, the owner's daughter; and Finnegan, a dim-witted regular. Each had to do material that fit their characters perfectly. I also had to write for the week's guest, always a major stage, motion picture, or radio personality. Edward G. Robinson, Dame May Whitty, Monty Woolley, Bob Hope, Fred Allen, John Garfield, Deems Taylor, Oscar Levant, Jack Benny, George Raft, and Tallulah Bankhead made appearances—anyone who was ever anyone visited Duffy's dump of a tavern.

ARCHIE   Welcome to Duffy's, John. What d'ya think of the place?
GARFIELD   Were there any survivors?
ARCHIE   Gee whiz, John. You ain't been here five seconds and already you've insulted the joint.
GARFIELD   What's the record?

With audiotape yet to be invented, radio performers in Hollywood did the show live for the East; then three hours later, they did it live once again for the West Coast. With no need for makeup and no need to memorize lines, it was a sweet time for actors—an even sweeter time for me.

And then it looked as if the party might be over. Upon turning eighteen, I got a fan letter from my draft board. It seemed the army couldn't get along without me. Having worked my way up to seventy-five dollars a week, I said to Ed Gardner, "For these last two weeks before I have to go into the service, do you think you could make it a hundred dollars?" That was the magic number. A hundred bucks a week was, to me, the Everest of earnings. Ed put his arm around me in paternal fashion and said, "Kid, I wish I could do it, it's just not in the budget." Had there been tape at the time, that statement could have been prerecorded. With Ed, there was never anything in the budget. "Tell you what," he said. "Forget about the raise and when you go in, I'll get you a nice set of military hairbrushes." I didn't get the raise. I didn't get the brushes either.

SCENE 5

CAESAR'S HOUR

From a transcript of *Caesar's Hour Revisited,* a Writers Guild of America, West, seminar, broadcast on PBS, 1996:

CARL REINER   (to Larry Gelbart) *I came into the room and you and Neil [Simon] said, "We've got something real good for you this week." They always got excited if they knew they had something that would tickle you. And they read it to me, my little part in this [sketch], and to this day, I think it's the funniest little sequence I've ever had.*

GELBART   *You were like a spymaster.*

CARL REINER   *A spymaster. I was saying to Sid, "You will go to Istanbul. And because a diamond is not expected to be in a brown paper bag, you will carry this diamond, the Cumbersome Diamond, in a brown paper bag." And it was a doorknob, the size of a—it was a doorknob. And I'm telling him, When you come to Istanbul, and you get off the train, a man will come up to you and say, "Give me the diamond." Don't give it to him. He asks everybody for their diamonds. However, however, however, a beautiful, beautiful blond woman, dressed in a satin dress, a tight-fitting satin dress, with a gorgeous body, wearing two long earrings will come up to you and she will say, "Give me the diamond!" You will give it to her. That woman will be me.*
And Sid said, "You'll be in disguise?"
And I said: "No. I'm in disguise now."

It was very much like going to work every day of the week inside a Marx Brothers movie.

There was Carl Reiner, whose very existence is some sort of anti-lull device. Much like nature, as well as my housekeeper, Carl abhors a vacuum. He views silence and calm as enemies to be vanquished, contemplation to be avoided at all costs. Say something, do something, anything at all, don't leave it to life to just happen. Technically Sid's Caesar's co–second banana (Howard Morris was the other), Carl was a very real part of the *Caesar's Hour* writing staff, functioning as cheerleader as well, whenever the room was in need of that commodity.

The staff boasted two Mels. The first, Mel Tolkin, is a phenomenally gifted, complex man with more tics than a flophouse mattress. Tolkin's family had fled to America to escape the oppression of their native Russia. It could only happen to Tolkin—fleeing from a czar to wind up working for a Caesar. Their association began when Tolkin, Lucille Kallen, and the other Mel, Mel Brooks, wrote NBC's *Your Show of Shows* for the founder/producer of that historic program, Max Liebman. Although other writers came and went (and I was not one of them), it was Liebman, Kallen, and the Mels, One and Two, who were responsible for setting a standard for the budding medium, their writing that influenced television, an influence that is felt to this day.

And it was this standard that Sid Caesar emulated for his own show, established after the breakup of the Liebman setup. It was the original program's success that caused the show to be dismantled, with NBC hoping to get three hits instead of just one by giving Caesar, his costar, comedienne Imogene Coca, and Liebman each a different show to grind out for the network.

The young Caesar, already a premature legend, was a man of mythic skills and almost mythic craziness. Imagine, if you can, how intimidating it was—how "interesting"—to work for a man who had once punched a horse in the face, knocking it to the ground because the animal had had the audacity to throw his wife off its back. I can only tell you that our knowledge of this fact certainly deterred us from ever thinking of doing the same to her. (Florence Caesar, as wives tend to do, knew her husband better than anyone. After his first appearance on television, Max Liebman told Florence that Sid was going to be a big star. To which Florence replied, "Couldn't he be a *little* star?") As the star he had indeed become, in yet another fit of rage (Sid and rages were a perfect fit), Sid yanked an offending washbasin out of a wall with his bare hands, and once threatened to pull a taxi driver out of his car via his wing window.

But when it came to putting together a writing staff for his own venture, Sid Caesar was all method and no madness. Hence, Mel Tolkin. Hence, Mel Brooks.

Before I was sentenced to spend two years in the same writing room with Mel Brooks, I was a devout atheist. But being present at the birth of countless comic miracles that this totally unique talent is capable of creating, being surprised and blindsided on a daily basis by his extraordinary and completely unique take on humor, I became convinced that no one could be Mel Brooks's kind of funny without some sort of divine assistance.

Other writers in the room who came and went during my stint on the show included Selma Diamond (along with Lucille Kallen, one of the few women comedy writers of the period); Neil Simon, working without his brother, Danny, for the first time; and a number of junior staffers, including Sheldon Keller, Gary Belkin, and Michael Stewart, a young man who served then as a lightning-fast typist-editor-amanuensis, capturing the nonstop, raucous pitching of jokes and ideas.

When he approved of a line as it was pitched by one of us, Caesar would nod subtly at Mike, in the manner of someone at an auction. Often it would be sharpened by someone else the minute the line took flight, and Mike, complying with the nod, would commit the new and improved line to paper. An invaluable aide, he was also a bright student of comedy, going on, post-Caesar, to write the books for such Broadway hits as *Bye Bye Birdie, Hello, Dolly!,* and *42nd Street.*

Neil Simon—"Doc"—went on to write every other hit that Mike Stewart didn't, including *Laughter on the 23rd Floor,* which recaptured the gleeful organized chaos that marked the writing of *Caesar's Hour.* (One of the toughest challenges any writer can choose is to write a comedy about funny people. It hardly ever works. Witty onstage characters are at the mercy of the talent and expertise of offstage writers to provide them with their wit. Few can service them as well as Doc, however, and *Laughter on the 23rd Floor* is a hilarious exception to the rule.) But all this was long before Simon wrote for the theater—long before he *became* a theater (the Neil Simon on Broadway's West Fifty-second Street).

Often the nod that Sid was giving to Mike was for a line that had been pitched by Carl Reiner. And as often as not, the line that Carl had pitched had been thought up by Neil Simon. Shy and noncompetitive, Doc would speak his ideas in a barely audible tone, while the rest of us sounded as though we were auditioning yodelers. Realizing this early in the game, Carl made it a point always to sit next to Doc and to act as a loudspeaker for him.

What helped us all a great deal was the fact that we were all young and largely unfamiliar with the word *can't.* We took it as a matter of course that we would assemble at the start of every week to write a new, one-hour comedy/variety show, with the accent on comedy.

First we said "Good morning." That was the last purely social moment of the day. Mel Brooks would come in punctually one hour late and start to read *The Wall Street Journal.* Mel we usually greeted with a "Good afternoon." Every Monday we began dreaming up and preparing sketches, monologues, pantomimes, movie and play satires, special lyrics, all to be put into rehearsal on Wednesday and performed live before an audience on Saturday. Sundays, we would rest. Rest and take calls from our friends telling us how much they liked the previous night's show (anyone who didn't call obviously had no taste), and then start the whole process all over again the following morning. And we did that thirty-nine weeks a year.

We didn't bat a thousand, of course, but I think even the poorest shows had ten or twelve stunning minutes. The weakest part of any of the hours was when Sid had to be Sid, when he had to appear as himself at the start of each program and welcome the audience, via the camera. Without a character to hide behind, Sid was lost. Without prepared dialogue, without a progressive story line, Sid simply did not know how to play Sid. One year, one whole year, he spoke with a Polish accent, *off-camera.* Despite his awesome talent, and whatever devices he employed, he has never been in any danger of winning a prize for being articulate. I'm sure that if Sid ever found himself drowning, he'd have to start yelling for help the night before. But write him someone he can lose—or find—himself in, and he communicates with a starburst that I've never seen matched.

To his writers, he was our heavyweight champ. He could and would do anything we asked of him. Our frames of reference became his. There was nothing he didn't understand, providing *we* understood it. Everything, every subject, was fair game. Nothing was too hip for the room. He had total control, but we had total freedom. We were satirizing Japanese movies before anyone ever saw them, fashioning material for him that sprang from our collective backgrounds, our tastes in literature, in film, in theater, music, ballet, our marriages, our psychoanalyses.

Most of the staff was second-generation American Borscht Belt people. People who had been to school. In the earlier generation, comedy writers had little or no formal education; a college was where they taught you to cut hair. I don't think there was ever a group so aware of their own psychological problems and others', and that awareness found its way into the writing. It went beyond street smarts. We zeroed in on the rough spots in life—there's no fun in happiness. Bliss is boring. Fortunately, none of us had that in abundance. One of the great engines for comedy is ambivalence, where you attack parts of something—or somebody—the worst parts of the human experience which, in total, you really love.

In my first days with Sid, he never said a word to me outside the writing room. And he was always there. (One advantage of his omnipresence was that by the time the show aired, he knew every line perfectly.) I was beginning to wonder if I was cutting it with him. And then, after the first show, at the wrap party, he put his arms around me, bent me back as if he were John Gilbert and I were Greta Garbo, and gave me a kiss on the lips. That gesture was his way of saying, "I appreciate what you've done." If I'd written him the compliment, he'd have delivered it flawlessly. Left to his own devices, he turned us into a scene from a silent movie.

When we, Caesar's writers, got together for a PBS special in 1996, for an hour of reminiscence—we do that every thirty years or so—one of us yelled above the others, "It's just like the old days. Nobody can finish a sentence."

It was as though we'd stepped out of the room for a quarter of a century and then stepped back in. If you've ever seen really proficient sidemen in a band who can sight-read, that's what well-qualified comedy writers do. You just pick it up. You sense the room. Except for the fact that we were all white and Jewish,* we felt like we were the Duke Ellington band. We had this great sound together. Everybody is valuable when you're writing that way. The *worst* line makes somebody think of something *instead* of that.

Damn! There's never a time machine around when you want one.

---

*Asked once whether there was a reason why all of Sid's writers tended to be "young and Jewish," I said it was probably because all our parents were old and Jewish.

M*A*S*H NOTES

FADE IN:

INTERIOR: A doctor's office—day

A psychiatrist, SIDNEY FREEDMAN, *admits* LARRY GELBART *on an initial visit.*

FREEDMAN   Please lie down on the couch.

GELBART   I don't usually do this on a first date. *(complying, looking up)* There's a mirror on the ceiling.

FREEDMAN   I treat a lot of actors.

GELBART   I'm a writer.

FREEDMAN   Of comedy?

GELBART   Drama. I can't help it if people laugh at it.

FREEDMAN   And that's your problem?

GELBART   *M*A*S*H* is my problem.

FREEDMAN   How do you do that?

GELBART   What?

FREEDMAN   Speak in asterisks.

GELBART   Comes from doing the series too long.

FREEDMAN   "Doing" it?

GELBART   Writing it, mostly. Stories, scripts, creating characters. I invented you.

FREEDMAN   *(suppressing a smile)* Oh, really?

GELBART   Sidney Freedman, the psychiatrist. You're a Sigmund of my imagination.

FREEDMAN   You actually believe that?

GELBART   All I have to do is backspace and you're out of this scene.

FREEDMAN   Please continue.

GELBART   I've been away from the series for eight years. It's been off the network for two seasons. And I'm still working on it. Still rewriting in my head; sharpening speeches, cutting dialogue, making fixes no one knows and not anyone needs.

FREEDMAN   Why are you doing that?

GELBART   I was always compulsive about the series. Wanted it just right, just so. When I was on the set, I'd bite loose threads off the actors' costumes. Sometimes I'd bite loose actors. I was rabid on the subject.

FREEDMAN   But, surely, now that the series is finished—

GELBART   Finished? With reruns? Now that it's off, it's on more than ever. It's everywhere. On film, on video, on T-shirts. It's a beer. It's a vodka. Who ever knew we were doing a show that people would see and hear and wear and drink?

FREEDMAN   Shouldn't that be a source of pride instead of pain?

GELBART   The pride is in what we did. The pain comes from no longer being who we were when we did it. Maybe that's why I keep performing my phantom rewrites, so that I can keep alive some part of the past that we—Gene, Burt, the cast and crew—shared together. That wonderful time when we were innocents, not an institution; when we were blissfully ignorant, yet to become icons.

FREEDMAN   Very perceptive. And alliterative, as always.

GELBART   You try to give pain a certain style. (*pause*) Maybe *that's* what the series was all about . . .

FREEDMAN   You're smiling.

GELBART   I've been searching for a definition of what *M*A*S*H*—excuse me, *MASH*—was all about for a long time. I may have just stumbled on it. Makes me happy.

FREEDMAN   A psychiatrist doesn't see a lot of happy people.

GELBART   Happy people don't pay the rent.

FREEDMAN   I always say that.

GELBART   I gave myself the speech instead of you.

FREEDMAN   (*amused*) You still think you're in charge here?

GELBART   Except for the book that follows this introduction.

FREEDMAN   What are you talking about?

GELBART   The part that follows us.

FREEDMAN   My dear fellow, we're in an office, not a book.

GELBART   Really? Watch this . . .

~~~

HAWKEYE   *Why can't the war stop, General? It's gone on for over two years now—surely the army must be in profit by now.*

What first struck me about the film was not what $M*A*S*H$ had to say about war or human folly; my initial impression had nothing to do with any of the movie's loftier themes. It was a particular song, written especially for the picture. The haunting "Suicide Is Painless" seems a simple composition, part sweet, part sad—and all the sweeter for it—and with swing built in. It got to me. As I wrote the TV series's pilot script with Dr. Richard Hooker's novel, which served as the basis for the screenplay, at one elbow and the perfectly executed screen adaptation of it at the other, it was composer Johnny Mandel's work that kept going round and round in whatever part of the psyche creative juices mix and marinate. After all this time, I still don't know the precise lyrics of the song, although they are obviously some sort of commercial for self-destruction. But it is that refrain, heard at the start of each seemingly perpetual rerun, that prepares me even now for what I am about to see, just as it prepared me then for what I was about to write. The flavor of the music had a great deal to do with the final work being unlike anything I had ever done before—comedy written in a minor key. However contradictory that seems, that is what finally evolved. I have always found it difficult to write to any sort of recipe, but I have always been aware that, for me, it was Mandel's melody that set the tone.

$M*A*S*H$ was that rarity for TV professionals, a show that you spent every waking moment working on that you enjoyed watching later as a viewer. Despite running hassles with CBS and Twentieth Century–Fox, those of us responsible for the series were allowed, even encouraged, to do our best work. Our labors brought a great deal of joy to a good many people. And some other people wound up making a good deal of money. I used to think I would be very happy if I got a nickel for every million dollars that Twentieth Century–Fox made out of *M*A*S*H*. And that's roughly about the way it worked out.

~~~

The opportunity to develop *M*A*S*H* for television was a matter of being in the wrong place at the right time. I was living in London when the chance came along. London is six thousand miles from where the action is in terms of the production of an American TV series.

We had moved to England in the fall of 1963—my wife, Pat, and our five children—because of my involvement in the British production of *A Funny Thing Happened on the Way to the Forum*. Our first idea was to spend a short time there for the rehearsal and try-out periods, and then return to America after the show opened. Even before we went to England, I had shown a talent for understatement. The short time turned out to be almost nine years.

The period was one of unintended, semi-, and quite premature retirement. I did little or no regular work at all, living off the royalties of *Forum*. To supplement that income, I would occasionally nip over to the States to do a quick TV pilot or two. It was not my favorite way to work, but my wife and five children and I were ensconced in a lovely, big house in Highgate, in North London, and while living abroad was a lot less costly than living in America would have been, cheap times seven can quickly turn into expensive.

There were two other major benefits to living over there. After working constantly for twenty years, a restorative process kicked in and, second, I was exposed, on a daily basis, to British television, which was then, for the most part, what we in America call public broadcasting, each household paying a yearly fee to the government for the right to watch TV programming of the type that offers a good deal of adult material. Strange that, of late, "adult" has come to mean suggestive or, worse, "adult movies, adult language"; the words no longer imply maturity, merely smut. In England I had the luxury of watching hours and hours of grown-up themes and grown-up talk, ingesting entertainment and information without titillation, programming devoid of censorship. From time to time, I did hear the odd four-letter word, even saw a few people *doing* the four-letter word, but the whole country did not go mad as a result and throw themselves into the Channel, or even switch to another one. They responded to adult programming in an adult fashion.

The revolution in American TV, the era that saw a freshness and boldness emerge on the small screen, had its foundation in the UK. *All in the Family* started life as a British series called *Till Death Us Do Part*, created by English writer Johnny Speight for the BBC. *All in the Family* owes a great deal to Speight and to Norman Lear, who imported it without sacrificing one bit of its irreverent boldness. Neither was interested in merely pushing the envelope; they settled for no less than ripping it right up the middle.

The American series *Sanford and Son* originated in England as *Steptoe and Son*; *Three's Company* was hatched over there as *Man About the House.*

Original programming has a greater chance of succeeding in Great Britain for several reasons. Chiefly it's because a series there consists of only six episodes. That's it, just six. Not twenty or more, as is the American way. Writing talents are not stretched to the point of breaking or becoming tedious or repetitious. English series are invariably the work of one writer, or perhaps a team of two—no hiring of writers by the six-pack, Hollywood style. (I am not such an Anglophile that I am blind to how much rubbish there is on British TV, but during the period I am talking about, the mid-sixties, it could boast an extraordinary amount of quality broad-casting—Benny Hill notwithstanding.)

In 1971, I made my one stab at British TV, producing *The Marty Feldman Comedy Machine* (importing two young American comedy writers, Rudy DeLuca and his partner, Barry Levinson). Visiting London at the time was an old friend, Gene Reynolds, a successful producer and director at Twentieth Century–Fox. We talked about the possibility of working together on a project one day. That one day began just a few short weeks later when Gene called from California to suggest I see a new Fox feature film called *M*A*S*H*.

William Self, then head of the Fox TV division, had sold CBS on the idea of picking up the tab for a pilot script based on what was proving to be a very successful movie. If the network liked the script, they would film it—as a possible series for the fall of 1972. It was an imaginative stroke on Self's part. It wasn't the practice then to put a movie still in distribution into play as a potential TV series.

I told Gene that, while I had enjoyed the picture, the thought that it might serve as the basis for an ongoing TV show would never have occurred to me. Spending as much time as I had away from California, it wasn't my practice to watch or read material with the idea of turning it into TV fodder.

Before you can say "expense account," Gene was back in London so that we could discuss the requirements of the pilot script before I began writing. I was working during the day on the Marty Feldman show, and Gene would visit the studio in Elstree, just outside London, where we would talk during lunch breaks, then continue later at my house, which sat beside Kenwood, an enormous, magnificent public park. There, we took leisurely strolls through the idyllic woods and winding paths, the unlikeliest of settings to discuss a series that would deal with the deadly effects of war.

From the beginning, Gene and I felt our chief obligation was to remain faithful to the spirit of the film, and as one eventual chronicler of the series, David S. Reiss, would put it, "not convert it into a more or less routine service-gang comedy or a high jinx war." We were determined to maintain the tone of the picture, although we knew we would not be permitted the freedom with profanity and sexual situations on the little screen, as had been employed and enjoyed on the big one. Living abroad, I wasn't aware of how far American TV had begun to nudge past the borders of permissiveness, established in the prehistoric days of radio broadcasting, with the new series *All in the Family.* Gene and I were keenly aware that, given the ongoing American involvement in Vietnam, it would be a terrible affront to the nation's sensibilities merely to turn out just another bunch of wacky people in uniform, to come up with another *Hogan's Heroes* or *McHale's Navy* or, wonderful as it was, even a *Phil Silvers Show* with Sergeant

Bilko. Fox and CBS agreed, never gauging the depth of our resolve or commitment.

The prevailing question about the projected series (although Gene and I never asked it) was: "How the hell is anybody going to take that subject—people at war—and make it at all funny?" It was too early in the game to be able to articulate my feelings, but I knew it was going to have to be a whole lot more than funny. Funny was easy. How not to trivialize human suffering by trying to be comic about it, that was the challenge.

~~~

My hitch in the army had lasted precisely twelve months and eleven days. Those few days more than a year saved me from being called up to serve when President Truman committed troops to the undeclared but still very real war in Korea. I managed to get shipped there anyway—as a member of Bob Hope's writing staff. (In the four years that I worked for him, I got to travel everywhere that Bob did to entertain our armed forces, including Berlin, during the airlift in 1948, and to Korea after hostilities started there in 1951.) My memories of the place stood me in good stead when fate (and Fox) gave me the chance to tackle *M*A*S*H*. I would be following in the footsteps of one of Hollywood's most accomplished screenwriters, Ring Lardner, Jr.

Lardner, who had picked up a paperback copy of *M*A*S*H* at an airport for some inflight reading, had served in wartime Korea, so he knew what he was reading and later would be writing about when he transformed the book into a screenplay. The book's author was Dr. Richard Hornberger (who disclaimed any racy connotation in his pseudonym "Hooker"—the reference, he claimed, was to his golf swing). Dr. Whatever would turn out to hate the series, making that more than clear in a letter to me in the fourth year of our run, in which his only comment on the show was: "I like the theme song; after that it gets kind of dull." Perhaps it was because the TV version tended to be a good deal more liberal, politically, than he was. He wasn't alone. A writer once described the series as "shrouded in a serious-minded liberal gloom." We certainly tended to be more serious than the film. Its director, Robert Altman, has always said that *M*A*S*H* was not intended as an antiwar film, but as one that was anti–prowar films, or any form of entertainment that made war seem acceptable because the people involved were able to be such good sports about it. To my great disappointment, whenever he could, Altman also made quite public his dislike of the series—so much so that when I met his wife at a party a few years ago and she offered to introduce me to her husband, I declined, saying I was certain he didn't have much use for me. "Nonsense," she said, and led me over to him.

"This guy thinks you hate him."

"Oh, no," said Altman. "I'm just jealous."

Our laughter melted a decade's freeze (although I've become aware that he continues his public opposition stance).

Before there was a series for anyone to like or dislike, there had to be a pilot script, one that would give the network the confidence that it contained the seeds of success. Gene and I set about deciding which of the movie's characters we wanted to retain. Clearly, there were too many for us to handle. Unlike the film, the TV version could run only twenty-four minutes and twenty seconds. (That seems like an eternity now. The content in today's half-hour shows runs just over twenty-two minutes. It won't be long before someone breaks the four-minute happy ending.) If CBS decided to go to the next step and finance the filming of the pilot script, there would be budgetary considerations. The next challenge was to come up with a plot for the test script, one that would have the qualities of the movie, and all of its production values, but at one third the storytelling time and one tenth the budget. That's basically half-hour television in a nutshell: a process of condensation and miniaturization—creation in cameo—and hopefully executed with a little grace under an awful lot of pressure.

Gene and I put in a call to Hollywood, to the CBS executive assigned to say "No" to people and told him the story line we had devised. Risking his job, he gave us an enthusiastic "Yes."

Gene then returned to the States, and I went back to turning out Marty Feldman shows, our *M*A*S*H* notes sitting on my desk, gathering fog. I was in the control booth taping one of the Feldman shows when a phone rang. Gene was calling from California. I remember clearly that the call came on a Wednesday, not the Wednesday after he left. It was exactly *eight* Wednesdays later. He had patiently, considerately, left me on my own for over two months. It was, unfortunately, a terrible connection: I could hear every word he was saying.

GENE   How's the script going?
ME   (*without a hint of hesitation, or any scruples either*) Great! I just mailed it!
GENE   Terrific! I should be getting it in a couple of days, then?
ME   Figure four or five. It's got a long way to travel.
GENE   Wonderful. Looking forward to it, buddy.

Having said that I had mailed it, I knew the time had obviously come for me to do so. All I had to do was write it first. Because the two of us had done such a detailed scene-by-scene outline, I was able to dictate the dialogue and the action to my secretary in two days. To my enormous relief, I sent the script off to California at midnight from an all-night post office in Trafalgar Square. I eased my conscience by saying I hadn't really lied to Gene; I had just been prematurely honest.

He liked the script very much. CBS liked it very much. Since CBS liked it very much, Fox, not yet the owner of its own network and eager to have any ongoing series on the air, naturally liked it very much as well. CBS committed to financing the filming of the pilot but asked for a few changes. My script had the leading man, Hawkeye, sleeping with Lieutenant Dish, an army house nurse also attached to the 4077th medical unit. They were married, only not to each other. Likewise, commanding officer Colonel Henry Blake was having an extramarital affair with one of the nurses, and Frank Burns was frequenting Major Houlihan's sleeping bag. The network felt that all the adulterous cot-hopping might prove a bit much for Middle America. Maybe I had been hanging around the royal family too much. Happily, writers have even more power than ship captains. We can not only marry people, but unmarry them as well, which is what I did in the case of Hawkeye and Dish in the rewrite that followed. In truth, it was more a polish than a rewrite, with me having gotten lucky in my first pass at the script. (Also lucky to have Lardner's screenplay rattling around in my brain. Lucky, too, to have reread Hooker's novel three or four or ten times.)

As I began the revisions in London, Gene and associate producer Burt Metcalfe started the casting process in California. The job they did revealed that the two men were obviously all thumbs—and each one of them bright green. Their choices were superb: the coup was hitting upon the idea of, and then being able to land, Alan Alda. Alan had starred on Broadway in a number of theatrical productions and given memorable performances in several television movies. The conventional wisdom was that he would not be interested in tying himself up with a weekly series. Gene and Burt, being unconventional fools, sent Alan the pilot script and he was ours. And how lucky we were. What is true of movies is also true when it comes to TV: what first grabs an audience's attention and later earns its loyalty are the faces they see on the screen and the positive emotions those faces evoke. Alan was our guarantee that that would happen; Alan, plus the balance of the ensemble, which reflected the flawless choices made by Gene and Burt.

With the cast and script in place and Gene set to direct, the pilot went forward. Happily, we were able to use the feature film's studio and exterior settings, which were still intact. These physical assets gave the series a unique, decidedly different look for a half-hour TV show—a look that had feature film production values (lighting, set dimensions, and details), providing the series with an atmosphere of permanence and reality, a visual grounding that was to add to $M*A*S*H$'s durability.

Two terrible possibilities loom before you after you complete the shooting of a television pilot. One, the network is not sufficiently impressed and you are not put on their schedule as a series. That's it. Over and out. It was great fun, or maybe it wasn't; but, in any case, it was just one, and only one, of those things. The other possibility can be just as upsetting: the network is greatly impressed and they are going to put you on the air. It's a seamless piece of good news/bad news. All your energy up to that moment has been channeled into the pilot; you've been thinking only in terms of minutes and seconds; now you have to start thinking in chunks of months and seasons. There is also the feeling that the pilot encapsulated completely what the series is all about, that the prototype has said it all. Now what are you supposed to do? The answer, of course, is you're supposed to do it over. And over and over. You are expected to re-create the pilot in endless multiples, constantly trying to top yourself, challenged weekly—with any luck, yearly—to find new ways to make your point, avoiding other people's clichés, always in danger of creating your own.

After viewing the pilot, CBS bestowed the better of the two evils upon us. They elected to put us on the air, scheduling the show for the beginning of the fall season of 1972, in the 7:30 Sunday night slot. Our competition on the rival networks was to be *The FBI* and *Wonderful World of Disney.* Our collective hearts sank. Not only was *M*A*S*H* going to be seen at an extremely early time in the evening for what was considered very un-Sunday, sophisticated, anti-Establishment material, but we would also be on opposite one program that seemed vaguely un-American not to watch, and another that you somehow felt might be watching you. But we were on the network's schedule. We were off and running. Sort of. We floundered, I would say, for the first six or seven episodes, trying to find our voice, our tone, the best way to enlist an audience to share with us our anger and resentment toward the sickening regularity with which ideological differences seemed capable only of bloody, military resolutions.

We finally found the form about seven weeks into our first season in an episode called "Sometimes You Hear the Bullet." Hawkeye operates, unsuccessfully, on a former friend of his who has been wounded on the battlefield, which he insisted on visiting as research for a book on the war. Having taken the time to establish this character and his relationship to Hawkeye, we felt the audience would be able to share Hawkeye's keen sense of loss—and understand when he cried at his friend's senseless death. (Tears on a half-hour show!) It was the first indication that a mixture of laughter and tragedy might be possible, without any heavy-handed manipulation of the audience's emotions. After this episode, there was a new confidence in our work. God knows we needed it, because the work never ended.

The first day of filming an episode always started with a reading of the script by the cast, the production staff in attendance, on the dedicated *M*A*S*H* soundstage, Stage 9, at the Twentieth Century–Fox studio in Century City. Once through, no stops, the actors not really trying to act; this was sight-reading, after all. But neither did they intone their lines in such a lackluster manner as to make the material seem wanting. This happens all too often, in all too many situations, sending the despondent writer off to redo material that has yet to be delivered in any plausible fashion, a case of script crib death.

The second time through anyone could stop at any time to comment or ask a question. Suggestions were made—some good, some less so; the same was true of the scripts. Each was roughly thirty-five pages long, neatly typed and bound, not a trace of midnight oil or blood on any of them. Series writers love people to know how hard they work, but it's hip to be very cool about it: appear unshaven (I don't know what women writers do), yawn occasionally, mention the beautiful dawn you noticed through your office window that morning, and never, never show up sporting a suntan.

Changes in the script would take place, if necessary, on the earliest scenes first, since the director would be rehearsing those minutes after the second read-through. Not rehearsing them for performance yet; the actors would still have to memorize their words and the moves he had planned for them. Those moves were his staging, his positioning of the actors inside the sets, his eyes acting as the camera with which he would later photograph them.

While this was going on, I would make the other script changes back in my office: a line here, a line there, perhaps a whole new scene, or on several nightmarish occasions, an entire script.

The rest of the day was taken up by looking at dailies (also known as rushes, they are the footage shot on the previous day of the episode in production); editing other shows that were in the post-production process (at times, as many as two or three at once); and looking at final cuts of still other shows. Then there were the mixing sessions for the purpose of balancing sound, incorporating music cues, and adding sound effects (including the cursed laugh track); meeting with writers to discuss new scripts; revising and polishing old ones, and working on whatever scripts I happened to be writing or rewriting at the moment; conducting endless research for story material and participating in promotion, all the while meeting or hand-wrestling with network and/or studio executives about one thing or another (more often than not about the hateful laugh track). It was all a bit like playing three-dimensional chess, against half a dozen other players, all at once.

Our schedule was: read and rehearse one day, shoot the show in the next three. Thirty-five pages in three days is an insane ratio. There are people today who will still tell you that what we did simply cannot be done. Perhaps that's partly true. I've been told that, a quarter of a century later, *M*A*S*H* is the only successful one-camera show that television has ever produced. The seeming impossibility of it all was what made it so much fun to do. Everyone connected with the series relished the challenge; the soundstage was charged with the electric enthusiasm generated by those in front, as well as behind, the camera. Despite that sort of spirit, we were not always able to get a show in the can within that three-day period. At times, something would turn out not quite as good as we envisioned it, and we wanted another crack at it.

Gene, overcoming the resistance of the studio, won us, one day each month, a pickup day, so that we could complete work on unfinished episodes and improve the overall quality of any others we felt we could help.

It all becomes easier and harder at the same time. Harder, because you keep trying to do better, keep trying to find new and original ways to make your point, to avoid turning new roads into comfortable ruts. With no desire to change the content of a series, you find yourself forever experimenting with the form.

There are countless obstacles to overcome in an effort to keep a series alive and challenging for those who labor at it and for those who will eventually watch it. The actors are waiting for the pages on the soundstage, the shooting is behind schedule, the budget has been exceeded, on and on it goes. Expediency becomes the enemy of ambition, compromise is in the air, you settle for easy ways—setting off land mines under your own best intentions.

For one of those, I take full responsibility. I tend to write a good deal of dialogue. In truth, I tend to overwrite a good deal of dialogue. I love spoken material, well spoken. I love to play with language; make it do tricks, turn a word inside out to see if it's got a hidden meaning tucked away somewhere, or perhaps find that it's capable of an extra entendre or two—a throwback to my radio training, obviously, where words had to do it all for an audience. I do, also, tend to write too many jokes. That's Bob Hope 101. Always leave 'em laughing. Always meet 'em laughing. Always keep 'em laughing. Working on a Hope script—whatever the medium—you always checked to make sure that there were five or six laughs to the page. If there weren't, you would put in a few more—and then a few more just for insurance. Some of the early *M*A*S*H* episodes suffer from that sort of cramming, that form of joke force-feeding that makes me wince whenever I catch examples of such wretched excess in a rerun.

Our first episodes didn't seem to completely measure up to our expectations. Invariably, we would shoot more footage than we needed, to give us more choices in the editing process. I came to realize that the only part of a show you cannot cut deeply, and still have it make sense, is the exposition, the establishment of the plot elements, the hinge upon which the whole piece swings. It became clear that the expository passages were not terribly funny, that the story points were made in rather straightforward, uninteresting chunks, as though the plot were some drudgery we had to plod through before we could get to the good parts. The answer was clear. Since the exposition was largely uncuttable, we were going to have to sugarcoat the medicine—to make vital information as entertaining as possible. It is probably the one and only "rule" I have ever consciously learned from my own writing experience. (That, and never get a suntan.)

Too much practice, however, can sometimes make you go way past perfect. Having learned how helpful it was for exposition to be painless or as entertaining as possible, I was often guilty of over-doing it. Instead of giving the audience what would ordinarily be a dry setup, I would try to make it so diverting that it sometimes ran the risk of being diverting to the point of becoming something merely amusing and instantly forgettable.

Of enormous advantage to us was the fact that many of our actors, for example Alan Alda, Gary Burghoff (Radar), and Larry Linville (Frank Burns), had stage training. Their respect for the text was exceptional. Nothing in a script—not one word—was ever changed without first asking permission, nor were changes suggested merely for the sake of changing. As invariably happens, a certain alchemy takes place when literature becomes drama, when written material is read aloud. Some combinations of words do not sit well on the tongue; what works for the eye works differently for the ear. If necessary, script adjustments would often continue right through the filming period, on into postproduction, where actors could read new lines in a recording studio, lines that would be put into the mouths of their onscreen images, or laid in on the sound-track, so that they were heard off-camera. I was grateful, on an hourly basis, for the thoughtful restraint shown by the cast, which saw each episode's script as the script for that episode and not as a springboard for improvement or improvisation. Our actors were always content to leave the writing to the writers, while they concentrated on the acting. That sort of behavior in an ongoing series, with its dozens of scripts subdivided by thousands and thousands of words, was a rarity. It still is. Too often, the initial reading of a script is the prelude to a fixing frenzy—everybody's got a better idea, a way to save a script that usually needs no saving. It becomes necessary for the people in charge to realize which members of the company truly have the ability to make a constructive contribution and to discourage those who fancy themselves pretend script doctors, rather than pretend medical ones.

More often than not, the idea for an episode would originate with Gene Reynolds and me. Gene has had a lifetime of experience in the picture business and possesses a sly, understated sense of humor. He began as a child actor (aren't they all, just a little bit?), working with gifted directors, writers, and other performers. While still knee-high to an agent, Gene very often played somebody as a boy: he was either Robert Taylor as a boy or Robert Ryan as a boy; nobody ever saw Gene in the second reel because the character always grew up to be the star of the film. A keen observer, he learned every aspect of film production and had a marvelous story sense, one that was a whole lot better than mine. We would constantly pan for a new premise in our research, and hitting on what we thought might be the basis for an episode, we would immediately do a step outline: work out a first act, a second act, and a "tag" scene, a filmed postscript to each episode. Gene had a rule of thumb, which we sometimes adhered to and, in the beginning, rarely abandoned: that each act broke down into five scenes.

We would then assign the outline to a writer, or I would write the script, alone or with someone else. If we gave the outline to a free-lancer, we expected a first draft in three weeks or so. After reading it over, we would meet with the writer and give him (they were predominantly hims in those days) our notes and suggestions—that is, if we felt he was going to be able to deliver an improved second draft. Sometimes it didn't seem as though he had grasped the series or the characters sufficiently (which was often true in the beginning, because neither had we, and it was unrealistic to expect that an outsider would have the clues to the mysteries that we hadn't solved or even defined yet). If we thought he could hack it (sorry about that verb), we would give him our notes and our prayers, and expect the second draft within a couple of weeks. If it was decided that that particular writer was not to go forward, I would redo the material myself, at no monetary or screen credit loss to the original author.

A two-act structure is automatic in a half-hour show because of the need to insert commercials. By the first-act break, we would try to create a feeling of suspense or tension, one or more cliffhangers, then head for the barn in the second act. We never waited to resolve the story in the tag, that half-page or so miniscene that followed the sponsor's final pitch, not trusting that an audience was going to stay tuned in or be all that attentive after the last commercial.

Our initial episodes were, like the plot, single-event stories, very simple, very one-note. It was around the third or fourth effort that my wife, Pat, complained that she felt a certain emptiness in the show. It seemed to her that the whole camp was devoted each week to just the one activity or problem with which that particular script dealt. Her criticism rang a nerve, as we might have said on *Duffy's*. I realized that one of the great attractions the movie version of *M*A*S*H* held for me was its kaleidoscopic look at the 4077th, different events happening in a lot of different places to a lot of different characters. I proceeded to write a script called "Dear Dad" that turned out to be the first in a series of letters from Hawkeye and others of the 4077th to their families and friends back home, an attempt to employ multiple happenings in a single episode. We were the first television show, to the best of my immodest memory, to use this multitiered storytelling technique in the half-hour form.

The episode marked the beginning of countless experiments designed to vary the show's structure. We devised shows that were all but plotless, meant only to convey a mood or an overall theme. We sometimes mixed black-and-white with color. One episode was devoted to a half-hour monologue delivered by Hawkeye in a semiconscious state. We delighted in throwing the show up into the air each week and seeing how it came down. There was an ongoing, healthy restlessness to avoid the risk of predictability—never tampering with the series's central statement, but always willing to change the way we said it, fully aware of how success can buckle tightly into a straitjacket. The show might have been set in wartime Korea, the doctors might have been experts in meatball surgery, but without this experimentation *M*A*S*H* would have been just another ensemble comedy show with a weekly problem that had to be paid off inside a half hour.

Plotting is nothing I did, or do, naturally. It is the hardest part of the writing process. No matter how many times you plot a script successfully, the next one, representing new and uncharted territory, convinces you that you were merely lucky the last time out, that you really don't know how to do it at all. It is simply the most time-consuming, the most taxing, the most frustrating part of the writing experience. The Roman playwright Plautus was really my plotting teacher, and I read his plays over and over, in adapting them for *A Funny Thing Happened on the Way to the Forum*, dissecting his masterful construction and his manipulation of the characters. Prior to that, I had written only short sketches and monologues, variety work, generally plotless pieces. I had never done anything that had a life of more than, say, twelve minutes or so, unless it was a parody or a satire of something that had its own structure, such as a movie or a play.

It was working with Plautus, my 2,500-year-old teacher, that I learned how to try to make a story work for two hours or more. It is not a lesson that simply gets nailed fast into your head. There is no quick and easy recipe. You still have to write to taste and to leave room for innovative ways to tell a tale. You think you are doing it correctly, you hope you are doing it correctly, but it's a constant process of tinkering, checking to make sure that your story has tension and progression and is working toward the resolution you have in mind for your characters and that each of them speaks in his or her own voice, except whichever one of them is serving as your surrogate (not that all of them don't, in some fashion or other, even the most unflattering of them).

Does fear ever sit on your desk, putting itself between you and the blank page, protecting its pristine whiteness? Yes. But after a time you stop thinking "What happens if I don't finish this?" and you start thinking about when you will. I have learned, after a mere five and a half decades, to trust the process, an untold amount of which goes on without the writer's knowledge or conscious participation. You know that if you have enough time, or even too little time, you are going to finish it. What you let yourself do after a while is allow yourself to do bad work, to put anything on the page, no matter how much you embarrass yourself. I'm talking about "dummy" lines, approximate or incomplete sentences, so you have some material to work with, to hone and polish to the near perfection that will only seem perfect until the next time you read it over. It's a matter of abandoning the notion that you have to start right off writing pearls, pearls that strung together will turn the finished script into a lovely necklace.

When we did our first multistoried show, "Dear Dad," CBS was concerned, feeling the audience would be confused as to which story to follow, that they would be incapable or unwilling to try to hold more than one idea at a time in their heads. The assumption was that they—the great unwashed "they"—would be put off by such storytelling. Those were the days when the networks not too secretly harbored the opinion that the average TV watcher had the mind of a twelve-year-old. Thanks to the role TV has played in our lives, the only viewers today with twelve-year-old minds are the five-year-olds. At any rate, we had no problem, nor did our audience, tracking the multiple stories and situations we began to employ increasingly. The device tended to make an episode richer and fuller. I was surprised to learn how many of our viewers thought that M*A*S*H was a one-hour rather than a half-hour show, packed with so many events as the episodes were.

Drunk with success, driven by momentum, we very quickly rid ourselves of the obligation to resolve every dilemma in which we placed our characters. A good many times we chose not to solve the problems they faced, letting some of them go unsolved, even allowing an occasional episode to come to that rarest of conclusions in commercial, half-hour TV—an unhappy ending.

This was another area of contention with the network. Networks are never comfortable parting with established, comfortable ways, nor are they advocates of leaving an audience sad—too sad to rush right out and buy a year's supply of deodorant. Bad enough, from their point of view, that the 4077th was rife with sexuality; that we introduced transvestitism to the half-hour vocabulary; that, in our never-ending life-and-death situations, we had medical people during surgical procedures constantly making jokes, often in questionable taste, unable to top the war, which was to them the ultimate in bad taste.

The one area in which I anticipated trouble and never received any made me so grateful that I could deal with the rest of the network's objections with a mere teaspoonful of outrage. To its credit, CBS never once asked us to tone down the political content of the show or deemphasize the humanism we tried to dramatize. For the first three years, we had the normal amount of flak from the network's Department of Program Practices—their euphemism for "censor," a word that scares them shitless (if you will forgive my childish delight in putting that word in such close proximity to "censor," without one of them being able to do anything about it). Checking each fresh script, they would register their objections to certain dialogue, certain situations. One they absolutely refused to allow us to film had as its premise two nurses, upset with Hawkeye's promiscuity, who pretended that he had caused each to become pregnant. It was the only show that Program Practices ever forbade. "Not a page of it," they memoed. "Not a minute." We never filmed it. The script was killed. *Memo mori.*

The rest of the valuable time consumed by them was pretty much SOP. Attrition by priggishness: "Please delete three 'hells,' on pages 2, 20, and 32, and the two 'damns' on page 17." They were especially vigilant about the two big S's: Sex and Sacrilege. No one ever says "Goddamn" on television. You can say "God" and you can say "damn," but do not ever try putting them together or there is Goddamn hell to pay. As for dealing with matters sexual, this was the early seventies. If it was tough to show a navel on TV, you can imagine the network's position about any other orifices farther south. But they did let us talk about the futility of war and they did allow us to be highly political. On lesser, sillier matters, we negotiated, script by script, on a daily basis since they would be reviewing several scripts at a time.

Our first censor was male and he was terribly uptight about a great many subjects. The second year, we had the flip side of the gender, and she was terrific, far more liberal than her predecessor. The fourth year CBS, along with NBC and ABC, instituted the infamous Family Hour, and network censorship immediately became inane times three. In an episode of that period, we had Radar stopped and challenged by a scared young rookie, on guard duty for

the first time in his life. When Radar bawled him out for danger-
ously pointing his loaded rifle at him, the militarily inexperienced
boy replied, "Sorry, sir. I'm a virgin." Program Practices would not
let us use the word *virgin,* even in this nonsexual context. (The idea
was that no language was to be used during the so-called Family
Hour time period—7:00 to 10:00 P.M.—that might be offensive to
any member of the family, whatever his or her age. That the word
virgin was considered potentially offensive to a viewer should give
you an inkling of how working in television often made you feel as
though you were Alice in Wasteland.) We were forced to cut the
word.

Vengeance was clearly called for. In the next episode I wrote a
character, a wounded soldier who, when asked by Radar where he
was from, said he was a native of the Virgin Islands. That they allowed us to say.

In the long run, censorship was not our biggest problem. Most
television writers are so conditioned by the restrictions of the business that after a while, they constantly engage in self-censorship.
While this keeps them from fighting time-wasting battles over trying to get such filthy words as *virgin* on the air, it also robs the
medium of unfettered ideas and the bold treatment of those ideas.
Nothing stifles creativity more than sitting at your desk with a head
stuffed full of don'ts, although you can argue that these obstacles
call for another kind of creativity that challenges you to come up
with acceptable alternatives. At any rate, as the show climbed in
the ratings and the network was generating higher and higher income from the sale of commercial airtime, they allowed us a good
deal more latitude. Money may be the root of all evil, but in television, it lets you do a good many "don'ts."

There were other areas of contention. CBS was not too happy in
the early years with the scenes we filmed in O.R.—the operating
room. Too much blood, they said. Any amount of blood would have
been too much, of course. Who ever saw blood, never mind that it
was the type that came from the makeup department, on a half-
hour comedy series? The network feared that any kind of gore
would be an audience turnoff. The last time I saw the series's O.R.

set, it was on display in the Smithsonian Institution in Washington, D.C.—a few steps from the original flag that inspired Francis Scott Key to compose our national anthem—along with a number of other *M*A*S*H* artifacts, and it was drawing record crowds.

Our biggest heartaches came with the network shifting the series from one time slot to another, using the show as a strategic device, a battering ram to combat the rival networks' counterprogramming. For all our ultimate success and prestige, it was as though we were living in a mansion with a day-to-day lease. There was the feeling that, no matter how well we had done for ourselves or for CBS, we had still not earned a permanent place for our efforts. However much freedom of expression they came to allow, the network kept us in a constant state of vulnerability and jeopardy; no matter how many homers we hit out of the park for them, they never let us forget that it was their park we were playing in—with their bat and their ball.

The first network requirement for each new episode was a typed, one-paragraph description of the proposed story line for their comments, i.e., their approval or rejection. I went along with this somewhat demeaning demand in the beginning, but by the fourth year, I was calling them saying, "Sorry, no paragraph this week. The dog ate my typewriter." That didn't create any waves. Once you're a hit, they begin to almost trust you. Then, too, they never really understood how we were able to make *M*A*S*H* work. All they knew was that we knew what we were doing, which was making them millions and millions of dollars, so they left us pretty much alone, except for the running battles with the censors and the violent time shifts from a Tuesday to a Thursday or a Thursday to a Saturday.

There is an all-too-common practice in TV, wherein a series has to submit a list of the writers, directors, and actors it wants to employ for network approval. We chose not to play that particular game. A network's estimate of someone's ability can differ radically from your own—especially in the matter of writers. Never publicly acknowledged, it is a fact of what passes for life in the television industry that the networks keep what is known as a "white list," the names of writers whose work they prefer using. It's not so much a case of favoritism or nepotism or any other -ism, unless it might be successism: they tend to trust writers who they feel have good track records. The Writers Guild of America won the right to be free of this kind of network intrusion into the creative process on paper; in practice, this kind of discrimination still goes on. It's an unattractive aspect of an already fairly unattractive business; if you're not one of the networks' chosen people, it can get extremely cold outside. Of the more than ten thousand members of the Writers Guild, 72 percent are generally unemployed. The list is not only white, it's also short.

A great aid in the writing of the series was our incessant research. Almost from day one, we began talking to doctors all over the country who had had medical experience in Korea, or the Vietnam version of it, people who had dealt with trauma surgery—surgeons, nurses, chopper pilots, former patients. Our stacks of big, black three-ring binders grew daily.

At the end of the second season, Gene and I spent a week in South Korea, visiting what had served in the war as a U.S. Army Mobile Hospital. No longer mobile, its designation was the 8055th, the real-life model for Hornberger's fictional 4077th. Billeted with the medical personnel, which included a Korean orderly whose length of service went back to Hornberger's days, we returned home with some twenty-two hours of taped conversations that were to prove enormously helpful, giving the series a deeper, even more solid foundation.

It was to prove somewhat difficult to keep up the show's quotient of comedy after seeing the real thing firsthand. South Korea is not a movie. It's not a series. It's a hard place, still not fully recovered from two very hard experiences: its war and warlike truce with North Korea and its invasion and occupation by the Japanese in World War II. We saw people who were hurt over there, people whose bodies had been insulted and maimed and whose blood did not come out of a makeup bottle. These were not battle victims, but victims of the war no less—Koreans, including children, who scoured the countryside for brass shell casings, stepping on land mines planted twenty years earlier. We saw one pathetic young man in a hospital bed for whom the price of brass was all four of his limbs.

Sometimes our research resulted in a page or two of dialogue or the premise for a whole show; sometimes a speech, or a word or two. I gave a line to the Father Mulcahy character that had been on the books, so to speak, buried in all our research for four years, finally finding the ideal place for an actual quotation that always struck me as a better line than any writer could ever dream up. In the last episode of the fourth year, we used the services of a professional war correspondent, Clete Roberts, whom we had interview our characters on-camera regarding their feelings about the war.

When asked whether or not the experience changed him, Father Mulcahy's response was, word for word, what one of our real-life interviewees had told us: "When the doctors cut into a patient— and it gets very cold here, you know—steam rises from the body, and the doctor will warm himself over the open wound. Could anyone look on that and not be changed?"

This episode, "The Interview," was, to me, the most satisfying of them all, the final product a combination of improvisation and prepared material. Unlike any episode we—or anyone in TV—had ever attempted, we did it largely by ear. Normally, you would dare not try this on a three-day shooting schedule. It is doubtful a network show would be allowed to do it at all. There was every chance that we'd fall on our collective faces trying to pull it off. That, of course, made the challenge irresistible.

The anxiety about the unknown, the untried, created its own kind of productive energy. The show, inspired by a real documentary, a Christmas trip to the Korean theater of war by CBS's Edward R. Murrow, had no real script, no plot whatsoever. The entire episode consisted of cross-cutting partially ad-libbed interviews with our actors discussing their participation in the war from the standpoint of the characters that they portrayed.

Several weeks before filming began, each actor was given a prepared list of twenty questions: What do you think about the war? What do you miss the most being so far from home? Do you see any good coming out of all this? That sort of thing. Each responded on audiotape. Using their transcribed answers, I embellished some of the responses, added some humor where it seemed appropriate, and enlarged upon the feelings that the cast had articulated. I also gave the interviewer, Clete Roberts, some additional questions to ask the actors once they were on camera together, questions they would be hearing for the first time so that their replies would be honestly spontaneous. Finally, I asked Roberts to spring some questions on them that none of us had thought of, so that even I, as director of the episode, would not know what was coming as the actors were forced to respond extemporaneously. I filmed the cast members in separate blocks of time; each had his own sitting, so to speak. I shot Alan for half a day, then Mike Farrell, then Larry Linville, and so on, right down the line.

The actors never saw one another during the entire process. They might have been out of one another's sight, but they were not far from one another's thoughts. When Harry Morgan, as Colonel Sherman Potter, revealed to the camera, as it came ever closer to him, "I've never worked with a finer bunch of people in my life," that was Harry talking about Alan and Mike, and all the others, his sentiments coming at us directly from his heart.

CBS was not able to see the script until after we put together our edited footage a few days before the show was to go on the air. That's because there was no script, per se. What we finally put together was a transcript of the words that remained on the final cut of film. It was a first for any series. I'm sure it was a last, as well. I do not believe there has been a similar situation since, in which a network does not see a script for an episode until after that episode has been filmed and edited. It took a great deal of faith on CBS's part to let a show go out over the air whose scripted content they had not approved in advance. Their chief concern was our insistence that the episode be broadcast in nonglorious black and white, instead of the usual Technicolor, so that it would have a grainy, gritty, TV documentary look. The worries of the network people-in-charge-of-worrying were allayed by Burt Metcalfe doing a written voice-over advisory at the beginning of the show stating that the following program would be seen in black and white, thus assuring America that it had not suddenly gone color-blind.

"The Interview" was the last of the half-dozen episodes that I directed, encouraged to try my hand at doing so by Gene. Gene, of course, directed a great many episodes beyond the pilot and was responsible for the selection of other directors. As with his casting choices, he was invariably on the money. His reliance on Jackie Cooper and Hy Averback to direct many of the formative episodes had a lot to do with establishing the quality and standard of the series. (There being zero degrees of separation in my professional life, Hy and I met when he was the announcer on the Jack Paar radio show and then we spent four more working years together when we served in the same capacity for Bob Hope. To add to the symmetry, Hy and I roomed together on the Hope junket to Korea.)

I didn't dare direct at all until the second year, I was so in awe of the process. By that time I realized that there just wasn't any way the cast or the crew was going to let me do anything stupid. I remember once wanting Alan to do another take on one of his speeches and struggling for a diplomatic, creative way to give him direction, and not being able to find the right words.

Alan cut right to the chase. "You mean you want me to do it better?" he asked.

"Exactly," I said. "Please do it better."

All you have to do to be a good actor's director is not try to direct good actors at all. Just point the camera at them and get out of their way.

Gene was, as always, generous with his time and experience, advising me on staging, editing, where to put the camera, or not. Directing offers writers a marvelous opportunity to realize their scripts. Any number of things happen when material is being filmed upon which you can capitalize. I knew, however, that I was needed far more at my desk than I was behind the camera, where half the time I said "Cut" before it started to roll, and "Action" when I wanted it to stop. As much as I enjoyed playing director, doing six was enough for me. There were a whole lot of other people who could do it much better—but no one else who enjoyed a better relationship with the cast, a cast that always made it seem as though we had all gotten together to make a home movie.

There was no way that any of our actors would allow any director to cause them to be unfaithful to the characters they portrayed. While they obviously never truly became these characters, a good many of the roles began to take on the attributes of those who played them.

Over a period of time, I began taking aspects of their own personalities, their professional, as well as personal, strengths and weaknesses, and folded the various bits and pieces into their characters. In time, the lines between who they were and who they were pretending to be began to blur, and each was able to behave ever more naturally before the camera, without the need to wholly act; but then, the best actors never ever let you catch them acting.

We always considered how much we could get from each of the characters, what else there was besides being heroic, or foolish, or in any way predictable. How would Frank Burns, the resident pest, for instance, act if he tried to buddy up to Hawkeye? How would Hawkeye react if he came upon easygoing Trapper John in the act of trying to murder a patient? (For the record, neither Frank Burns nor Trapper John succeeded.) It was not as though we had a checklist, but there is a kind of comfortable, too-comfortable rhythm in creating for the same people when you're grinding out a series. The fear of doing it by the numbers created a restlessness and a curiosity about finding new and surprising avenues of human behavior that we never explored before.

Certainly there was no precedent for the last episode of our third season, in which the character of Colonel Henry Blake died. Naturally, CBS did not want us to "kill" the Henry Blake character, played by McLean Stevenson. They were most upset about that, and so was sentimental, dear old Twentieth Century–Fox. Killing a character in a half-hour show had never been done before. That was all the reason Gene and I needed to know we would have to do it.

*M*A*S*H* was a fast track for actors. It was a highly skilled group, but the late McLean Stevenson, who played Henry, was not an actor in the classical sense. He was a personality, and a terrific one, to be sure. Although he had done a lot of work in television and appeared in a good many commercials, I don't think he ever felt completely comfortable working with experienced actors, which is not to say that he didn't do a marvelous job. I think that after three years as a costar, he felt the series had done a marvelous job for him, too—that it had served as a showcase for his talents and he would move on, get his own writers, producers, and directors, and do for himself what we had all done for one another. *M*A*S*H*, however, was a once-in-a-career confluence of collaborators, an experience not likely to be repeated simply because you hoped it would. Though Mac was under contract to the series for five years, the consensus was that it was in everyone's best interest to let him leave after the first three. An unhappy actor in a group effort becomes a tremendous emotional burden for all concerned. It was hard enough cranking out show after show even when we were happy. (Perry Lafferty, one of the good guys among the executives at CBS—the best one, in fact—has said that whenever he looked at me in those days, he thought I was on the brink of death. Now, all I can remember is what a great time I had; that's the upside of masochism.)

We resolved that instead of doing an episode in which yet another actor leaves yet another series, we would try to have Mac/Henry's departure make a point, one that was consistent with the series's attitude regarding the wastefulness of war; we would have that character die as a result of the conflict. After three years of showing faceless bit players and extras portraying dying or dead servicemen, here was an opportunity to have a character die that our audience knew and loved, one whose death would mean something to them.

Gene and I worked out a story entitled "Abyssinia, Henry"—"Abyssinia" being a twenties expression, meaning "I'll be seeing you." The phrase struck us as very breezy, very Henry Blake–ish. We asked two writers, a pair of *M*A*S*H* stalwarts, Everett Greenbaum and his partner, Jim Fritzell, to write the episode. We distributed the finished script to the cast and various production departments, but removed the last page, which called for Radar to enter the O.R. and read a Defense Department communiqué that informs everyone that Henry Blake, who had been discharged and was flying back to his family in the States, had gone down in the Sea of Japan. "There weren't no survivors," he concludes.

I kept that one last page under wraps, locking it in my desk drawer. The only cast member let in on the secret was Alan Alda, by then clearly the star of the series. We planned the production schedule for this episode so that the O.R. scene would be the last one shot. There were, in fact, two O.R. sequences in that show: one at the top of the show, in which Henry is informed by Radar that he, Henry, is going home, that he has received his discharge orders, whereupon everyone in the room breaks into raucous song; the second, of course, was the final scene in which Radar enters to read the communiqué announcing Henry's death. After we shot the first scene, the one in which Henry gets the good news, the cast and crew, understandably, began to wrap, pulling the plug on the episode and for that matter, the whole season.

There were a great many visitors on the set: spectators, press, family, friends, easily a couple of hundred people. We asked every-one to wait a few minutes before joining us in the traditional wrap party, that we had one more piece of business to finish. I had a couple of words privately with Billy Jurgensen, our cinematogra-pher, told him what was up, and asked him to position his camera for the one additional scene. I did not want to rehearse it; we would shoot it only once. Then, Gene and I took the cast aside and I opened a manila envelope that contained the one-page last scene, telling them I had something I wanted to show them.

"I don't want to see it!" Gary Burghoff exploded. "I know you! You've got pictures of dead babies in there!"

Assuring him I didn't, I gave each a copy of the scene to read to themselves. Each had a different reaction.

"Fucking brilliant," said Larry Linville.

"You son of a bitch," Gary said to McLean. "You'll probably get an Emmy out of this!"

Mac, who had stayed to watch the filming of what he knew was his last *M*A*S*H*, was speechless. But that doesn't begin to say it.

We returned to the set. For once I said "Action" instead of "Cut." We began to shoot the scene. Gary was unbelievably touching as he entered the busy O.R. and read the message to all the doctors and nurses. Extras in the scene, performers who had been with the series since day one, reacted with a kind of heartfelt sincerity that was stunning—their performance based on their real surprise and lingering shock, their awareness of how much Mac meant to them. The crew, hearing of Henry's death for the first time as the cameras were rolling, stuck to their chores; they did all one could ask of them.

Unhappily, there was some sort of technical glitch. Either the boom mike or a light or whatever could go wrong did (because in filming, whatever can, does), and we had to shoot it again. I was heartsick. Gary would never be able to do a second take as beautifully as he did the first. I still knew nothing about directing. He was better. And on the second go, a totally unexpected thing happened. After Gary finished reading his message, there was a hushed silence on the set as B.J.'s camera panned the stricken faces of the cast (still genuinely shaken by the context of the scene), and then someone off-camera accidentally let a surgical instrument drop to the floor. It was perfect, that clattering, hollow sound, filling a palpable void in a way that no words could. I could not have planned it better; I wish I had—whenever I happen to hear it again, I marvel at how perfectly it fit. Mac left the stage without a word to anyone. He couldn't stay for the wrap party. The scene destroyed him. I learned later that he sat in his dressing room crying for hours.

I donated to the Smithsonian all the letters we received after the final Henry Blake episode was aired. There were hundreds of them, mainly from viewers who were irate over the way we dealt with the death of the character. Many of them accused us of hurting their feelings needlessly. These were people who thought of the series as simply a comedy, and as such, no place to be asked to face the subject of a character's—and, by extension, their own—mortality. Gene and I responded to each letter with individually handwritten responses of our own. In replying in this personal and time-consuming way, we hoped to convey the seriousness of our intentions and the responsibility we felt toward our viewers, even those who disagreed with the choice we had made. We explained that having Henry die was not a show-business decision; we were not punishing an actor for leaving the series. We were trying to make his departure one that would be apt, as well as memorable. Last, we reminded our correspondents that the same week "Abyssinia, Henry" was shown, a planeload of Vietnamese children perished in a horrible plane crash while taking off in Saigon. These children were being evacuated to the United States in advance of the imminent Viet Cong takeover of South Vietnam. I remarked in my letters, without irony, that I hoped as many people wrote protesting the deaths of these innocents as took the time to write protesting the death of Henry Blake.

~~~~

Finally, so that we can play "Taps" over this backward glance at the series, how to explain its popularity over all the years? Let's start with the cast: a group of most attractive women and men—not just in the physical sense, but in the way that they behaved. And when they didn't behave all that well, they were never permitted to get away with it. You couldn't be foolish or pompous or arrogant at the 4077th without someone commenting on it or making you pay for whatever harm you caused to the system or the senses. Our characters were heroic at a time when America was woefully short of heroes. The then current, real-life war in Vietnam was terribly divisive. The people of the Four-O-Double-Seven were able to articulate many of the sentiments that the increasingly antiwar public felt about being trapped in a place and a situation from which they could not honorably extricate themselves. We tried to make our characters act in a benevolent way under the most malevolent of conditions, something we'd all like to be able to do. We never stopped trying to improve the writing, always striving to give the cast members material they could get their teeth into, instead of using actors just to charm the camera. The camera, too, I believe, is another reason for the series's long life. We used only one, as noted, contrary to the three or more that most half-hour shows use to shoot their episodes. They, however, use tape. We, in the manner of a feature movie, used film. This difference permitted our actors to work in an entirely different, far more intimate style. The *M*A*S*H* cast was able to relate to a lens just a few feet or sometimes inches from them, not to an audience of several hundred people seated before them in bleachers, to which they would have had to project their lines and attitudes in an exaggeratedly theatrical, bigger-than-life fashion. They were able to remain completely cinematic in their technique. Their voices never had to be raised in order to reach the back row of the audience; a small, simple facial gesture aimed directly at the camera could become more telling than the proverbial thousand words (even if it took me two thousand to convey the same thought).

When you are involved in a series, you are involved twelve months of the year. You are forever running somewhere, thinking you should really be going somewhere else. It doesn't stop when you get home. Your family thinks that's you, carving the Sunday roast. Instead, that's a totally preoccupied series person figuring how to trim another two minutes out of a show that he thinks is perfect (and stands a far better chance of being perfect if two minutes come out of it). All of your energies are channeled into finishing an episode, making it as good as what you have defined as the best you can do. The fact that an audience is going to see it is almost secondary. You forget that someone will actually be sitting in front of a set one night and watching. All you want to do—all your exposed nerve ends, held together with bicycle tape, care about— is to be able to know that that one's in the can and you can get on with wrapping up the next.

I have not seen any wars averted because of *M*A*S*H*'s success or what we tried to say. One young man wrote us, "God, I love your show. I can't wait to join the Army." So much for our message. I don't know what lasting positive effect the show has had. Whoever said television is bubble gum for the eyes was right. I have watched terribly moving material on the box—sensitive dramas, assassinations, children starving by the nationful—and the next thing I know, someone is trying to sell me a frozen chicken. Sad to say, though, it may be that the series is better remembered than the costly war that inspired it. Invited to speak before a veterans' association, I tried to redress this imbalance.

In 1990, *The New York Times* pointed out that "to date, *M*A*S*H* has been the only memorial to those Americans who served in Korea. Happily, that situation is soon to be remedied."

Proud as we were of our efforts on the series, we never quarreled with the premise that those men and women who, in real life, faced real death, deserve to be part of the national memory in a manner that doesn't have to stop for commercials, one that doesn't obscure the enormity of their sacrifices with a laugh track.

The series was antiwar. That was our intention from the beginning. But we were not anti the more than thirty-three-thousand U.S. troops killed above and below the Thirty-eighth Parallel or the more than one hundred thousand who were wounded or the five thousand one hundred and seventy-eight captured or missing in action. They, all of them, not as statistics, but as human beings, were surely antiwar as well, and for far better and immediate reasons than those of us who fought the Korean conflict once a week in prime time, twenty years after it ended.

We are in their debt forever and proud that the series helped to act as a memorial for them until the real thing finally came along.

If I have sounded too self-congratulatory a note (or perhaps an aria) in all that I have written about this series, it is, I suppose, because being part of the enterprise remains such a prideful experience for me. I am amazed to find it still running in syndication. For my part, I finally learned to stop looking at reruns. I discovered that episodes I once thought were wonderful were perhaps not all that wonderful at all, while episodes I thought were failures had at least a scene or two that redeemed them. The worst aspect of watching reruns is compulsively, mentally rewriting the material, trying to write better lines to rush over to Stage 9 to make changes in an episode that was irreversibly imprinted on film twenty-five years ago.

On the eve of the series's last telecast—ten years and 251 episodes after the pilot, and just one week after all of the show's exterior sets in Malibu Canyon mysteriously caught fire and burned to the ground—the *New York Times* Sunday Arts & Leisure section asked me to provide them with a hail-and-farewell to the 4077th. I took a jeep ride down Memory Lane and wrote the following valedictory. The *Times* generously, but somewhat inaccurately, described me as the creator of the series. A more precise attribution would have included Dr. Hornberger, Ring Lardner, Jr., Robert Altman, and, most certainly, Gene Reynolds. My own credit, which appears on-screen at the end of each episode, is the correct one. It reads: "Developed for TV by Larry Gelbart." I did not create, I developed the series. I worked from elements in the original novel and the subsequent screenplay it inspired, molding them into the half-hour form. I have always found it clumsy to refer to myself as the developer—it makes me sound as though I am someone who will have your snapshots ready in an hour. Being referred to as "the creator" really makes me uncomfortable. There has to be some limit to ego.

At any rate, whatever I did, whoever I am, I did write the following piece.

The piece, which ran on February 27, 1983, was nonetheless headlined "ITS CREATOR SAYS 'HAIL AND FAREWELL' TO *M*A*S*H,*" and the byline read: "Larry Gelbart is the creator of the *M*A*S*H* television series and was co-producer for its first four years on the air."

Here, at some risk of repetition but with new details added (and slightly edited), is Gelbart's farewell. It is characteristic of its author, good-tempered, with the same slight "needling" quality he described as his mother's, funny, serious, bordering on eloquence which he fights off with humor. —Ed.

Tomorrow night at eight, *M*A*S*H* leaves prime-time television after presenting 251 episodes dealing with life—and death—in the

4077th Mobile Army Surgical Hospital during the Korean War; the two-and-a-half-hour special depicts the final days of that war and their effect on the characters portrayed by Alan Alda, Mike Farrell, Henry Morgan, Loretta Swit, David Ogden Stiers, Jamie Farr, and William Christopher—actors who have spent more time in our living rooms than some of our own relatives.

It is not true that the series ran longer than the actual conflict. The real war was not on for only a half hour once a week, and real combat rarely stops for commercials. My own involvement ended after the first ninety-seven episodes, at which point I had to have the pencil in my hand surgically removed.

Over the course of its run, $M*A*S*H$ was undoubtedly for some viewers simply a traditional service comedy with the usual mixture of gripes about army housing, clothing, food, and life by the numbers; all the red tape generated by the green machine. And, of course, there were the insults: Radar's height, or the lack of it; Klinger's nose, the sheer length of it; Frank's ferret face; Henry's gift for ineptitude. All stock comedy. And, for those who had no interest whatsoever in the political or philosophical content of the series, reason enough to tune in.

But on a more serious level, $M*A*S*H$ always tried to get the viewer involved—right from the opening credits, underscored by Johnny Mandel's haunting "Suicide Is Painless," with the airborne wounded being transported on choppers (which, to this day, still appear to me to be flying backward), to the nurses running to their stations, their faces etched with determination. We always wanted the viewer to care as much as those nurses did.

Indeed, whether any particular episode, scene, or line took the high road or the low, or tried sometimes to combine both, the show always adhered, without any conscious reference, to the words of the director Rouben Mamoulian: "We must affirm and insist that the ultimate goal of a film, no matter what subject matter it deals with, is to add to the beauty and goodness of life, to the dignity of human beings and to our faith in a better future."

War is hell. So is TV. $M*A*S*H$ and the medium were made for each other. Although turning out a mini-movie on a three-day shooting schedule for ten and a half years, battling compromise and complacency all the way, is not, of course, in any sense as dangerous or serious as risking one's life in combat, the pressures of making the series gave those of us responsible for it something of the sense of madness, the feelings of frustration and fatigue shared by the surgeons and nurses of the 4077th.

Stage 9 at Twentieth Century–Fox is a wonderful place to visit if you need a crash course in claustrophobia. Tiny and cramped, it was built when the movies were young, actors much smaller, and people apparently didn't breathe as much as they do now. (Gene Reynolds, *M*A*S*H*'s original producer, as a child once worked on a film on Stage 9 with Shirley Temple. Gene was a child actor, not a child producer.) Stage 9 is a miserable place to have to report for work for more than a decade, therefore the perfect environment for the *M*A*S*H* cast to convey, through their characters, just how miserable they actually felt.

On the plus side, Stage 9, jammed as it was with sets, props, and people, had very little room for ego. We had to send out for praise. And, mercifully, there were occasional trips to the Fox ranch in Malibu Canyon where we shot the exteriors that allowed us to let some light and air into the series. But mornings at the ranch could be bitterly cold; high noon, blistering hot and dusty. Nature is not interested in film schedules. It was a matter of life intimidating art.

While the cast and crew fought the elements (to say nothing of the lice and rats all around Stage 9, despite a large sign that read: "Positively No Visitors"), Gene and I fought two of life's most unnatural forces, the network and the studio, for the right to deal with bolder, more serious subjects than they were inclined to allow. In the early seventies, the effects of violence, pro- and antiwar attitudes, adultery, amputation, derangement, impotence, homosexuality, transvestism, and interracial marriage were not considered fit subjects for the home screen.

Most of these battles we won. As our ratings climbed, corporate resistance fell. But before the ratings came the rantings. Gene and I argued, cajoled, behaved like statesmen or stubborn mules, whatever it took to convince "them"—the network brass—that we had to push back or erase boundaries that held in other half-hour series. . . .

For me, the least satisfying episodes were the ones that employed techniques we knew would work, as opposed to those in which we took risks. What we wound up with is, I believe, anything but what *M*A*S*H* was frequently labeled: a sitcom. Of course, we went for laughs. We constantly strove to be funny. Hippocrates himself gave us the prescription when he wrote, "The doctor must have at his command a ready wit, as dourness is repulsive both to the healthy and to the sick."

But we were not afraid to play it "straight," to sacrifice laughter when it seemed appropriate. There was always a conscious effort to give the audience either a laugh or a lump in the throat, to create a form of emotional whiplash wherein you freeze the smile on someone's lips. Indeed, from time to time, we tried to upset the viewer. (The British playwright John Osborne, once accused by a member of the audience at one of his works of going too far, said he only knew he had succeeded whenever he was told he'd gone too far.)

Whatever its label, the television series could be enjoyed on several levels. Some viewers shared its outrage at those who think life and dignity are expendable in the name of patriotism or ideological superiority. Some subscribed to the series's notion that people are basically decent and well-meaning, yet somehow never completely in charge of their destiny. These viewers could think while watching *M*A*S*H*, they could even feel—a rare experience for members of the television audience.

It is estimated that the vast store of *M*A*S*H* episodes to be rerun in syndication will keep the series around well into the twenty-first century, long after I am gone. A nice compilation, to be sure, but I'd give anything to have it the other way around.

Thinking of the possibility of *M*A*S*H* playing so far into the future leads me to hope, paraphrasing Winston Churchill, that if America and its television audience should last a thousand years, people will say this was their finest half hour.

FIRST INTERMISSION:
THE COMEDIANS

Gelbart admits to a "ridiculous, lifelong fondness for comedians." He turns next to a few quieter reflections on the manners and modes of funny performers he has known. If at times his tone takes on the feel of the eulogy, it may be because he has been asked so often to speak for a person's life where a sudden absence has created a great void. And he does it with grace and, yes, relieving humor. Not very long ago, Gelbart sat on a dais at the Hillcrest Country Club in Los Angeles, "famous as the stamping, eating, and quipping ground for the legendary comedians and entertainers of this century: Groucho, Harpo, and Chico Marx, Al Jolson, Jack Benny, George Jessel, Danny Kaye, Eddie Cantor, and George Burns." Next to him sat Milton Berle, next to Berle, George Burns, next to Burns, Danny Thomas. It was, noted Larry, "Mount Rushmore—with cigars."

That "inner glow" he referred to is no tan. It may be something like love. —Ed.

UNCLE MILTIE

Finding himself in a new medium, one with no past at all, Milton Berle simply gave television his own.

What a stroke of luck for us all that this once unexplored and most powerful means of communication should find the one performer in all the entertainment world whose energy, dynamism, and sheer gall (the kind you can see through) would turn a television set into a good deal more than a mere piece of talking furniture.

All of his brash, ballsy years of experience in vaudeville and nightclubs, every trick he ever learned or purloined Berle brought to TV, and sure-footedly, light-fingeredly, single-handedly gave us, as viewers and future contributors to the medium, our first ideas about what television should and could be.

First, he taught us that it had to *move.* Berle had no intention of using TV as though it were only radio with a window. Berle moved. All the time. Upstage, downstage, from wing to wing. Like all well-schooled vaudevillians, he knew it is always harder to hit a moving target. Even standing still, Berle moved. He radiated action; and his incessant internal movement generated a like response.

The opening of each show was charged with energy. His on-camera entrance, different every week, never subtle, invariably crude, was kinetic, electric. The sketches, the stand-up monologues, the guest star appearances moved. So indelible was the pace the Berle show set, its sense of animation and rhythm, it is the standard for TV variety and comedy as it enters the millennium.

Before tape or film, Berle faced live studio audiences and unseen millions with the guts of a burglar. Working at Rockefeller Center, in NBC's 6B, a radio studio with matchbox proportions, on a first-year budget of $15,000 per show (that's probably less than the per-show budget for drugs on the original *Saturday Night Live*), Berle was inexhaustible. And there are a great many exhausted people who will attest to that.

Week after week after week—a TV season in those days ran thirty-nine of them a year—there was the peripatetic Berle, serenely doing the undoable—calling the camera shots, conducting the orchestra, directing the cast, remembering the script (as opposed to writing it: there were no writers that first year; it was Berle's awesome memory that supplied the material—jokes and bits of comic business he'd done before, and which he knew by heart, as well as reams of routines other people had done before— he was famous for also knowing theirs by heart).

Though his competition in the early days was nil, the biggest threat to Berle (then and now) was allowing an audience to catch its breath. Containing all of his relentless efforts to capture and keep the crowd's attention and laughter transformed a simple TV set into a pressure cooker. Berle held his early viewers in thrall as he burst into their homes with a wildness and a spontaneity that remain unmatched. He was all over the place. He ran into the audience. He ran into the cameras. Doing his famous impression of Owen McGiveney, the quick-change artist who used to play a half-dozen characters seemingly simultaneously, Berle almost ran into himself.

There was just one catch: in order to watch him, you had to buy a television set. You couldn't take your shoes off if you watched him in front of an appliance store. In a fairer world, Berle would have received a royalty on every TV set ever sold from the early forties on. It was the public's enjoyment—and the education in entertainment he offered—that helped create the demand. What Berle meant to television was far more paternal than avuncular. He was more than Uncle Miltie. He was, in fact, the medium's founding father. Our video George Washington. Actually, our Martha as well. He was, to mix a metaphor, the king of drag.

If it's true that behind every great man there is a great woman,* Berle was very often both of them. Female impersonation, as a theatrical device, predates Christ (which might explain why so many frocks were worn at the Last Supper) and was a staple on practically every Milton Berle show. Fifty-inch Z cups, high heels, blacked-out teeth, crossed eyes—you name it, it all went into the hopper, as Berle constantly wedded, without bothering to ask anyone's consent, a modern technological miracle with the kind of bits that must have caused Nero to giggle.

From the beginning Milton understood the need to weld old material to the new medium. It was too static to simply photograph a monologue, to take one long picture of a sketch. He sensed that

---

*There really was a woman. See Gelbart's tribute to Ruth (Mrs. Milton) Berle, p. 77. —Ed.

close-ups, two-shots, changes of angles were necessary for vigor and visual variety, and for directing the home audience's attention to someone delivering a line or to the reactions of one of the players to that line (frequently, both of them Berle). While his studio audience was watching the show being performed live (their vision unobstructed—Berle had the savvy to keep the bulky, view-blocking cameras off the stage and at the back of the house), the home viewers were seeing only what he wanted them to see.

Berle was no stranger to the lens. He had appeared as a child actor at the age of five in dozens of silent movies—it may have been the last time in his career he was ever silent at all—and went on to appear in almost forty more films. A performer who never stopped learning, he was, from a tender age, as aware of what people were doing behind the camera as he was about what he wanted you to see him doing in front of it.

It is ironic that for all of his exposure on the big screen, it was only on the small one that Berle assumed such heroic proportions. In motion pictures, he had to follow the script, stay in character. That was no chore for him. A highly disciplined actor, Berle has a great sense of dedication and is always respectful of the text when performing in a film or a stage play. It was in television, happily for us, that *he* was the script; that whatever character he played, whatever the situation, he was always Milton Berle, the epitome of the fast-talking, hip, flip, urban wise guy.

If Berle's impact on the public was phenomenal, consider his effect on other performers, performers frightened and/or intrigued by yet another way to reach an audience, to enhance or extend a career. It is customary for new forms to be snubbed by practitioners of the old. Yet here was one of their own, a headliner, a proven success, who was daring enough to crawl inside this strange little box every week, to act as a canary in a coal mine while learning how to master the medium in full view of millions. Berle was everybody's New Haven—and TV's first recruiting officer. One by one, other artists began to appear beside him as cautious, curious guests, and who among them didn't eventually wind up with shows of their own? How many hundreds of thousands of television entertainment hours were spun off because of their exposure to this walking, running, jumping encyclopedia of comedy craft and technique?

He was a pioneer. A brave scout. A fearless leader. Why is it we only think of the John Waynes and the Ronald Reagans as the best and *real* representatives of this country? Why is it that the West is supposed to say America to people?

To me, Milton Berle, with his eastern cheekiness, his resourcefulness, and his courage, are as American as a stage mom and apple pie.

JACK BENNY

Thirty-nine was a very good year.

Before that, Jack Benny had been thirty-everything—several times. When he was fifty-one, a number totally unacceptable to the vanity of the character he had so painstakingly constructed for his audience, Benny, in a radio sketch, gave his age to an inquiring nurse as thirty-six. And so began the longest-running lie in show business.

In the next season, being faithful to his contrived chronology, Benny became thirty-seven. Two years later, he turned—and was to remain, endlessly, shamelessly—thirty-nine. It was a good year, a great year, forever set on rewind, for two reasons: thirty-nine suited the public, fictitious Benny ego, while it revealed the perennially youthful anxiety of the private, real Jack Benny, in his desire to excel. Benny always needed, more than anything, to win our laughter and approval.

He was justly proud that he was able to do so for well over fifty years. That pride did not precede any personal pratfalls. Despite his popularity with his legion of fans (his peers idolized him as well), he remained, to the end, a kind, thoughtful human being— no small trick in a business where power corrupts, and absolute power is never enough.

It was the case of Dorian Gray in reverse. The vain, penny-pinching nickel-nurser was a pathetic mess, the offstage Jack Benny an ageless prince.

So complete was his achievement, so convincingly had he painted himself as a giant of pettiness, a miser of mythical proportions, that the world paid him the ultimate compliment of accepting the artist as his own creation. It was tantamount to believing that both of Picasso's eyes were set on the same side of his face.

Benny's broadcasting career began in 1932. It ended in 1974. He was a man for all forty-two seasons, each of which bore his stamp of excellence, each pegged to the lofty standard he set for himself and left as his legacy. By challenging the accepted comic conventions of early-thirties broadcasting, which were for the most part rooted in and carried over from vaudeville, Benny changed the nature of radio comedy altogether, making the humor far more character—and situation—oriented—which, in turn, influenced the most durable of all television forms, the sitcom (so named, one increasingly suspects, because to sit through most of them is to become comatose).

It was the Jack Benny radio program that pioneered "gang comedy," with a resident company of players, each given the license to assassinate their boss's, Jack Benny's, character, their common complaint being that he had none.

And what a gang they were. Mary Livingstone, Benny's in-life wife, his on-air girlfriend, who was forever embarrassing Jack by relating one tale or another about his cheapness or piddling behavior; Eddie "Rochester" Anderson, Benny's sandpaper-voiced "butler," to whom Benny was anything but a hero; Dennis Day, the show's tenor (which also described his IQ); Don Wilson, the program's jovial announcer (Benny's was one of the first radio shows to inject comedy into its commercials); and Phil Harris, Benny's high-living bandleader. The material prepared for them by the writing staff was mercilessly critical of their star—and what listener did not enjoy hearing the fantasy of ridiculing the boss played out without being fired for it?—a star who was shrewdly willing to play straight man in a company of straight men. Their barbs drew howls, never blood. This was a gentler time and these were gentle folk, allowed to ply their playful trade long before broadcasting had to warn viewers about degrees of unacceptabilities that are about to come their way (along airways that belong to the viewers). Let it be noted that the most often uttered four-letter word on the Jack Benny show was *Well!*

Benny's grandest and most enduring invention was, without doubt, Benny himself. Born in Chicago in 1894, on Valentine's Day (right from the beginning, he showed a flair for timing), he was giving violin concerts and being hailed as a prodigy at the age of eight. Benny, through diligence and application, rapidly went downhill from that early age to become a consummate musical failure, the horrible violinist's horrible violinist. Happily, the man himself became a Stradivarius. While he honed his craft for years as a stage comedian, it was in radio that, as his own best instrument, he went beyond potential to perfection. He picked up instinctively, knew in his marrow, as did Edward R. Murrow, the intimate nature of broadcasting, knew that the microphone was not just a piece of mechanical equipment, but that the microphone was the listener's ear.

Acting upon that perception, he brought to the air the performing style he had developed earlier, working before theater audiences. While he put the maximum effort into preparing for a performance, during the course of that performance he was a minimalist. If most funny men worked with a broadsword, Benny needed only a hat pin. If most needed a dozen or more words to get a laugh, Benny could earn one with only three or four, the difference being made up by the audience's understanding of his attitude in any given situation. And often those few words would be replaced by a mere look, a look that said it all.

His great and good friend, his co-legend George Burns, called Benny a "quiet laugh riot." Benny could, in fact, be funny being totally quiet, absolutely mum, as he demonstrated during the most celebrated radio passage of his career, in that memorable, seemingly endless wait, while he very carefully thought over his response to a stickup man who demanded Benny's money or his life. What other comedian before—or since—was ever able to use silence as a punch line? Before Jack Benny, who would have believed anyone could succeed as a mime on radio?

What courage he displayed as a performer, what supreme confidence not only on that occasion, but time after time, waiting until what often seemed a moment after the last possible moment before he would come in with his line. It's not that he was working without a net, but rather that his net was maybe a sixteenth of an inch from the ground—and Benny knew to the millisecond just how long he could wait before he delivered the payoff.

George had Gracie, but Jack had grace.

And elegance. If Bob Hope's machine-gun-like delivery made him a Cagney of comedy, than Benny was its Astaire, and like Astaire, Benny was able to make his exquisite expertise seem entirely effortless, despite the fact that he was a world-class worrier, a sure sign of someone who knows that others expect the best of him.

Above all, he exuded an incredible sweetness. Many comedians exhibit this quality, but who among them, other than Benny, portrayed themselves so relentlessly as tightfisted, selfish peacocks and still won our affection? And never, not once in his career, did he ever drop the pose, or offer an apology or disclaimer, never stooped to telethonic sentimentality to pander for some approval of the decent man behind his character's petty persona.

On March 29, 1932, on Ed Sullivan's celebrity radio show, his first significant broadcasting appearance, Benny began his routine by saying, "Ladies and gentlemen, this is Jack Benny talking. There will be a slight pause, while you say, 'Who cares?' "

Happily, just about everyone finally did:

• Everyone who ever heard him on his radio program make change for a guest star visiting the mythical Benny house who wanted to make a call on Jack's pay phone, located right next to the cigarette vending machine in the Benny living room.
• Everyone who ever watched him stare into a TV camera with that incomparable put-on of a put-upon face, that look of pained innocence, the expression of a calf who has just found out where veal comes from.

How could anyone not care for a man who was a walking inventory of all of our failings and foolishness, who spent a lifetime holding up a mirror in which he substituted his image for ours to show us our shared pretensions and shortcomings and, in making us laugh at his all-too-human frailties, allowed us to forgive them in ourselves?

On December 26, 1974, eighty years after he was born, Jack Benny passed away at the age of thirty-nine.

The good, indeed, do die young.

BOB HOPE

I see where General Eisenhower has decided to run for president. Boy, what some guys will do to get out of the army.

—written for a Hope monologue, 1952

Time always has the final cut. As capricious as it can be cruel, time, moving from one moment to the next of its own creation, determines with supreme indifference who in life will be bent and bowed; which of us will retain the ability to walk and who will need a walker; who will remember and who will have no idea what it is that they've forgotten.

Time, for nine decades, was very kind to Bob Hope. In truth, it was downright lavish. After successful careers in vaudeville as a hoofer and a monologuist and as a musical comedy performer on the Broadway stage, Bob Hope became what fully half the world wants to become: one of the movie stars that the other half of the world buys tickets to see. Mine was the generation that waited breathlessly to catch the next Hope and Crosby "Road" picture. How we ate up their smooth, improvlike antics in those blissfully innocent days—when we thought that it was only golf balls that Bing drove, instead of driving his family to drink and, sadly, to suicide. Whether they were headed for Morocco or Bali, wherever the road or the gags led them, Bing was always Bing, no matter if he was called "Chuck," or "Scat," or "Duke," and we could always be certain that Bing would get the girl in the last reel instead of Bob, who would always be Bob, even if he was called "Ace," or "Chester," or "Fearless Frazier," and that Bob would always be ready, willing, but seldom able—except for his effortless timing and masterful clowning, which he put at the service of his bravery without heroics, his cowardice without apologies.

And in a parallel career, he became one of the kings of radio royalty. It's no coincidence that Bob Hope's name consists of two verbs. Generating incredible bursts of brio, he made the family Philco crackle once a week with his staccato, snappy delivery. As a kid, I'd put my high school homework aside on Tuesday nights to listen in wonderment to the Hope show, not knowing that in a few short years, at twenty, I would be writing for him—that my next homework would *be* the Hope show.

Joining him in the fall of 1948, I was one of a staff of six. For Hope this was almost a skeleton crew; in previous years, he had employed up to a dozen or so writers, all working at the same time turning out his material. Hope, knowing full well which side his career was buttered on, paid his writers well and treated them respectfully.

Every Hope broadcast followed the same pattern: an opening monologue—it was the "mono" to Hope, never the monologue, and never distributed as part of the show script. Only in Hope's copy did the treasured material reside. The jokes we wrote were rotated much as a farmer's crop is. Tax jokes at tax time ("I always like to go to Washington, D.C. It gives me a chance to visit my money"), the annual opening of Santa Anita racetrack ("I don't want to say that my horse was slow, but you could bet him to Win, Place, or Live"), Academy Awards jokes, smog jokes, the world was our straight-line. Crosby jokes were always in season ("Bing had a bad accident the other day. He fell off his wallet").

The monologue was linked to a few minutes of chat with the program's regulars (in my day, singer Doris Day, announcer Hy Averback, comedian Jerry Colonna, bandleader Les Brown), followed by an exchange with the week's guest star, and finally, an extended sketch that would include the whole company.

But what it mostly was, as noted, was jokes, jokes, jokes.

There is no distinctive kind of Bob Hope joke. There is a certain Hope style when he's coming on to a woman, or when he is in an awkward situation (often one and the same), and there is an unmistakable brashness in his delivery, but there is no typical Hope material beyond a good, sharp one-liner, sharp but rarely barbed. So much of Hope's success is that whether his target was a president or a peer, he was always nonthreatening.

His writers, like so many sport-jacketed cobblers working at their benches, continually fashioned Hope's material for his radio shows, his personal appearances, and his movies, peppering screenplays written by others with countless additional lines for whatever character Hope was playing, with, sad to say, little or no regard for the context of the script, or his fellow performers, or even the wishes of the director of the picture. We were only following Bob's instructions: make him as funny as possible, as often as possible. Had Hope talked in his sleep, I'm sure we would have been called on to provide him with material for that purpose as well.

The most exciting thing about working for him was his unfailing ability to provide everyone in his orbit with the element of surprise. For openers, he was not Bob Hope at all. Arguably the most American of America's comedians, Bob was born in England, coming into this world as Leslie Townes Hope. The other surprise was that, with Hope, you literally didn't know from one day to the next which corner of the planet you were going to be hurled to, with only moments to unpack your bags before you began banging out a monologue filled with topical references.

Telephoning you at home, at almost any hour of the day or night, was a favorite pastime of his. Conducting what seemed like a routine conversation, Hope would suddenly inform you that you were about to join him on a monthlong tour across the country, or that you'd better check to make sure your passport was valid because he was expecting you to accompany him on a trip to entertain the military personnel on duty with the Berlin airlift—or that you'd be spending Christmas in the midst of the war in Korea by way of Alaska and Okinawa, pausing to attend a lunch in Tokyo as the guests of General and Mrs. MacArthur.

Traveling with Hope almost nonstop for four years provided me with the invaluable experience of being able to turn out pages in all sorts of places: on planes, sometimes commercial, sometimes cargo, quite often military; in train compartments or on ships' deck chairs; in bouncing jeeps and kamikaze taxis, in elevators and dressing rooms, in Quonset huts and rest rooms.

It was in 1950 that Hope invited his writers to take a trip with him to a place that seemed the most foreign—and without question the most mysterious of all—television.

When vaudeville died, television was the box they put it in.
—written for a Hope monologue, circa 1949

Bob had agreed to stick his head into this voracious new medium, to make his national debut on TV with a one-hour Easter Sunday revue—they were called "specials" in those days—to be aired on NBC on April 9, 1950.

He was smart enough to hire a group of people who were already television veterans even at that early date: Max Liebman and his staff and crew. Liebman gave everyone from his regularly scheduled *Your Show of Shows* the week off, including stars Sid Caesar and Imogene Coca, but held on to the services of Carl Reiner. (Checking into my life forty-eight years ago, Carl has yet to give up his room.) For his guest stars, Hope hired the comedienne Bea Lillie, actor Douglas Fairbanks, Jr., and singer Dinah Shore. The form we chose, naturally, was the revue. In terms of freshness the writing team came up empty, writing more a static radio show with cameras aimed at it rather than tapping into the potential of an exciting new medium. The humor, and it is an act of more imagination than the script contained to call it that, was almost entirely verbal. It was as though we were trying to make words *look* funny. Without any Broadway or stage experience, we couldn't write a theatrical sketch to save our lives—or Hope's either. We put him into silly costumes, surrounded him with our ideas of comic props, stuffed his mouth full of one-liners, and then tried to close each routine with the biggest joke that we could think of—a pratfall, a gunshot, or anything noisy. Truly prehistoric TV.

Reviewing the effort, *Variety* wrote: "[Hope's] Easter Day program was an object lesson in how lack of good material can thwart the best of intentions."

That was my first foray into television, my trial by misfire.

Once he overcame his writers' stage fright, once he began combining the skills he had honed in his early days with a know-how about the camera that no lens could keep its eye off, Hope spawned a TV career with legs that a centipede would envy.

Sometimes I wake up in a cold sweat. If only I had done my homework, if only I had applied myself and concentrated on my school studies, instead of listening to Hope and Benny and Fred Allen, and all the other comic giants who lived inside my radio— my God! Think of what I'd have missed.

GEORGE BURNS

Just on the cusp of the twentieth century, 1896 was a very good year, too. That year saw the first exhibition of a revolutionary new invention, the motion picture. In 1896, the Klondike gold rush began; *The New York Times* was purchased for the grand sum of $75,000; and—on January 20 of that year—Mr. and Mrs. Louis Philip Birnbaum, of 95 Pitt Street on Manhattan's Lower East Side, brought home to their tenement flat their newest born, a son. Born to Jews forever playing catch-up with pogroms, he was the ninth of what would eventually be their family of twelve children.

The Birnbaums named the infant Nathan. And Nathan Birnbaum he was to remain until the age of ten when, with three years of performing experience already under one of his older brother's cinched-up belts, Nathan Birnbaum decided to rename himself George Burns. Already the man inside the boy knew what his calling in life was to be. His razor-sharp mind was set on his ultimate goal. He knew that "Nathan Birnbaum" would require far too many of the lightbulbs in which he expected to see his name spelled out.

There was, of course, no mention of young Nathan's birth in the young *New York Times*. If that announcement had appeared anywhere at all, it would surely have been in the yet-to-be-founded show-business bible, *Variety*—his arrival listed under "New Acts." All but congenitally predisposed to a life in the theater, nestling in the womb was, for George Burns, a form of waiting in the wings. Programmed as he was to take his place in the spotlight from the beginning, it's a wonder he didn't take a bow at his own bris.

It is a daunting assignment to try to coin any fresh praise for a legend. Where does one search for a surplus superlative or come up with some original thought on this wholly original being? This vaudevillian whose life, and whose act—if, in fact, there is any discernible difference between the two—were held over for nearly a century? This was George Burns. This man for four hundred seasons.

There is born-again—and there is born-again and again and again. Who, other than George Burns, could boast a career so unique and unpredictable that, when one phase of it played itself out, another, newer one instantly began?

He was a star in every field of entertainment in which he'd ever danced a step, croaked a tune, or gotten a laugh—sometimes accomplishing all three simultaneously. Outliving vaudeville, he nimbly moved from its center stage right onto the invisible apron of radio. As quickly as a new medium came along, George had his best suit pressed (he had no bad ones), ordered another batch of 8 × 10's, gathered up his sheet music, and hung his star on the door.

On TV, the breadth of his talent gave the small screen a surprising largeness. In movies, his distinctive style gave the big screen an unexpected intimacy.

As an author, a lecturer, a philanthropist, a star of concert halls and nightclubs, George became a major contributor to the popular entertainment and culture of American society for nearly ninety years. He was truly a legend in his own time and a half.

I'd like to be able to write that thinking of George to play the title role in *Oh, God!* was an inspiration, perhaps the result of a divine whisper in my ear. Of course, I can't dismiss the possibility. If God, the originator of the Final Cut, isn't entitled to casting approval, then who is? The truth is, the thought of George required absolutely no thought at all. He was, at once, the natural, obvious choice. Who better to play the Almighty's stand-in than a man who embodied such dignity, who himself commanded respect without ever once demanding it?

Who better to portray the Supreme Power than a man who had used his own so well? Who more plausible as a maker of miracles than a survivor of open-heart surgery in his seventy-eighth year? An Oscar winner at the age of eighty? The recipient of a Grammy award at ninety-five? Who better to play the character of the Creator, with a mixture of humility and chutzpah—who did not become wise because he got old, but got old because he was wise—than that gravel-voiced smoothie?

As we learned in the third act of his life, George meant a good deal more to us than a mere provider of laughter. Reviewing a nightclub performance of his in 1988, the critic Martin Gottfried wrote: "You come ready to laugh . . . what you're not ready for is to be touched. In George Burns you have the essence of entertaining, everything rolled into seamless, artless character, pure humor wedded to pure style. Warmed and awed by this foxy grandpa in a natty tuxedo, we want him never to leave—not just the stage—us."

George's professional idol was the vaudevillian Frank Fay, a man renowned for his quick, often scathing wit. His sharp tongue also earned him a great many enemies. Once the object of a lawsuit, Fay was warned by his lawyers to say as little as possible when he took the stand, to take care not to offend the judge or the jury.

Sworn in to give his testimony and asked to state his name, he answered, "Frank Fay."

Asked his occupation, Fay replied, "World's greatest entertainer."

Later, his lawyer, furious, asked him why he felt it necessary to answer the question in that way.

"I was under oath," said Fay.

I, too, am under oath. To write implies a contract with one's reader. Therefore, I'm compelled to say this: the graceful, seemingly effortless durability George Burns demonstrated from the turn of one century to the turn of another—all the more remarkable in a society so obsessed with the new and the novel, where people are considered over the hill almost as soon as their skin clears up, and where for too long, leader after leader, hero after hero, has fallen from grace or been cut down in mid-bloom— proves that his life was a gift to us. One that kept on giving. And giving. With a bloom that seemed eternal.

Numbers had nothing to do with it.

His accomplishments and legacy are totally secure.

Now and forever, George Burns belongs to the ageless.

Next, Larry turned his appreciation to one of the people backstage, or at the side of the star—to Mrs. Milton Berle. His heartfelt commentary on one of the women who made it all work, when it did, or stood by but not helplessly when it didn't, reveals to us the importance of the supporting role. —Ed.

RUTH

She could swear like a sailor, but she had the dignity of an admiral.

It was a dignity grounded in confidence, supported by savvy and displayed with poise and sophistication. The sum of these qualities made Ruth Berle that rarest of women: the kind who can be one of the girls, and also one of the guys.

And, in that latter role, she sacrificed not an ounce of femininity, or the near-patrician bearing that was as much a part of Ruth as were those marvelous cheekbones, or those perceptive eyes that took everything in, that viewed and reviewed each of us in her own distinctive fashion and whose expression was such a clear, outward indication of the shining intelligence that resided behind them.

That intelligence was the essence of Ruth, an intelligence that sparked her never-ending interest, her curiosity about what was happening in the world. And a passion for dealing with and trying to correct whatever wasn't.

Ruth was never content to leave bad enough alone. Hers was a curiosity that was mixed with concern.

She cared about her country. Cared enough during World War II to sacrifice the comforts of civilian life and join the WACs, the Women's Army Corps, the military; a source of enduring pride to her family, and a badge of honor for Milton, making him probably the only member of the Friars Club ever to be married to a veteran.

Ruth cared about the role and the behavior of our government. And when she didn't care *for* a particular government, she did all she could to help change it. She was a tireless campaigner. In retrospect, one wishes she had run for office herself.

She was a sports fan, and, as with everything else in her life, she didn't dabble at it. She knew the stats, the odds, and again, Ruth being Ruth, she always knew the score.

She was an avid reader, invariably halfway through the last chapter of a book whose reviews I was just reading.

A friend in need was Ruth's cue to pitch in and try to bail someone out. To help someone deal with a loss through either of the dreaded "D"s—death or divorce—Ruth was there. If you had a kid in trouble, or *you* were that kid, Ruth was there. *Really* there. She made house calls. In the middle of the night, jumping into her "Superfriend" costume—babushka and boots, a raincoat over her nightgown—she'd drive to your side, no matter how far the distance between you. She'd pull strings, she'd pull them through the night, she was there—to lend a hand or an ear or a shoulder. And not just to lend, but to give. And most often quietly, unobtrusively. Grandstand plays were for Dodger Stadium.

Ruth's personal code contained a third D-word: *discretion*. A confidence was safe with Ruth. Others would only know what you wanted them to know. You could choose to give your secret away. But not Ruth, who might be a better friend to you than you were to yourself.

She had a fierce honesty—which is probably *why* she never ran for office. Her inability to sacrifice principle for approval would never have been acceptable. If there's a punch that Ruth ever pulled, or a fool she ever suffered, lightly or otherwise, I don't think any of us was aware of the event.

There are many who feel it necessary to think, to speak, to behave in conformity, finding comfort and safety in numbers. Ruth was comfortable being Ruth. She knew her own mind. And very often yours as well. Ruth never needed a consensus. She never needed to shop for opinions. If her feelings on a subject made her a minority of one, it didn't matter. Her primary goal was never to be unpopular with herself.

For her, there was no bending in the wind. How she was was how she was. Like the best-drawn figures in life, or in fiction, she never stepped out of character. If Ruth Berle ever surprised you, you hadn't been paying attention.

The chief component of that character was the personal gyroscope she had that helped keep her on an even keel. She had the kind of radar that led, first, her mind, and then her tongue, with the sort of speed that all great wits share, that enables them to go directly to the truth.

Who else but Ruth would have responded when Milton suggested, after an exhilarating ride in a Learjet, that they should buy one of the million-dollar planes for themselves: "Don't you think we ought to paint the kitchen first?"

She could use that same sharpness to soften a hurt, to heal a wound. Some years ago, Milton opened in the starring role on Broadway in a Herb Gardner play, *The Goodbye People.* At the opening-night party that followed, the show's press agent brought in the first of the critics' reviews. It was crushing. Clive Barnes, of *The New York Times,* didn't like it. He didn't like it a lot. The show was doomed. Without missing a beat, Ruth turned to Milton and said, "Darling, is it okay if I take off my lucky dress now?"

On Broadway, the Broadway of old, the Lindy's Broadway, the euphemistic way to report the unhappy news that someone had died was to say that he or she had taken a cab. When the newspaper columnist Lee Mortimer, who had a highly publicized preference for Chinese women, died, it was Ruth who announced that Lee had taken a rickshaw.

When her time came, Ruth took a Rolls-Royce. We call it class, the British call it style. Call it what you want, Ruth had it in spades.

Remembering, I think of the years that my wife, Pat, and I shared with Ruth and Milton, that our sons Adam and Billy spent together since boyhood. That past doesn't come back in any visual sense, not as so many snapshots. It's rather a sound I hear. The sound of laughter.

Our society seems to have trouble assigning the proper role to women. That's regrettable, yet inevitable, since our society is for the most part governed by men. And men are notoriously reluctant to grant women the public power we so gladly surrender to them in private.

It's an ongoing struggle for women to achieve not only the recognition of their rights, but horror of horrors, equality as well. There was an unmistakable something about Ruth that made her seem *born* equal. Not so much a woman who had the same rights as men in terms of potential and position or of expression and aspiration, but more as a person who was equal to the best in our society.

Ruth was the officer who turned Milton into a gentleman. And into her biggest fan. He took pride in her appearance, in her commitment to causes. He quoted her endlessly, far more than he did himself—no small tribute from a comedian. He did more than share the spotlight. He gave her center stage.

Who would have thought it? Milton, with a lifelong reputation for borrowing bits and pieces from others—Milton pulled off the biggest switch of his life. He married an original.

Ruth had a low tolerance for people who went on and on. "At ease," I can hear her saying now. "At ease." Her way of saying, "Enough said. On to whatever comes next."

In the final moments of this Intermission, Mr. Gelbart finally owns up fully, if any further proof be needed, to the importance of the men and women who deliver the lines, bend them to their will, or will them to come across, who give life to what writers create.

Many writers lament the downtrodden, lonely life of the writer. Implic-

itly, Gelbart suggests that the difficult public life of their key collaborators, the performers, often makes it possible for that lonely life to be more
comfortable.   —Ed.

SEND OUT THE CLOWNS

Take my life. Please. There was a time long ago when, if I wanted
to see a comic working at his trade, I would have to go through the
trouble and expense of traveling to a nightclub, or a vaudeville
house, or a house of burlesque. I would sit through endless hours
of aerialists and acrobats, hearing brassy G-chords and ogling sassy
G-strings until the band would strike up "Fine and Dandy," and the
guy with the padded shoulders and the porkpie hat finally made his
way to center stage to tell the audience all about the funny thing
that happened to him on his way to the theater that night.

As it would affect and reshape so much of modern life, from religion to politics, from sports to the justice system to the act of creating life itself, broadcasting also changed the world of comedy. No
longer did the members of an audience have to assemble after leaving their homes to be in the presence of clowns; broadcasting delivered them to the audience—first via radio, where we found them
in our ears, then later on television, where we continually find
them in our faces. If broadcasting delivered the comedians, the comedians more than delivered for broadcasting. Were it remotely
possible to quantify such a fact, the profits, the staggering zillions
that the providers of laughter have generated for network and cable
companies, for syndicators and affiliates, would offer ample evidence of the power of the punch line to have an impact on the bottom line.

Comics, that gifted, exclusive society of professional fools, have
proved to be the most durable commodity on the box. The most
popular of western heroes have come and gone thataway. The most
famous of prime-time doctors eventually find their viewers refusing their house calls. Meanwhile, the comic is a constant. Clearly,

we need laughter more than we need a sheriff; a smile far more than surgery. With apologies to my friend Stephen Sondheim, comedy tonight is not what it's all about. Comedy is forever.

A television comedian bestows upon the viewer watching from and with all the comforts of home, where any seat is the best seat in the house, a unique gift. Comedians elevate their viewers, upgrade them to the status of royalty. We watch, as so many kings and queens, in our robes or in our underwear, as these supplicants do their shtick, each a petitioner for our approval, each our personal court jester, wanting only to please, asking only that we tell others of their skills and proficiency in the art of funniness when we assemble around our various royal water coolers, hoping we will grant them, in time, perhaps, a sitcom of their own so that they, too, might one day achieve their own tsardom. And we, who will spend billions to attend gargantuan movies with eye-boggling special effects, spend much more time simply watching an appearance by a single person, whose only special effects are language, body and face, and a distinctive point of view. (Although it should be noted that comics such as Robin Williams and Richard Pryor can, in themselves, be a cast of thousands.)

It seems the most inevitable and fortuitous of marriages: television and the practitioners of comedy. The TV monitor forms the perfect frame for the comic's face; in close-up, the scale is life size. That is not a picture of a person talking to us—it seems a real person. A real person performing on a stage in New York to someone sitting ringside in California. Or it's the other way around, or in any other possible direction, for the medium has turned the entire country into one vast comedy club.

Having a performer literally at our fingertips makes for an intimacy that allows our comics to deal with the one subject in the world that we can never get enough of. That subject is, of course, ourselves. What we look like, how we grew up, how we didn't, how we relate, how we don't, our sex lives, our sex deaths. Comics are journalists, instigative reporters. They are the self-assigned correspondents of our common experience, the cruise directors of the same boat that we're all in. They goad us with truths we would rather ignore or deny. They update us on the human and all too often inhuman condition. The stand-up spot is a soapbox, a telly pulpit, a confessional. The best comedians hold up a mirror to themselves, permitting us to see not only their reflection but also our own. They address our fears, our dreams, they examine bits and parts—the ones under our clothes, the ones under our hats. Using comedy as anesthesia allows them to deal with life's pain, its embarrassments and its frustrations. As you've learned for yourself, it isn't easy being royalty.

Not long ago, as the legendary comedy stars' contracts with life started running out, a premature wake began for the death of comedy itself. Without the age-old training grounds for American comedians—live variety shows, the Catskill Mountains, the tank towns—where was anyone ever going to get the experience and confidence to eventually get a shot on TV? Where were they going to come from? The answer, as it turned out, was from everywhere. From out of the woodwork, from out of the colleges, from amateur improv groups, from TV itself, with the various incarnations of *The Tonight Show* and *Saturday Night Live*, among others, acting as beginner slopes for the budding comic talent, the diamonds in the rough as well as the hopelessly zircon, those whose careers often turn out to be far shorter than the limos that picked them up for their trip to the studio.

The truth is comedians, in any age and in any technological environment, come from only one place. They come from themselves. What they present for our benefit is the external performance of the routines that constantly play in their heads—their view of the world and its cast of fools as formed by their childhood experiences, and their never-ending desire to capture our approval, either because we represent the world to them or because, even in our millions, we take on the aspect of a single, surrogate, hard-to-please parent.

The comics' compulsion is our gain. Their seemingly frivolous nature belies their incredible bravery. *You* try, as a novice, facing an almost faceless crowd that can turn hostile on a bon mot's notice, armed only with your wit. However many might be deterred or discouraged, others never stop filling up the four corners of our screens. We may have a choice about whether or not they have elected the right career for themselves, but they do not. They have to do what they are doing. And they will do it if tens of millions are watching, or if, after counting the house, they find that the audience, plus them, equals two. On and on, they come. On and on, the band hits their intro and they make their entrance through the curtain in a tradition predating the building of the road that the first chicken crossed; and, whether they stand before us in a suit or a dress, in a tux or in drag, they are naked. Working without a net, flying solo.

Of course, we are not talking about life and death here. A comic is not a matador. Then again, when a matador enters the ring, he is assisted in his performance against the bull by two armed picadors atop two horses, and three banderilleros wielding deadly barbs. Six men and two animals to master and subdue one beast. The comic faces his terror alone. Unaided, often blinded by the spotlight he or she is so desperate to bask in, the comic must dominate and control with no help from anyone at all, with the possible exception of an agent praying in the wings.

Wait. Perhaps we *are* talking about life and death here. Listen closely to their language. When comics talk about having a good night, they talk about how they killed the audience; how they slayed them, how they put them away. Or if they, the comics, failed, how they really died last night.

Vast amounts of resentment mingle with comedians' love for and dependence upon their audiences. The crowd is, after all, the obstacle or the gateway to the performer's success. This total reliance upon total strangers who tune in to catch your act, some of whom might possibly be just a little too high, while others might just possibly be all too low to appreciate the routine that you have worked so long and so hard to perfect, makes for an understandable and altogether maddening ambivalence.

So, next time you pass a home for old comics (you can always tell one by the rubber chicken nailed to the mailbox), pause and offer a quiet round of applause. Someone very small and gray and barely able to stand up, let alone be one, is just liable to appear in a window and tell you the funny thing that happened on the way to the home.

LOCATION SHOT 1:
LESS ANGELES

Mr. Gelbart, in addition to writing movies, plays, etc., and writing *about* movies, plays, etc., has occasionally written on places, notably in a series he undertook (he hasn't done Forest Lawn yet) for *Harper's Bazaar*, this one in March 1994.

We call these glimpses of places he's lived—or lives—Location Shots. They are part of his story, too. (We've seen his affection for London earlier.) Here, it's L.A. itself, and he hits it so hard you know that he cherishes the place. —Ed.

Last month, as I celebrated what I sincerely hope was not my last birthday, I realized that this year marks the fiftieth anniversary of my arrival in Los Angeles. As it happens, my present age (and at this point in my life any age is a present) matches precisely the number of the fabled route (66) that carried me from the Chicago of my childhood to the West Coast on which I was to pass unerringly from puberty to adultery.

Now, most American cities are afflicted with urban blahs—and worse—and Los Angeles is certainly not the only place where things have gone wrong. But for years Los Angeles was the place where people came to get away from what was wrong with all those other places. L.A. was where life, where your life, was going to shine.

Ah, but that was before L.A. lawlessness set in. Before the town hit the murder charts at number 4 (with a bullet); before we went from the brothers Marx to the brothers Menendez; before drive-in dining was replaced by drive-by dying, gang warfare having mixed L.A.'s famed mobility with murder, so that death is now delivered piping hot, right to your own front door. ("Carjack-in-the-Box? Five homicides to go—hold the fries.")

Crime is a natural by-product of racism. However much a social cancer afflicted L.A. fifty years ago, there seems to be fifty times more of it today. The attitude here is very much "I'm all white, Jack."

To fortify themselves, the privileged go to sleep (or try to) with handguns on their nightstands, steel bars on the windows, closed-circuit TV, security systems that somehow never seem to offer quite enough, and Dobermans and Alsatians—German dogs to protect their German cars. (Hitler promised the faithful that one day there would be a Volkswagen in every garage. Turns out he meant every garage in L.A., and instead of a VW there's a Mercedes or a Beamer—unless, of course, there's a Lexus or an Infiniti. The Axis powers wasted all that money investing in tanks and bombers and concentration camps. It was your *cars* we wanted, you schmucks!)

Onward and downward. What has happened to Less Angeles? When I first came to town, there was, instead of water, fresh orange juice on restaurant tables. Free. Now you pay if you want orange juice. If you're smart, you pay for water, too. These days a lot of deadly stuff is coming out of our faucets. They don't call them taps for nothing.

Those crystal-clear, perpetually Technicolor days, when it seemed that the sun had chosen L.A. as its primary residence, ended in the early fifties. To the rest of the country, smog was just a joke word in a Bob Hope monologue, but not to the residents of L.A., who were discovering that the puffy white clouds on what they thought would be a field of blue forever were being replaced by a skyful of sludge. It was an eye-opening (and watering), breath-shortening, and, for some, life-threatening experience. When L.A. is really having a bad air day, people are warned to stay indoors, and parents are urged to keep their children from going to school. We all came to L.A. to be stars; we've wound up as extras in a science-fiction movie.

Why is the sky, if not falling, most assuredly failing L.A.? Largely because two thirds of the pollutants that plague the place come from its citizens' favorite means of conveyance and, very often, conception—their cars.

On any given day, the eleven million people who live in the city of axles are filling the air with megatons of noxious fumes and traces of lead and rubber—to say nothing of ear-shattering stereos—all of it trapped by the gorgeous mountains that attracted so many of us here to begin with. While there have been some recent victories in the battle against this overhead dreck, L.A. still holds the distinction of having the worst air in the nation. There is really only one way to survive in this city: never inhale.

Why, incidentally, even a half-century later, does Los Angeles still seem a noncity to me? Why does it still feel like a municipality without a middle; a collection of fringes, all bordering the outskirts of some invisible center; suburbia without any place that it's sub to; an exurbia that isn't ex of anywhere?

And never more so than today. Angelenos view their periodic riots (Rodney King, Watts—pick one) on television with the feeling that the madness is happening someplace else altogether. From the Sunset Strip we watch the civil disturbances as though they were coming from the one in Gaza, all the looting as though it were on cable, on some Shoplifting Channel. Nobody from the smart, up-market Westside ever goes downtown—again, exactly what town is it down from anyway? It's all very disturbia.

Just as the country ends at the Pacific, so have a good many expectations. Dreams, no matter how far west you dream them, don't always come true. The once-inviting beach, seventy miles of tans and vans, where you could mingle with all the pretty people without being invited, has deteriorated miserably since I first went there half a century ago, half hoping to find Norman Maine's bathrobe at the water's edge. Go there today. See those rubber-clad surfers, those blond sandroids so symbolic of the old golden L.A.

image? Every one of them whose head hasn't yet been baked by the sun into brains Benedict has been inoculated against hepatitis, well aware that, these days, when someone wades out into the once-pristine Pacific, he's apt to be up to his waist in hospital waste.

The sea, refusing to OD on all the syringes and sewage, keeps giving people who live on the coast—on the very *edge* of the coast—an occasional reality check. Now and then it batters the shoreline, sucking a few condos and cottages loose. It's just one of the ways nature has of reminding folks that although the meek may one day inherit the earth, the earth, in turn, will inherit everything. Between tidal waves, freak floods, flash floods, brushfires, firestorms, landslides, mudslides—to say nothing of the quakes (the fear of which has me writing this sitting *under* my desk)—it's no wonder that many a house in L.A. has left home without leaving a forwarding address.

And yet, hardly anyone is deterred. In the last half-century, more and more Frank Lloyd Wrongs have built any number of houses that stand atop stilts that are poised upon precipices or jutting out over bluffs, or they've balanced them on rocks or set them deep inside inflammable, inaccessible canyons—houses whose walls, if they could talk, would say, "What the hell are we doing here?"

It takes unceasing hubris to live in L.A., given the experience and evidence that at any moment this place can either shake, slide, or burn. Or maybe do all three at the same time. None of us is forced to stay. The choice is ours. The San Andreas is nobody's fault but our own. And yet, we all go on about our lives, ignoring/denying the fact that we are living them on top of that awesome geological perforation that lies below like some great dotted line to facilitate our being detached from the rest of the continent.

Basta. Bashing L.A., and especially L.A.'s la-la-ness, is as easy as shooting duck confit in a barrel.

I will be leaving town one day, of course. Everybody finally runs out of birthdays. And I know just how I want to go.

Every now and then, when some part of L.A. is going up in smoke somewhere, no matter how far from the fire you are, your car will wind up covered with a fine layer of ash.

Well, sir, I came to L.A. by car, and that's exactly the way I want to leave. I don't mean in a hearse. When my number's up, when I finally take the Big Off-ramp, I've made arrangements to be cremated and for my ashes to be spread all over the hood of my Jag, my theory being that, while there may not be life after death, even after you're gone it is still possible to get stuck in traffic in L.A. just a couple more times—or maybe even be carjacked posthumously.

But if my wife stays true to form, I'll be going through the car wash before I ever know what hit me.

ACT TWO

TV INTO MOVIES

UNTIED STATE

My experience with the short-lived TV series *United States* taught me, among other things, that labeling entertainment offerings on television has a great deal to do with audience and network perceptions of what any particular program is all about. The notion and promotion of *United States* as a situation comedy served it very badly—in the same way that that label, applied to *M*A*S*H*, trivialized what we considered a radical departure from what was expected of the half-hour form in television. If not a sitcom, what were people to call a comedy about the effects on people of combat? A comcon? *United States,* a half-hour series dealing with marriage—the state of being united—unfortunately was also promoted as a sitcom. But anyone tuning in to watch the series expecting to see yet one more variation on "Hello, honey, I'm home!" got a whole lot more than they bargained for. As a series about married life, *United States* went a good deal further, wider, certainly deeper, and infinitely darker than that. The writing resulted in scripts that turned out to be emotional X rays. *United States* was not a series you watched with your feet up on the coffee table, a beer in hand—unless you intended throwing it at the set.

(On the subject of mislabeling, I was unquestionably the prime offender. Calling the series *United States* gave a good many people the mistaken notion that the contents were documentary in nature, rather than comic-dramatic. Having cast the first stone, I found it ricocheting and hitting me right between the eyes.)

The program was the result of my collaboration with a gifted young writer I had first met when he was six years old and I was about to marry his mother. His name is Gary Markowitz, his surname being the same as my wife's former mate, or my ex-husband-in-law, as I've come to think of him. We tried to cover a good deal of domestic territory in the series, intending it as an examination of the one marriage in two in America that doesn't end in divorce— not because such marriages are fairy-tale unions, but because the participants manage to withstand the stresses and strains of wed- lock, the pressures from within and without by a combination of determination, hard work, humor, and the strong desire not to find themselves and their children on the sad side of the divorce statis- tics.

It was a far more challenging series to write, far harder than *M*A*S*H*. *United States* was closer to the bone, the heart, the mind, and the spleen, and all of them mine. For the first time in my writing experience I was prepared to be a good deal more candidly autobiographical than ever before, to use my own life as an inkwell. I had never been a surgeon, in or out of the army, but I had been in the husband and father trenches for almost thirty years, and so my own marital experiences constituted my research, consisting mainly of one wedding license and one family album—in addition to impressions of other married couples I've known. After all, as Richard Chapin, the husband in *United States,* observes: "All mar- ried people are married to all other married people."

For starters, Gary and I did away with the idea of peppy, feel- good theme music to introduce the show, an aural promise to the viewer that a happy-go-lucky time was about to unfold. Each episode began with an off-camera duet between a trombone, rep- resenting the male voice, and an alto sax, chosen for its feminine quality. Performed by Bill Watrous and Bud Shank, it was an im- provised jazz theme, reflecting how so much of married life is im- provisational. We did away with the laugh track, rejecting outright the suggestion to the viewer that there were three hundred people living in the same house as our couple, going from room to room with them and laughing their heads off at their intimate and/or hi- larious exchanges, while some of them weren't hilarious at all. In- deed, a good many of them were painful, and constant discussion between our married pair about what it was that caused that pain.

Originally we had tried to sell the idea of *United States* to CBS, in the late seventies, when that network was looking for a series to star the actress Linda Lavin. Linda chose to do another CBS projected series, *Alice,* based on the successful motion picture *Alice Doesn't Live Here Anymore.* Why anyone would want to do a successful series that went on to have a run that lasted for years, and earned her a queen's ransom, instead of starring in one that lived for eight weeks and then was forced to submit to electronic euthanasia, I'll never know.

Next, I talked to Grant Tinker and Mary Tyler Moore about Mary playing the wife, a role she was to stop playing in real life with Grant himself just a short time later. Mary was intrigued with the idea. Unfortunately, my plan included having a whole season's scripts written before going into production, and she was not prepared to wait the year that that would have taken.

Enter Fred Silverman. Or rather, enter me, into his office. Fred liked the idea of allowing a series its full complement of scripts written in advance of actual production, and all the benefits that would accrue from that sort of preparation. He committed NBC to underwrite twenty-two of them—a highly innovative and bold step in a medium where it is difficult to find a fresh footprint anywhere at all. Fred deserves a lot of credit for the risk he accepted for the network. They, in turn, got a good deal of favorable PR for giving the series a chance. Signing *United States* suggested that NBC gave their audience a bit of credit for wanting something different.

Gary and I were left alone to get the scripts ready. Totally alone. No creative notes from the network, no interference whatsoever. It was a dream situation. While we were to prepare twenty-two of them, the series had an on-air commitment for only thirteen episodes. The idea was to be ready with the additional material in the event of a mid-season pickup. At one point, the network offered to give us a full, on-air commitment of twenty-two episodes, but since we did not have all the scripts ready at the time, we resisted. Hugely profitable though it would have been, going on the air in advance of having all the scripts written was exactly what we were trying to avoid.

Part of our plan, from the beginning, was to employ highly mobile tape equipment to emulate the same production techniques that are used when shooting film. We did not want the typical three-camera studio sitcom setup, with a lot of bright lighting and our actors emoting for the benefit of a live audience. We were after a more intimate kind of dramatic interplay.

The show was produced at a landmark Hollywood location, KTLA, site of one of the oldest studios in the industry (and owned by Gene Autry, another of the industry's oldest). Working a few yards from where Hollywood's first talkie, *The Jazz Singer,* had been filmed, we found it to be not only one of the oldest, but one of the creakiest places to work. Over the years, the studio's once-tight soundstages had been used primarily by TV giveaway shows, performed before audiences who are generally whipped into a frenzy to give such programs their own particular sense of excitement and delirium caused when total strangers win bedroom sets and inflatable swimming pools. We quickly learned that it is extremely hard to get absolute silence in a soundstage that is no longer used as a soundstage but rather as a broadcasting studio.

While we dealt with technical challenges, NBC launched an expensive, impressive campaign to tell the public that they would soon be treated to something rather special. For the show's premiere episode, they launched the advent of the series with a proud, extravagant ad in *The New York Times,* in the *Los Angeles Times,* and in every big city *Times* or its equivalent in the country. By our fifth episode, it was impossible to find any evidence of any promotion for the show at all. The hype, the trumpeting, had become muted. Silence at last. We were still on the air, still on the TV screen, but we had dropped off the radar altogether. Missing in action. From full-page pictures in *The New York Times,* we had become candidates for guest appearances on milk cartons.

The last words I remember anyone at NBC saying about the series were spoken by a program executive who, in announcing the cancellation of the series, said that it had proved to be much too visceral.

I suppose by that he meant that the series had guts. Which, of course, is a prime crime in prime time. You can *show* guts on TV—

showing fake slaughter is fine—or even the bloody results of *real* violence, but depicting marital strife was considered overly visceral. Fred Silverman's spokesperson at NBC (the last network Freddie was to run, having by then run out of networks) had joined the chorus of critics of *United States* who said the show was too unfunny—or that it was too funny—or that it was simply too much or perhaps too little: that it was way too sexy, too cool, too tense, too laid-back, too brittle, too dull, and, for others, just simply too-too. I never had so many too's applied to anything I've ever been connected with—including those professional and lay reviewers who found the show too good to be true, too good for the masses, and too far ahead of its time when the show debuted in early 1980. Its premiere performance was delayed several times. NBC simply did not know what to do with the show after viewing the first few episodes we had completed.

What had caused the dream to crash and burn? When Fred Silverman and company got to see the scripts we delivered, the timpanilike sound that echoed through the halls of NBC was due to any number of hearts sinking in unison. *United States* was nobody's idea of a pussycat sitcom. The characters were real, their problems were real, the scripts were—all together now—too visceral.

The network felt (an oxymoron, if ever there was one) that perhaps the show's husband and wife, Richard and Libby Chapin, did not fit an audience's expectation of a married couple. This was the eighties, remember, a full decade before *Roseanne* and *Married . . . with Children*. Richard was written as a well-meaning man, not always able to be everything he, and his wife, meant or would have liked him to be. Libby was sharp, with a woman's intuitive quality and a need to know more about things than her husband did. Richard was an optimist, he wanted everything to be tidy and good; he wanted *people* to be as good as he needed to think they were. Libby was more analytical, a bit slower to accept facts and faces. They complemented each other. When they didn't, there was trouble.

The network feared the Chapins weren't likable characters. In truth, we had no intention of making them likable every minute of every half hour an audience would spend with them. We meant to show them in unattractive ways when the situation called for it. The reward for displaying their warts was the mail we soon received from viewers who wrote asking such questions as "How did you know my husband and I had gone through last night's situation?" Or said, "It's as though you're looking through our bedroom window, listening to us in our own bed." Some said they could not watch the show sitting in the same room as their spouse—that they found a good deal of the material painful, but compelling all the same.

Less impressed with our vision than our viewers, NBC put us on the air at 10:30 P.M. An unheard-of placement for a half-hour show, it was more a detention cell than a time slot. Not only were we hung out to dry where it was virtually certain no one would watch us, they next put us on in such an irregular pattern that audiences would have a choice of which night of the week they might ignore us. First we appeared on Tuesday night. Rescheduling us, they put us on Thursday night. Then they put us on *twice* on Wednesday night. They were trying to use up their commitment by airing the show as quickly as possible. One result of never allowing an audience to know where the show was in any given week was near-zero ratings. At one point I had the distinction of having the number-one series, *M*A*S*H*, on the air, as well as the number-sixty-nine show, *United States*. The week they put it on twice, I had the number-seventy show as well. *United States* was not simply dead in the water—it was dead, in a ratings sense, before it got *into* the water.

I don't remember many details regarding the end. Time inevitably cauterizes most of the worst wounds (time and the recurring compliments from viewers who continued to express their approval of the series, mixed with their regrets that it died so quickly). Through all of the obviously waning interest exhibited by the network, I was constantly, privately assured by them that "We're behind it," "We believe in it," "We're moving it," "We're saving it," "We're selling it." It was, to be sure, a hectic time at NBC, quite unlike the atmosphere that followed some years later when shows that demonstrated some quality but started slowly were allowed to live and eventually gain an audience. During the short days and even shorter nights of *United States*, the network was still using problem shows for target practice.

They were in an especially unusual spot for a network: with so many episodes written, shot, and in the can before it ever went on the air, they couldn't say fix it, make changes, give the couple a funny neighbor or a talking dog, or have them adopt black twins perhaps. They—we—were locked in. NBC had become a corporate Ahab, lashed to a great, thrashing white whale of a show. Though we had completed taping eight of the thirteen shows NBC had guaranteed us, we were canceled after those eight were aired.

Regardless of its fate, I don't think of the series as a failure. In terms of being able to work under self-imposed conditions in a pressurized industry that continually imposes its own will upon you, it was a breakthrough. Given a second chance, I would probably make many of the same mistakes all over again (no laugh track, tough marital exchanges, respect for the audience's intelligence, among others). I'd probably make a good many new errors as well.

On a final, fiscal note, I learned a valuable lesson by taking on the responsibility for delivering the series through my own production company, OTP (its initials based on the old saying about writing in the theater business, "If it ain't on the page, it ain't on the stage"), getting a crash course in how much waste there is in television—and motion picture—production. Despite the fact that *United States* was not a success, it earned a tidy profit for the company and the show's profit participants. I discovered that you have to try really hard *not* to make money producing a show—although people on top do try hard not to earn any, at least formally, in the sense of the first few years of balance sheets, so that they don't have to share their assets with any other eligible participants. An artistic loser or an audience lost, or never found, can still be a financial winner.

Being canceled had at least one other benefit. I was spared what little network nutwork we did have to endure. A case in point: our opening episode, entitled "All Our Weapons," was based on the idea that when married folk engage in heated exchanges they use every emotion possible to inflict damage upon each other. It concluded when Richard, in order to make peace with Libby and bring a miserable evening to a happy finish before going to sleep, tried to make her laugh by donning one of her nightgowns. As we were taping the scene, the shoulder strap of the gown dropped, revealing one of Richard's pectorals.

"We can't have that," said the NBC censor, whose job it was to sit in the control booth during the tapings. "The shoulder strap can't drop that way, not in that revealing fashion."

I thought he was putting me on.

He assured me he was completely serious.

"You realize this is a *man* in a woman's nightie," I said.

"I know," he replied. "But within the context it's very provocative."

Maybe for him it was.

As the man said, for a good many people *United States* proved to be just a little too much . . . too visceral.

An excerpt follows from the television series *United States,* not exactly a sitcom. This episode, the series's premiere, "All Our Weapons," is, to be sure, not "All Our Laughs," though it does have its wry twists and rapier thrusts, like any happy marriage.   —Ed.

CAST

RICHARD . . . . BEAU BRIDGES

LIBBY . . . . HELEN SHAVER

INT. BEDROOM

FADE IN:

INT. THE CHAPIN BEDROOM—NIGHT

LIBBY *and* RICHARD *in bed. She is watching the TV beyond their toes; he is reading a book. Only her nightstand light is on.*

After establishing, the bedside phone rings. Libby, closest to it, answers.

LIBBY   Hello? (*pleased*) Hi! . . . No, no, I was just watching a movie. Wait. (*remotes the volume down; resumes eagerly*) Well? Did you get it? (*listens, frowns*) But I thought it was all set . . . You're not serious. Right in his office? I don't believe it. Didn't he just have open-heart surgery a few weeks ago? . . . I didn't know he was such a lech. I'm supposed to see him about getting a donation for Nicky's school . . . Yeah . . . Maybe I should take a little something along to unscrew his pacemaker. That ought to keep his hands at his side . . . What now? Any other prospects? . . . Uh-huh . . . Or listen, why don't you try my bank? Frontier Savings. They might have an opening soon. I know two of the staff are pregnant . . . Yeah . . . (*laughs*) Must be something in the money. Try. Give 'em a call. Let me know, huh? . . . Right . . . You, too. Good night.

(*She replaces the receiver and readjusts her pillow, getting set to watch the film again.*)

RICHARD   (*eyes still on the book, mutters*) Beats the hell out of me.

LIBBY   I beg your pardon?

RICHARD   I said it beats the hell out of me.

LIBBY   Meaning?

RICHARD   (*still looking at his book*) Meaning it happens every time. I could set my clock by it.

(*By now, it is obvious that there is a fair amount of tension between them.*)

LIBBY   I liked it better when you smoked.

RICHARD   (*turning to her*) What does that mean?

LIBBY   You used to blow beautiful smoke rings. Two at a time. Once, I remember three. Now, it's word rings. Circular sentences, one after the other, substituting symmetry for sense.

RICHARD   Can't you say anything simple once? Just nice and simple?

LIBBY   You can have one or the other, but nice is out.

(*She turns up the TV sound, puts the remote down.*)

RICHARD   (*irritated*) *That* is what I'm talking about.

(*He picks up the remote and turns the volume down.*)

RICHARD   (*continuing*) With your friends, it's all smiles and sweetness and light, the royal treatment. They call you on the phone and you roll the red carpet right into their ear. But the minute you hang up, the minute it's back to us, every look you give me is a four-letter word.

LIBBY   Sometimes five.

RICHARD   Being snide doesn't help.

LIBBY   It doesn't hurt.

RICHARD   Yes, it does.

LIBBY   Then it helps.

(*Silence, then:*)

RICHARD   Just once, I'd like to be treated like a friend instead of a husband.

LIBBY   That's a lousy way to put it.

RICHARD   Put it any way you like. It's no thrill lying next to you like I'm some accident the dog had on the bed.

(*Silence again. Until:*)

LIBBY   You want to know what beats the hell out of *me*? The way *you* act as though nothing happened tonight, or last night, or that this whole week hasn't been World War Twelve. That I'm supposed to forget everything that led up to this pathetic, little boy lost plea of yours.

RICHARD   Whatever it was, it's over.

LIBBY   How can you minimize it that way?

RICHARD   Don't you know us by now? I minimize, you maximize. Between us, there's a nice kind of middlemize. (*a pause, then*) Come on, babe. Didn't we promise we'd never go to sleep angry? Didn't we? Didn't we make up that rule once?

LIBBY   And didn't you promise you'd never raise your voice again? That you'd never again use that rotten, abusive tone?

RICHARD   I didn't. I couldn't help it.

LIBBY   Don't *you* know, after all this time, how *frightening* you get? Richard, you're a man.

RICHARD   Thanks for the promotion.

LIBBY   Now, who's being snide?

RICHARD   (*sighs*) Making up with you is almost as hard as fighting.

LIBBY   You're incredible. The way you can go from first gear right to nasty.

RICHARD   You don't do too badly.

LIBBY   I learned from the master.

RICHARD   Meaning your last husband?

LIBBY   If only he had been.

RICHARD   Cheap shot.

LIBBY   Sweets for the sweet.

LIBBY   God, we're boring. We have had this fight so many times, I bet it goes on when we're not even here.

RICHARD   Can we just discuss the specifics?

LIBBY   Oh, we both know the specifics. Let's just jump down to where you say maybe the whole thing's been a mistake, and maybe we ought to try it apart for a while while you rethink your life in a hotel room somewhere where the rethinking comes to a dead stop at the sight of the first pair of tight jeans at the ice cube machine.

RICHARD   That's not what I'm about.

LIBBY   Oh? Then why the threat lately, the constant threat, no matter what the argument, that you've had enough, you've had it, good-bye and good luck?

RICHARD   It's just a thing I say, that's all.

LIBBY   Just the ultimate weapon in this age of the disposable marriage, that's all. Wham, bam, and you're ready to be the summer soldier and the Sunday father.

RICHARD   The truth: don't you ever feel that way? That you'd like to chuck the whole thing aside, that you'd like to be free?

LIBBY   I *am* free. I thought you felt that way, too.

RICHARD   I do, but do you think there is one married man alive who doesn't secretly wish he could be as untied as he once was?

LIBBY   Absolutely. As long as his marriage didn't slam shut behind him.

One TV project that *did* work, post-*M*A*S*H,* was Gelbart's inventive, imaginative, dramatic, and yes, at many moments, funny adaptation of an unlikely story for the medium. With no pertinent background in the world of business, L.G. tucked into the best-selling nonfiction book he was offered—and made of it a new success.   —Ed.

BARBARIANS

Ray Stark is one of an all but vanished breed of Hollywood producers. Long before he gets to the last page of any book he's reading (in Hollywood, reading itself is a vanishing pastime), if it has sufficiently stimulated him, he's already thought of the writer he wants to sign to do the screen adaptation, the leading actors he'll cast in it, exactly what the ads should look like, and what its first-week grosses will be at the box office.

So it was with a work that appeared in 1992, written by two *Wall Street Journal* writers, Bryan Burrough and John Helyar. *Barbarians at the Gate* was an account of the sale of the RJR Nabisco Company to the firm of KKR for the astronomically unreal sum of $25.7 billion. Closing the covers of the book, Ray Stark swung into action. He got Columbia Pictures to option it, and then, because he saw the story of high finance as the basis for a low comedy, asked me to adapt it as a screenplay.

It proved to be a difficult assignment. I really have a hard time giving two fives for a ten. But the one thing I've learned from adaptations is that if it's too easy or too pleasant a job, then I've probably not done a very good one. It means I've used too much of the source material, that I haven't rethought it enough in either cinematic or theatrical terms. Adaptations should, of course, retain the spirit of the original work, but they cannot simply be an elaborate retyping job. (A notable exception: Roman Polanski shot *Rosemary's Baby* straight off the pages of Ira Levin's novel.)

I approached Stark's invitation with not a little trepidation. If there is any challenge I find irresistible, it's the one I suspect will be the most likely to resist me. *Barbarians at the Gate* was a masochist's dream come true. I knew absolutely nothing about

junk bonds, leveraged buyouts, Wall Street dealspeak. The assignment, as I saw it, was producing a script that dealt not with
numbers but with people—and dozens and dozens of them populated the book's 515 pages. The book, like life itself, had far too
many lawyers. Following Shakespeare's advice, first, I murdered
them, at least as many as I could. I kept only the protagonists,
Ross Johnson, CEO of RJR Nabisco, and Henry Kravis of
Kohlberg, Kravis, Roberts, and the men and women closest to
them. A good deal of weeding and compressing had to be done before I could get down to the plotting, staying true to the book's account of events. I wanted to invent as few of these as possible.
What had actually happened was what made the story of the RJR
Nabisco deal so unbelievable. I wasn't about to try to improve
upon reality. My biggest task was to make it all comprehensible.
Especially to me.

Equally challenging was the prospect of putting words into the
mouths of real-life human beings, people who actually existed—all
represented by high-powered lawyers who existed as well. A good
many of those concerned, the people I would be writing about, offered to meet with me, to give me their version of the events in the
book. Curious as I was about them, I resisted any face-to-face en-
counters, preferring to take the book's word for their roles in the
drama. If drama is the right word. From the beginning, Stark and I
had the goal of making *Barbarians* a bedroom farce—substituting
money for sex, people getting paid instead of laid.

By the time the final, the shooting script was placed atop the
pile of all of my earlier drafts (a stack standing nearly two feet
high), Columbia Pictures was no longer involved, the company
having admitted they didn't have a clue as to how to market the
project.

Thanks to Stark's undiminished enthusiasm for the screenplay,
Barbarians found a home on HBO. It was on that cable channel
that audiences saw the following scene, in which Ross Johnson vis-
its the Reynolds Tobacco laboratories to get the word on the first
test results of Premier cigarettes, a new product on which he is bet-
ting the company's—and his own—future.

INT. RJ REYNOLDS—LATE AFTERNOON

Before a huge cross section mock-up of a Premier cigarette, Ross, Horrigan, and a group listen to RJR executive TRAVIS GAINES.

WARNING: In dealing with a drama depicting real-life tobacco company executives, a certain number of four-letter words is inevitable to achieve TV-verité. —Ed.

GAINES   Of those we interviewed, eighty-six percent approved of the idea of a smokeless cigarette. Forty-one percent said they'd try at least two packs before deciding whether to switch brands. Of those who had given up cigarettes, seventy-three percent responded favorably to the idea, saying they'd seriously consider smoking again, if they could be positive that the cigarette they were smoking was absolutely smokeless.

(Ross loves those numbers.)

GAINES   Eight percent of *that* group sampled at least one Premier to give us their opinion of the product. Which means that, of all those we interviewed, eighty-one percent sampled anywhere from one or two to an entire pack. Their reaction to Premiers was almost uniform.

(Silence. Gaines seems reluctant to go on.)

HORRIGAN   They all said they tasted like shit.

ROSS   Like shit?!

HORRIGAN   Like shit.

ROSS   They *all* said that? *Nobody* liked them?

GAINES   Fewer than five percent.

ROSS   *(to Horrigan)* You said you heard the results were terrific.

HORRIGAN   Nothing wrong with five percent. I'll take five percent of the smoking market any day of the week.

ROSS   Jesus Christ! How much are we in for up to now?

HORRIGAN   To date?

ROSS   To date. To here. To now.

HORRIGAN   Upwards of seven-fifty.

ROSS   We've spent seven hundred and fifty million dollars and we've come up with a turd with a tip? God Almighty, Ed. We poured enough technology into this project to send a cigarette to the moon, and all we got out of it is one that tastes like it took a dump.

HORRIGAN   You want to talk about the smell?

ROSS   What'd they say *that* was like?

HORRIGAN   What's first cousin to shit?

ROSS   What does that mean? A fart? Is that what you're saying?

FIRST SCIENTIST   We've got an awful lot of fart figures, sir.

ROSS   Tastes like shit and smells like a fart. Looks like we got ourselves a real winner here. It's one goddamn unique advertising slogan. I'll give you that. I don't believe this! *(using his lighter on one)* What the hell's wrong with that? I don't smell anything.

FIRST SCIENTIST   That's not the way to find out. If you light a Premier with a match instead of a lighter—*(pointing to the model)*—the sulfur reacts badly with the carbon in the tip.

ROSS   Do we have to have the carbon?

FIRST SCIENTIST   That's what makes it smokeless.

ROSS   Well, how do we get it shitless?

FIRST SCIENTIST   Hard to say. Given enough time—

ROSS   We haven't *got* any time! We've announced it's coming out this year! *(to Horrigan)* You insisted on it!

HORRIGAN   Because *you* did!

ROSS   Because *you* said they'd be ready!

HORRIGAN   They *are* ready! We just need some adjustments.

ROSS   Jesus, Ed, I don't have to tell you what's riding on this— *(taking a drag)* And what the hell's wrong with the draw? You need an extra set of lungs just to take a drag.

FIRST SCIENTIST   It *is* a little difficult.

ROSS   A *little* difficult?

SECOND SCIENTIST   It's what we call the "hernia effect."

ROSS   Oh, is that what we call it? There's *another* great billboard. What do we do? Give away a truss with every pack? "Warning: This cigarette can tear your balls off"?

(Horrigan tries one with a match. Ross winces at the odor.)

HORRIGAN   I don't think it's so bad.

ROSS   No parent can smell what's in his own kid's pants, right? Stop jerking off, Ed. Who the hell'd sneak into a john to smoke one of these? *Wherever* you light one up, you're in the shithouse. And I'm beginning to get that same feeling myself!

For all that Gelbart can turn barbed, or scathing, he turns sunny in his enthusiasms. This burst of kudos for Garry Shandling's first bit of original television, *It's Garry Shandling's Show* (1986–90), is an example of the respect of one pro for a group of them.   —Ed.

SCENE 3

SHANDLING

Despite nearly a half century of effort, be it sitcom or stand-up, TV comedy has barely changed. By and large, the forms are frozen. In the case of sitcoms, fossilized. Page 13 of any series's weekly episode is frequently interchangeable with page 13 of many other series' weekly episodes.

Yet every so often, though not nearly often enough, a show appears that, while not reinventing comedy, does alter the form and manages to change the presentation of humorous material in such a way as to delight and surprise. Surprise is essential to humor. When was the last time you were surprised watching a TV comedy show?

It's Garry Shandling's Show is, to me, that refreshing breakthrough. Combining elements of variety, talk shows, sitcom, audience participation, fantasy, reality, you name it, the show defies comparison with any other program on the air today. It is audacious, satirical, hip, sophisticated, and wonderfully, miraculously, silly.

It is, in addition, that rarity of rarities, a TV effort that has the uncommon goal of appealing to the highest common denominator.

There is a spirit of freedom on the Shandling show that reflects one of the major reasons for its quality and uniqueness: it is not seen on network television. It is not seen on NBC, CBS, or ABC. It is not a product of the ceaseless and essentially joyless cloning process that gives us so much repetitive programming (the two major escapees being David Letterman and *Moonlighting*'s Glenn Gordon Caron).

Why do our TV sets seem like copy machines with moving pictures? Everything we see on the box represents choices made by network executives, who tend to be young. Experience for the job is not necessary. In fact, it's quite often considered a handicap. A blank mind provides a much cleaner slate. What qualifies them for their positions is their, however brief, lifelong familiarity with the tube. Exposed to television even before they're in the womb (not inconceivably conceived during a commercial break on Johnny Carson, resulting in a form of tubal pregnancy), network mavens are chiefly concerned with perpetuating what they've been programmed to believe a TV program should be. Their standards and criteria were formed by thousands and thousands of hours of pre- and postnatal viewing.

Whether by shrewd choice or happy accident, Shandling and his collaborators come to us courtesy of cable. It is one of two comedy series that suggest a hands-off attitude on the part of the powers-that-be.

The second series with a difference is *Brothers*, the show that treats the subject of homosexuality with such gay abandon.

Because it's on cable, the Shandling show enjoys another tremendous advantage. No commercials. When you watch this show, all you see is the show. There are no pauses in the action (although most of Shandling's action consists of Shandling turning from one camera to another), no unwelcome breaks in the entertainment so that viewers can be reminded that they can and should drink as much beer as they possibly can if they want to get the most out of life.

This freedom from free enterprise allows the viewer to watch each episode in one go—especially important in the case of this series since its story lines are almost nonexistent and so fragile that any pause, any mandatory break, could prove fatal in terms of maintaining the audience's acceptance of what is going on. Being allowed to present each episode nonstop allows the half hour to develop a rhythm, a momentum that never has to be arrested and then regained after this message from Detroit (or more likely, Tokyo).

These slender story lines offer no complicated plots, little or no tension or surprising twists. Rather, the surprises come from the way the half hour passes.

There is, of course, the obligatory opening theme song. The obligation stops here. It's not a tune you're likely to leave the room humming. It is, like the program it introduces, filled with self-mockery and is a warning to us that what we're about to see is the result of some lively, mischievous minds at play.

Shandling talks directly to the audience at the top of each show and at numerous other times during the course of the program. This, of course, is not a new device. George Burns did it years ago when he starred in his own series, and Roman comedies that pre-date the birth of Christ always featured actors' asides to the audience. (Burns also starred in several of these.)

But Shandling carries the device to new and original heights. He not only addresses the studio audience, taking them into his confidence or sharing some information with them unknown to the other actors in the show; he will, on occasion, step out of whatever set he's doing a scene in to invade the studio bleachers and include the audience in the proceedings, soliciting their opinions as to how to proceed. Standard fare for a Donahue or a Winfrey, totally unprecedented for an actor appearing in a scripted show.

He will also engage his crew, camera operators, stage manager, whoever, in his wanderings, whether on foot or in his electric golf cart, and work all these normally behind-the-scenes people very much into the scenes.

These departures are all planned, naturally. Shandling is not improvising on the job. What's so refreshing is that the writers of the show *are*. Clearly, they are trying, and equally clearly they are succeeding in turning a cliché form on its head, inside out, upside down and backward. Each week's show is charged with a kind of restless energy, an impatience with predictability, a gleeful assault on convention, a willingness, a *need* to experiment, to juggle all the tiles and come up with a different mosaic each week.

Form is not the only element of the Shandling show that is treated with such gleeful disrespect. Least sacred of all is Shandling himself. With a long face that seems to use up half his height, Shandling's looks, or lack of them, and his awesome strikeout record with women make him the chief butt of the show's humor, which ranges from simple one-liners to the surreal.

In fashioning what can best be described as television of the absurd, Shandling and his fellow Shandlers offer us testimony and hope that, even on TV, there can be something new under the sun—that imitation is the sincerest form of laziness.

The producers of the series are Bernie Brillstein, Brad Grey, Jeff Franklin, and Alan Zweibel. The director is Alan Rafkin. The writers are Shandling, Zweibel, who are credited as the show's creators, Jack Burns, and Ed Solomon. Hope I haven't omitted anyone. I'm grateful to them all. And to cable, as well. If they can come up with a few more as good as this one, I'll happily throw away my channel changer.

In what follows, Gelbart nominates certain persons, programs, and events to make his own version of a TV top ten list. He shows that the most powerful creators of television are, at times, events themselves. And so too with certain "real life" figures who become willing or unwitting actors in dramas larger than life.

He concludes the segment with a brief remembrance of one such actor whose appearances on the screens of our minds and memory have become, despite everything, untouchable and unforgettable. —Ed.

SCENE 4

TEN OUT OF FIFTY: SOME PERSONAL CHOICES FOR A HALF-CENTURY'S HIGHLIGHT REEL

1. TEXACO STAR THEATER

Television arrived a virgin—one that Milton Berle claimed as his own on their very first night together.

The magical invention came to us as a blank screen. There was no handbook, there were no rules, not a clue as to how to make it more than just a curiosity. For Berle, the red light of the camera was a green one for his masterly chutzpah, which allowed him to define a new and alien appliance as he went along, pulling the new medium up by his boot—and brassiere—straps. In its formative years, Berle *was* TV.

2. EDWARD R. MURROW

What Uncle Miltie was to entertainment, Edward R. Murrow was to television journalism. (There was a time when you could tell the difference between the two.) With his dark, drooping eyes and signature cigarettes—which would, eventually, close those eyes forever—Murrow's standard for no-nonsense professionalism was just a few inches short of Mount Everest, which accounts for why so few of his peers and followers were ever to join him there. In taking on the fearsome, and then some, Senator Joseph McCarthy, a demagogue so powerfully in and out of control at a time when even

President Eisenhower was loath to engage him in public, Edward R. Murrow gave television one of its proudest moments; one that has yet to be approximated. Unimpeded by the then courageous CBS, Murrow was allowed to focus his courage and his camera on someone so dangerous to the republic, he already had an -ism named after him. The electronic banana peel that Murrow placed in the senator's path created the start of the slip that saw McCarthy go from omnipotence to oblivion. In attacking so powerful a leader, Murrow demonstrated that television could act on behalf of the electorate far more effectively than many of the leaders it sees fit to elect.

3. *YOUR SHOW OF SHOWS*

A few comedy sketches, a monologue, a bit of mime, some special material, a ballet number, some modern dance; a little opera, a bit of swing, a classical soloist, a popular song rendition, and guest star appearances. No, not an entire theater season; just the typical ingredients of any one airing of *Your Show of Shows,* the Golden Age of television product that had the distinction of being pure platinum. For over four of television's infant years, viewers were treated to a brand-new hour-and-a-half live variety show of Broadway caliber, all under the guidance of producer Max Liebman. The succeeding years rarely produced anything better in the field of light entertainment than *Your Show of Shows,* which was a template for all that followed in the field of TV variety.

4. RICHARD NIXON

A three-way tie with himself as provider of one of the most compelling programs of the past fifty years. How to decide between the Nixon-Kennedy debates, which shaped all future presidential campaigns, or his "Checkers" speech, or his farewell address to his White House staff: whether he was playing Elisha Cook, Jr., to Jack Kennedy's Henry Fonda, or doing an infomercial for cloth coats with his hapless wife, Pat, at his side, or finally leaving Washington after he had double-crossed the Potomac—in all three performances, Richard Nixon provided the American public with more drama than any political figure or professional actor has ever rendered on the small screen. His upper lip acting as a sweat gutter, his dark whiskers growing almost visibly as he spoke, he had a way of making even his enemies wish he could make a better showing. Only television was able to shine the light on him, right through him, it seemed, to give us such a close look at such a distant figure. As with all of the very best television, the camera did not comment. It merely recorded what was, without trying to shape the outcome. When will it ever again find such a fascinating, dark star?

5. THE JFK TRAGEDY

As the medium assumed the unassigned task of covering the awful moments and days after Dallas, people of all ages realized for perhaps the first time that America was the name of a family as well as a nation. Providing an ongoing connection to this vast land which, indeed, felt wasted, the lens was everywhere we didn't want to be, and yet could be nowhere else. Without a hint of intrusion, engendering compassion without stooping to sentimentality, television helped us fumble our way toward some sort of comprehension of our loss and our shame. Its constancy, its reassuring way of just *being there*, offered not just comfort but a very necessary sense of continuity. For a much, and all too often correctly, maligned medium, its service to the country in the wake of November 22 was perhaps television's finest hour—for hour after hour.

6. THE LANDING ON THE MOON

Was his name really Armstrong? Just like Jack's? Was it really happening at all? After rocketing from Earth, was this real-life Buck Rogers climbing down the ladder and actually putting his foot on the surface of the moon in that giant leap for all of us-kind? And were we really watching it *live*!?—watching, as in seemingly effortless fashion, television demonstrated that it could go anywhere it wanted to go, anywhere *we* wanted to go, in—or out of—this world? By accompanying those who were determined to arrive at seemingly unreachable goals—astronauts or athletes, artists or ambassadors—television has taken each of us along to share in their adventures and take joint pride in whatever their accomplishments. All boundaries disappeared with the moon shot. Jupiter and Mars now appear on the local news. Because of television, we now even know what home plate looks like. Earth is a picture book, fluffy white and baby blue, from way out there. So beautiful from afar, such a cock-up up close. How nice it would be if we weren't just another pretty planet. Given that complimentary image of ourselves via TV, how nice if we could be as wonderful in person as we are on the tube.

7. PUBLIC BROADCASTING

It is no less than a national treasure—an institution unique in its awareness that broadcasters are accountable to broadcastees. While regularly scheduled, live, original network drama has long gone the way of the test pattern, PBS continues to create or import productions that connect its audience through the commonality of our experiences and our emotions—and without sensationalism or violence. (I daresay the body count on PBS is far lower than anywhere else on the air.) It is a place where impressionable children are treated with some care for their innocence, where kids are thought of as kids and not as midget consumers. On the never-ending hunt for *something* to watch, PBS is a God-sent pit stop, a place to stock up on sanity, on civility, or to get an updraft of optimism and pride in our species, while sharing the excellence of some enlightening thought or performance on display. A favorable reaction from a viewer means a lot to the people at PBS. It is to them, after all, a word from the sponsor.

8. CNN

Any hour, any day—every day, every hour—concentrating solely on the reporting, analyzing, and anticipation of news events, CNN is also a public hot line, allowing world leaders, aware of the scope and impact of Mr. Turner's brainchild, to communicate directly with one another—shaking fists or shaking hands, all for the benefit of the camera. And we, potatoing away, witnessing it all, get to watch history along with those who are making it. The true genius of CNN is its awareness that what most people care most about is other people. In a box crammed with fantasy and escapism, CNN is a twenty-four-hour-a-day reality check. Murder, mayhem, heroes, bimbos, conflict on a global or domestic level, CNN reminds us that for pure drama, truth is far stronger than fiction and that reportage can in itself be a remedy for the evils it reveals. Had it been in existence during the rise of the Third Reich, would Nazism have gone as far as it did? How much stronger might the lessons have come home to us if, without ever leaving home, we could have been present at Nuremberg? (Hyperbole aside, that was the *real* Trial of the Century.) Having slept right through the revolution, the networks have finally decided to create their own version of CNN, proving once again that in television, nothing succeeds like someone else's success.

9. ALL IN THE FAMILY

In the beginning—of television comedy—in the beginning was the word. And the word was *Don't*. Don't show life as it is, don't show people as they are, and don't, under any circumstances, allow anyone to talk in any way that resembles how anyone actually talks. Polish 'em up, button 'em down. The less human, the better. Call them Peepers, call them Beaver, call them Partridge. Let none of these navelless wonders ever utter a discouraging word—or ever go to the bathroom and, if they did, these Americanoids were never to reach behind them and flush. And then it happened. One amazing night, Archie Bunker went to the can. And from off-camera—could it be true?—we heard him flush! The gurgling of the plumbing at 704 Hauser reverberates to this day; flushed with a vengeance forever were network and sponsor timidity about human imperfections and all manner of hypocritical detritus. The seat went down and the lid was off. The moment television comedy was allowed to reflect the human comedy—that was the moment the fun really started.

10. JENNY JONES

And so it came to pass after half a century that the pursuit of ratings engendered a mind-set so mindless that *anything* went as far as programming was concerned, that nothing was too foul to be fair game. Accordingly, the providers of mass distraction, indifferent to the shredded sensibilities of the masses chained to their sets like so many channel serfs, and convinced that the end justifies the means, even if the final result means someone else's end, treated us to the spectacle of one talk-show guest, his manhood threatened, murdering a fellow talk-show guest, the horror forgotten as speedily as it had been committed. Rendered near-numb by the constant displays we have witnessed of rudeness to one another in what has become the American uncivil war, the masses—minus the murder victim, of course—continued to tune in on the never-ending parade of degradation, of the shameless exponents of emotional mooning. Competition, crowding out common sense and content, has created a market-driven morality. Like the whimsical species that created it, television's unblinking eye makes no distinction whatsoever between soaring through space or splashing in the sewer.

And here endeth the sermon.

JFK

One way or another, he was going to win you over.

He was going to charm you.

You never had a chance.

He would do it with his logic.

Or his grin.

Or his wit.

You could be seduced merely by a photo of him.

At the tiller of a boat.

Strolling barefoot on the beach.

Wearing tails or with his shirttail hanging out.

Now, gone these far too many years, he continues to captivate us by the indelibility of the memory of him.

Who, sitting in the place of power that suited him so well, has since endowed that space with such a sense of style, of unerring civility, of being so offhandedly regal?

One blink or two in a gun sight, and all that turned out to be too good to be true.

All that we are left with is an image of a smile that will not fade and of all that princely promise never to be fulfilled.

What a mixed blessing it is to see him in snippets of film we've come to know by heart.

To still thrill to his bringing down the house, before they brought down the wall, in Berlin.

To still empathize with a father denied the joy of lifting his own children in his arms.

To still somehow hope that the motorcade will make it safely to the underpass, its occupants whole and unhurt.

From a long time ago and from a place far beyond far, he wins our hearts still.

We are his forever.

We are eternally charmed.

Written for *JFK Remembered,* by Jacques Lowe, Random House, 1993.

Eventually, Gelbart's career segued deeper into motion pictures.

The following is a short account of an early experience in making the bumpy transition.   —Ed.

SCENE 5

FAIR GAME
(AND WAS I EVER)
AND
THE NOTORIOUS LANDLADY
(AND SHE WASN'T THE ONLY ONE)

My basic training for the perils of the rewrite wars began in 1960, when Charlie Feldman, a Hollywood agent-turned-producer-turned-legend, hired me to do a screenplay for him. Better it should have been *about* him (except he was too unbelievable).

In a city of technicolorful characters, Charles K. Feldman was a standout. Handsome, dashing, he had an eye, and several other body parts, for the ladies. The back story on Charlie was that he and his brother spent their earliest years in an orphanage, their birth parents dropping their option on the boys, and a visiting couple, unable to decide which of the Feldman frères they would adopt, hit on a novel, somewhat Dickensian idea. They would have the boys run a footrace in the orphanage yard. The winner would get a lifetime of home meals. The loser would go back to his gruel. Charlie won the race and received the first prize of a mother and father. Apparently people of modest means, his adoptive parents found a real winner: Charlie provided them with all they could hope for, once he became one of the movie business's most successful talent agents. Upon their deaths, they left the surprised

Charlie a pile of money, money earned on investments they made
from Charlie's help to them. Okay. Reel two:

Visiting in L.A., staying at the Chateau Marmont (the site of
John Belushi's suicide, his last picture being my screenplay *Neighbors,* an experience that left me slightly suicidal as well), I was invited to meet with Feldman in his house in the lush Coldwater
Canyon area of Beverly Hills. (I *think* it was Charlie. His habit of
surrounding himself with men who, to me, looked uncannily like
him—with his round, handsome face, Gable mustache, and toothy
smile—made me hope I wasn't talking about signing to do a picture
for Charlie's butler.) Charlie proposed that I write the screen version of a sliver of a Broadway play called *Fair Game.* Written by
Sam Locke, it had run for 187 performances, chiefly because of
the popularity of its star, *Guys and Dolls'* original Nathan Detroit,
Sam Levene.

Charlie's instructions were for me to forget the Sam Levene,
Seventh Avenue garment district approach to the lead character,
which the play had required. Charlie, wanting to anglicize the
property, had in fact signed William Holden for the part. And it
would no longer be Seventh Avenue. "Make up something . . ."

Going to work in an office at Columbia Pictures on Sunset and
Gower (coincidences continue: directly across Sunset were the
same CBS studios where I had started with Danny Thomas), I
began working on adapting *Fair Game.* My first inspiration was to
turn the Sam Levene character into a safely non-Jewish executive
in a Revlon-style cosmetics firm. My second inspiration never
made it through the ozone. I knew next to nothing about how to
construct a movie. My chief experience had been shoehorning the
odd joke into Bob Hope screenplays, but jokes do not a screenplay
make. Using Sam Locke's theater piece as a blueprint, I cobbled together a progression of scenes, took a deep breath, and went on.

I sent my first twelve pages to Richard Quine, the man who was
going to direct the picture.

"I'm in love," said Quine. My twelve pages had put him in a
swoon. He wanted to get together and discuss where the script was
going, what my ideas were (so did I, but I didn't have the foggiest

idea), only he was in the middle of preproduction activity on another Columbia picture, *The Notorious Landlady,* which he was
getting ready to shoot.

I went ahead and somehow finished the draft of *Fair Game.*
Quine may have been smitten by my first twelve pages, but love
would have had to be legally blind to find anything romantic in the
next one hundred. They were awful. In any case, Quine never saw
them. Charlie Feldman did, and to my surprise, he wasn't terribly
concerned with their lack of quality, to say nothing of cohesion.

"You've got to do it all over again anyway," he said. "I lost William
Holden, but I've managed to get Jeanne Moreau, the enchanting
French actress, to play the part."

Having reconstructed the play so that the role of the male lead,
as originated by Sam Levene, was no longer Jewish, I now had to
go back to the drawing board since the male lead was no longer to
be played by a male. As I sat there, wishing that Charlie's brother
had won the race at the orphanage, Quine was on the line, asking,
"If I can spring you from Charlie's picture, can you come over and
work on *The Notorious Landlady?* I'm having trouble with the
script."

All too glad to jump ship, I let Quine get me out of *Fair Game,*
which, in turn, never got made. Not with a Frenchwoman, not with
a Gentile or a Jew. I didn't have another meeting with Charlie Feldman until many years later, and given the Charlie Feldman clone
syndrome, who knows if I actually met him then either?

~~~~

So, *The Notorious Landlady.*

Richard Quine was unhappy with the writer, rewriter actually, of
the suspense comedy. The original writer on the project had been
Blake Edwards. Quine was in a bind. He needed new pages, lots
of them, and he needed them the day before yesterday. His actors
were assembled and he had to start shooting right away. Jack Lemmon was the male lead, Jeanne Moreau apparently not being available, and Kim Novak was his leading lady. The third star was Fred
Astaire, in a nondancing role. (But then, I, the once-and-never

Future Fred Astaire, was also involved in a nondancing capacity.)

The work went well. I thought so. They thought so. At least, they thought to tell me they did. I was enjoying the sensation of actually working at a motion picture factory, one of the places that used to ship the boy I had been fresh dreams and fantasies for my Saturday afternoon delectations. I dined alongside famous faces in the studio commissary. I met other writers. Important writers, writers who actually knew how to do what I was only beginning to know. I met S. N. Behrman, for Christ's sake.

I was having a very good time. I know you're way ahead of me, so just let me connect the dots for you.

One day, working on the last few scenes of the script, I heard gales of laughter coming from the office next to mine, the office of the producer of the picture, Fred Kohlmar. Putting a drinking glass to our common wall, a primitive but time-tested way of eavesdropping, I soon realized that the laughers were Kohlmar and Richard Quine. There was a third laugher in the room. It was S. N. Behrman. What the three men were enjoying so heartily was Behrman's rewrite of a portion of *my* rewrite—the one they kept telling me was going so well. Without informing me, Behrman had been working behind me, improving my improvements, with Quine billing and cooing in *his* ear.

I was a young, trusting writer when I listened in on the wall to the everyday run-of-the-mill betrayal going on behind it. I was a good deal older and smarter by the time I put my glass down. Also, really crushed.

I've had similar experiences since, when I'm on the other side of the drinking glass, when *I'm* rewriting somebody else's rewrite. It's never pleasant, either way.

Flash ahead now, about ten years later, to a new episode of Writer, Writer, Who's Got the Writer?, a game for adults who cannot forget they were children. —Ed.

NEIGHBORS (ALTHOUGH NOT ALL THAT NEIGHBORLY)

In the mid-seventies, or roughly about where my waistline seems to be heading these days, I put aside reading Thomas Berger's then latest book, a darkly comic novel called *Neighbors,* to take a phone call from someone asking me if I would like to write a screenplay based on Thomas Berger's latest book, a darkly comic novel called *Neighbors.* The story of suburbanites living next door to each other, one a sort of model citizen, the other entirely unbuttoned, not to say unhinged, it would require a measure of subtlety if the novel was not to be sacrificed to the picture. The caller was the diminutive agent and producer Irving Lazar, who I always felt proved that good things came in small packagers. Swifty Lazar thought I'd be the perfect choice to do the work. So did I.

I knew Tom Berger from my London years, when we saw each other socially for some time. Not only was I a fan of his work, I admired the quirkiness in anyone who had, as a pet, a canary purchased at Woolworth's. The idea of adapting one of his books was most appealing. (Thanks again, God, for giving me something I wanted, as a way of reminding us yet again what a clever devil You are.)

I didn't do a lot of original writing in adapting the book for the screen. I liked the source material far too much to want to "improve" it. (There were countless drafts of the screenplay of *The Maltese Falcon* before Warner Bros. signed John Huston to write and direct the filmed version of Dashiell Hammett's classic. To aid Huston in adapting the work, his secretary typed all the dialogue directly from the book in screenplay form. To Huston's dismay, a copy of the secretary's work was sent to the powers-that-were at the studio and they complimented Huston on his script by greenlighting the project.)

Lazar functioned as executive producer on *Neighbors,* which means his phone call to me was the last I ever heard from him. The men who would be in charge of the production were the renowned independent producers—an independent producer being someone who is dependent upon everyone—Richard Zanuck, son of the legendary Darryl F., and David Brown, who is somebody's son, I'm sure. (People in the entertainment industry are extremely aware of their heritage. I recall an actor accepting an award saying that all that he was he owed to his parents, especially his mother and father.)

In my first meeting with Zanuck and Brown, we kicked directors around—always a pleasant pastime—and they came up with the name of John Avildsen, fresh from the first of the *Rocky* sap operas.

Five minutes into a conversation with Avildsen, and I knew he was all wrong for the picture. Our senses of humor were 720 degrees apart. I was appalled at what he found funny, starting with the movie *The Blues Brothers,* which I considered a complete mess. I know a lot of people think *The Blues Brothers* is a funny film— good God, a lot of people think *Neighbors* is a funny film—but Avildsen and I had such obviously different takes on comedy, I knew we were going to be in trouble.

Zanuck and Brown assured me everything was going to be fine.* It was a great script, they massaged me, and Avildsen was hot—and in Hollywood, hot equals great. They assured me that Avildsen was the perfect egomaniac to direct my work.

To my second horror, the comedians John Belushi and Dan Aykroyd, even twice as hot as Avildsen, were signed to play the leads. If the screenplay had any distinction, it was that, like the book on which it was based, it was a quite lunatic chamber piece.

---

*Lili Zanuck, Dick Z.'s wife, was reported to have said, after an early meeting with Avildsen: "Do you think this guy is right for this picture? I don't know whether I trust anybody with comedy who is so fucking rigid" (Bob Woodward, *Wired:* New York, 1985).

I was certain it could not support Belushi and Aykroyd's rock-and-roll approach. Again, Zanuck and Brown asked me to have faith in their judgment, presupposing that I had any faith left after they had signed Avildsen to misdirect the picture.

For their part, or parts, our two stars couldn't decide who would play which character in the film. Who would play the straight role and who would play the fiend? To everyone else, the logical choice was as clear as the nose on Belushi's face—that feature often obscured, however, by the little spoon that constantly protruded from it. (If I appear to speak disrespectfully of the dead, it is only because I am trying to write this in the context of the time.)

In the end, Belushi played the straight role and Aykroyd played the fiend. It was a kind of inside joke, the kind that keeps audiences from going inside a theater.

I flew to New York for the first reading of the script with the stars and the director. I remember the reading was on St. Patrick's Day because it was the first time in my life I ever got a green migraine. To be sure, it was not the best day it had ever been to be me. When is a writer more vulnerable than the first time he hears his work read aloud by others? Actors generally have no intention, nor are they prepared, to give a performance. So a reading of a screenplay—or a theater piece—is just that. A reading. Words that are not meant to be literature but rather dramatic dialogue accompanied by action are read—often sight-read—as something they were never meant to be. And the writer can only think: *Who wrote this crap?* Who could be responsible for these joyless, listless, endless reams of drivel? My own impulse at first readings is to rip the scripts out of the actors' hands, set fire to them—the scripts *and* the actors—and use them as kindling for my own immolation.

The actors cannot really be blamed. Naturally, they do not want to be judged so early in the game. Better the writer should look inept. Still, after a while (over half a century in my case), you begin to understand that before you go back to your room and rip into the script and redo it completely, you've got to have a semireasonable reading of it, with the actors trying to convey *some* sense of what you had in mind.

That was not to be on this occasion—chiefly because not only was Belushi an extremely popular and sought-after performer at the time, he was also, on the day we read, extremely loaded. Constantly stopping the reading for trips to the men's room made him even more so. What he was ingesting, I have no idea—I'm a writer, not a chemist—but whatever it was was making him highly creative. Every time he returned from the men's room, he had a few more thoughts for improving the screenplay. I was beginning to think that, instead of a dealer in the toilet, he had a writer in there. He couldn't stop spouting his ideas. It's a pity he wasn't there to hear them. He was as generous with the substance he was abusing as he was with his ideas, and he was childish in refusing to read with even a tentative sense of what I had spent months writing, good or bad.

Aykroyd, too, had a lot of ideas he wanted incorporated into the script. My gratitude not only knew no bounds, it was positively stillborn. Having John Belushi and Dan Aykroyd help with a script was like throwing a party and having the Borgias as your bartenders.

Alone with Avildsen later, I asked him how in the world he was going to be able to handle Belushi.

"What's the problem with Belushi?" he asked.

Belushi had spent the afternoon higher than the ceiling fan and the director hadn't noticed?

Avildsen assured me he would have no problem controlling Belushi. It turned out he couldn't, of course. No one, including poor John Belushi, ever quite managed to do that.

The finished picture, containing countless embellishments provided by Belushi and Aykroyd and Avildsen and who-the-hell-knows-who-else, inspired by God knows how many trips to the john, turned out to be as awful as I thought it was at that first reading.

After that first session, Avildsen dropped me at a restaurant, where I ordered a martini and a refill even before I got out of his car and then put in a call to Zanuck and Brown in Hollywood to tell them how disastrously the day had gone. I warned them that the movie didn't have a chance of being made properly, maybe not even at all.

David Brown, clearly detecting my condition, turned to Zanuck after the call and said, "Jesus, get me a drink. We've got a drunk calling someone else a dope fiend."

This I learned upon reading Bob Woodward's account of John Belushi's life in his book *Wired,* which devoted a chapter to the making of *Neighbors* since it was the last film his subject was to make. Mad as hell at Brown's description of me, I began taking steps to sue him. Bob Woodward, acting as peacemaker, talked me out of it. He was right, of course. Things balance out.

The day after I'd been drinking, I was sober again.

But Zanuck and Brown were still independent producers.

~~~

To hopefully cement over the memory of this experience forever, here is an excerpt from the final screenplay of *Neighbors.* Unchanged by anyone—unembellished, unimproved, and totally drug-free—here are what I considered the best and most fitting words I wrote in the entire script:

"FADE OUT."

In what later will seem a preview of a movie worked on, or at, by Joan Didion and John Gregory Dunne, Gelbart takes us to the summer of '77, which, however much it may sound like one, was not the title of the movie in question—questionable as it was from the start. —Ed.

SCENE 7

THE ROUGHEST CUT
OF ALL

Summer of '77. I'm on the beach in Honolulu, when the phone that always rings, even when you're on the sand, rings. I am asked by stage and occasional movie producer David Merrick to write a screenplay called *Rough Cut,* which he is putting together for Paramount Pictures. Blake Edwards is to direct. (If you're beginning to feel as though you're trapped in a house of mirrors, welcome to my world.) Burt Reynolds will star. It's a sophisticated diamond caper movie, in the Cary Grant mold. Terrific.

A word of advice: never take a job that's offered to you while you're sipping mai tais in the noonday sun.

Someone, in fact, has already written a screenplay based on a novel whose name escapes everyone. I'm told I can use whatever I want of either. While I read both, my manager makes a deal with Merrick, whose name is on file at the U.S. Patent Office as one of the inventors of the slippery pole.

I look forward to meeting with Blake on my return to L.A. We hadn't met since we didn't meet on *Notorious Landlady.* The next day, my manager calls back. Merrick does not want me to write the film. Why not? To this day I don't know. One day he loves me, the next day he hates me. What I also didn't know was how lucky I was, being out of the picture, figuratively and literally. Also temporarily.

A few days later, another call. Merrick *wants* me to do the picture. I begin to feel I have a three-picture deal with Merrick—all to write the same picture. I was later to learn that a team had been hired to write the screenplay after Merrick called off my first deal. Burt Reynolds, who had writer and director approval, insisted I write the script, and so the team was dropped. As of that moment, nine writers—if you count me three times—had been at work on the film. (I take life one déjà vu at a time.)

Back in L.A., Blake can't meet. He's off to Europe to scout locations for that major epic, *The Pink Panther's Revenge*. We begin the first of many trans-Atlantic, trans-Pacific, trans-Sylvania phone calls in which I invariably wake him at three in the morning from any number of noons of my own. Finally, we make a date to meet in Paris to work out the story line of the film. He'll be able to spend two days with me. Two nights, actually. Turns out to be more like two hours.

Blake is staying at the Bristol Hotel in Paris. In a duplex apartment with its own elevator. Very appealing to deposed dictators and movie directors. By the time we meet in his private dining room, I have a galloping case of Napoleon's Revenge. After a superb dinner, which I wash down with Mylanta, we go into his study and chat for about an hour about the screenplay. Same thing, the next night, minus the gastrointestinal follies. Blake being totally absorbed with *Panther* matters, we decide that I should return to L.A., work out my own outline and begin to write the screenplay. Blake is very tired. He's had a long day. He expresses complete confidence in me. Mainly, I think he just wants me to go. *Vite.*

So I do. I go and I write it. I deliver the screenplay to Merrick in January of 1978. He immediately sends it off to Blake, who is now in Hong Kong (naturally), scouting locations for who the hell cares what anymore?

In February, I'm off to Fort Lauderdale for a month of rehearsals with the Jackie Gleason company of my play *Sly Fox*, which is preparing to go off on a national tour. (That's another story—I'm giving you only one nervous breakdown at a time.) Via phone, Blake and I try to figure out when would be the best time for me to meet him in Hong Kong. We decide the best time would be never but agree to get together in several weeks in London.

The meeting takes place in Blake's suite in the Dorchester. The suite is the only one on his floor—he's roughing it. I'm feeling rotten again, terrible jet lag—the Wright Brothers' Revenge. Merrick is there, too, back from or on the way to somewhere. Blake has read my script. He loves everything up to and including the main titles. That is to say, he loves the first page. After that, he doesn't love it at all. He tells me how he sees the rest of the picture. He begins to describe a completely different movie, not the one I wrote, nor one that I can or want to write. An honest disagreement.

This is the movies. Directors are the money. Merrick honestly sides with Blake. I'm off the picture. I've been in the business a long time. I'm a pro. It always hurts.

I learn a few weeks later that *Blake* is off the picture. Merrick is looking for a new director. It seems Burt Reynolds wants to do another picture before starting *Rough Cut.* Merrick is willing. His one condition is that Burt has to give up writer and director approval on *Rough Cut,* to which he readily agrees.

There follows a long period during which I have no idea of what is happening with the screenplay. In June of 1979, Merrick asks me if I will go back to work on it. I learn at least four other writers have added their fingerprints to the pages. I then do three rewrites of the screenplay, working closely with Reynolds and the legendary Don Siegel, who had replaced the legendary Blake Edwards. It wasn't long before Merrick fired Siegel. But that was only so he could re-hire him again a few weeks later.

After the first couple of weeks of actually shooting the picture in England, Siegel was once again taken off the picture by Merrick and replaced by a British director. When the British director was fired shortly thereafter, Blake Edwards flew to London from his home in Switzerland to offer his services to Merrick. One of *his* conditions was that he be allowed to do a rewrite of my rewrite of all of the various rewrites. By now, very few of us know what the picture is all about, except that it's a cinch to be a disaster, if we can get it that good.

First, director Blake was turned away and Merrick rehired second director Don Siegel as the picture's third director. The English playwright Anthony Shaffer was hired to work on my script of the various scripts. Eventually many others were to contribute to the screenplay. Don Siegel wrote some. His assistant and future wife, Carol, wrote some. Merrick himself rolled up his French cuffs and wrote several versions of the ending, one worse than the other. Someone named Tuttle came and went, as I remember. Other names I happily forget. Or never knew. It's just possible more people worked on the script of the picture than ever went to see it. Given a look at *Rough Cut*'s unholy mess of a final cut, I withdrew my name from the credits and substituted a pseudonym. The movie was what people in Italy call a whorehouse. It's what people in a whorehouse might call a movie.

SCENE 8

MOVIE MOVIE

FADE IN: New York cinema marquee—COMING WEDNESDAY, "MOVIE MOVIE."

PAN TO: Coauthor of *Movie Movie,* a comedy that recalls the double features of the thirties. He turns to camera and speaks:

I don't know about you, but for me, the most excitingly dark, enjoyable, and nourishing place—after the womb—is a movie house. And whereas we enjoy only a nine-month run in the former, you can go to the movies anytime you like. Which is exactly what I did every single Saturday afternoon of my whole life as a child. What a joy it was, the ritual of seeing the same actors in virtually the same situations, often in the same sets, the men rarely hapless, the women barely able to get through the doorway with their Adrian shoulder pads that cried out for CinemaScope.

Who knew then that Bogart's dangling cigarettes were killing him or that Joan Crawford used to put her kids to bed with a right cross? They were gods and goddesses, teachers and models. A

Charles Boyer movie was a training film on suave. It was Cary Grant who first made me decide to become handsome.

This schoolboy crush on the movies had for years made me want to create one of those ceremonial Saturdays at the pictures, where for pennies you could see a double feature, several short subjects, a newsreel, a few cartoons, and the weekly chapter of whatever serial was playing. Those were the days when an afternoon at the movies was like a month in the country.

SHIMMER EFFECT (as they say in film school): Flashback to mid-1975, when I pitched the following idea to a major Hollywood studio, a studio where a lot of disaster pictures are made—on purpose. Would they finance the writing of a film to be called *Double Feature,* made up of two scenarios, each a condensed satire of a thirties-type movie, whose combined running time would be no longer than a present-day conventional film?

The screenplay would also include an opening newsreel, using stock footage of the period; a short takeoff on a serial chapter à la Flash Gordon; and a pair of trailers for "next week's" double feature.

It would employ a small cast, which would appear in both films. The same sets and props would be used wherever possible, so that a character in a very serious situation in the second feature might get a laugh merely by entering a room that the audience would recognize from the first feature.

Additionally, both films were meant to be shot in black and white so that they would be technically faithful reproductions of those early films that can still give your heart a Pangborn every time you see one.

The studio reaction to the proposal was immediate. They loved it. But since people who make deals in Hollywood move like icebergs, it took six months to sign the contract. And then it took Sheldon Keller and me all of six weeks to write the script.

The studio's reaction to the script was also immediate. They didn't love it.

First, they didn't think that the kids who buy records would lay out three dollars to see it. I pointed out that we had written a movie, not an album. In any case, young people have been fed a steady diet of thirties movies on TV for years and are quite familiar with their conventions. (And whatever happened to movies for us middle-aged kids? The idea that the only target for entertainment has to be the very young is a difficult one to accept.) Second, the studio complained that they found themselves, in the midst of a comedy script, *caring* for the characters. They didn't think the mix would work.

They missed the point by a mile. The film was and is meant to be an affectionate satire. The audience is *supposed* to care. And laugh. People have been known to do both at the same time.

So the studio allowed me to take the script into the marketplace. If I sold it elsewhere, all they wanted was their original investment back—plus interest. I left with their blessings, at 7 percent.

DISSOLVE: A few other studios read the screenplay. They loved it. But not that much. Martin Starger read it. Once an executive at ABC—in the days when you didn't admit it—Starger now runs the American end of Lord Grade's operation. He loved it and didn't send regrets. I began to love Martin Starger.

Lord Grade, Baron of Elstree. Don't let the title fool you. Lew Grade is a doll, a pussycat peer, a lot like the lord next door. I'm having a sign made for his desk: THE BUCK STARTS HERE. His is the fastest checkbook in the West. Grade was the principal backer of *Sly Fox,* which I'd written for Broadway, and since we had a one-hit roll going, Starger convinced him to put up the money to produce *Double Feature.*

We all agreed that this film was not meant to be only another movie spoof. In addition to reproducing the form and style of the period, the goal was also to convey, through language and image, the innocence of the times, the simplicity and morality that influenced a generation of moviegoers.

CUT TO: Mid-1977. The budget is set at $6 million. Stanley Donen is to produce and direct. There is a marvelous cast that boasts three Oscar winners—Art Carney, Red Buttons, and, as the top-of-the-bill, George C. Scott. (Scott is my choice to star in anything; if they ever film my life story, I want Scott to play me. And my father. And my mother, if he likes.) So much for the easy part.

A question arises. Should the picture be shot in black and white? Will an audience feel "cheated" if it's not in color? Worse still, will they think that it is an old movie? The decision is to shoot both features using color stock, which can be printed as black and white and allows us to make our choice later.

The next thing anyone knows, it is later. The film is finished and ready to be previewed.

Along the way, we change the title. The original, it is felt, might prove confusing to the public. GEORGE C. SCOTT IN "DOUBLE FEATURE" on a theater marquee might make one expect to see Scott in two of his earlier films. *Double Feature* became *Movie Movie,* a phrase I hope suggests the kind of film that an audience likes to curl up with.

Other changes: the picture will be sneak-previewed with the opening faux-newsreel; the first of the two mini-features, "Dynamite Hands"; and two trailers in black and white. The second mini-film, a musical titled "Baxter's Beauties," will be in color. (The Flash Gordon serial never got written. Length problems. A pity; I love those thirties rocket ships that looked like an empty living room with a steering wheel on one wall.)

~~~~

CUT TO: June 30, 1978. Sneak preview in San Francisco. The newsreel obviously confuses the audience. They don't even know that they're going to see two movies since there's been no publicity or advance word on the film.

The newsreel is never seen again. Other tightening suggests itself. Over the side goes one of the two trailers. More laughter would be useful. Additional lines are written in the next few days, the actors record them, and they're incorporated into the film. Donen has a wonderful idea for a new ending for the pugilistic segment, "Dynamite Hands." It can be shot in one day. It's expensive. A starving family in India could make films for a whole year on what that one scene costs. But we do it. (I also send a CARE package to India.)

There are three more sneak previews in September. The first includes a specially written prologue to replace the newsreel in the hope that it will prepare the audience for what is coming. "Dynamite Hands" is shown in black and white and "Baxter's Beauties" in color. Next time out, both are shown in color. The last time, both in black and white. In the end we go back to the original Solomon-like notion of showing half the baby in black and white and the other half in color.

One piece of business remains. In deciding on the prologue, we had discussed an alternate idea: having a well-known screen personality appear just after the opening titles to talk directly to the audience, leading it in an entertaining and informative manner into the picture proper. George Burns was considered the perfect choice. Warner Bros., the film's distributor, was eager to follow up on the Burns idea. Perhaps they felt an audience would be comforted by having the man who played the title role in *Oh, God!* blessing the film they were about to see. Anyone who enjoys the film will need no explanation for why this is so. Those who don't get it just never will.

The finished film will take up two hours of your life. It took up two and a half years of mine. That's why you don't get a percentage of the profits and I do.

When Gelbart was approached to work on a movie about a man impersonating a woman, he didn't know that it would turn out to be (excuse it) such a drag. Or that he might be arrested later, after the usual humiliating experience, for impersonating a writer. Certainly, as it turned out, a number of other people should have been.

Nevertheless, he is credited, rightfully, with much of what survived as a tattered script. Making this movie is the story of a mess. Naturally, given the usual runarounds, rewrites, hirings, firings, and conflicts of egos and uncertainties, the picture was a success.   —Ed.

TOOTSIE

161. INT. THE SOAP OPERA TV STUDIO—CONTROL BOOTH—DAY
DOROTHY MICHAELS (MICHAEL DORSEY) *in full drag and woman's makeup can be seen on several monitors as "she" stands before the cameras, getting ready to audition for the occupants of the booth.* GLORIA, *the soap's producer, clearly not thrilled with the way Dorothy's less-than-telegenic face is coming across, presses a speaker button, so that she can communicate with a camera operator on the studio floor.*

GLORIA   (into a microphone) *Camera Three—can you pull back a little?*

162. SHOT—CAMERA THREE OPERATOR
OPERATOR   (into his mike) *How do you feel about Cleveland?*

"Larry? George LeMaire at Columbia. Is this a bad time?"

Since I was hard at work when LeMaire's call interrupted me, it was a perfect time.

"We've got a project in the works called *Tootsie*. It's Dustin Hoffman in drag. Does that sound like something that would interest you?"

"You calling me from square one or have you got a script, in which case, how much trouble is it in?"

"You tell us."

The notion of Hoffman in a dress was irresistible.

The messengered screenplay was at my door in less than an hour. It is a maxim in the movie business that sick scripts are delivered at a much faster pace than the money one is paid to make them well. Sick scripts earn no interest at the banks for studios; withheld payments do. The *Tootsie* screenplay, which ran a hundred and twenty pages or so, became the scenario for the next year and a half of my life. A year and a half, at that point in my life, was petty cash. Now, finding myself chronologically challenged, it seems a minor eternity.

The draft I read was the fourth incarnation of the screenplay, the second draft written by the third writer assigned to work on the project.

The first was Don McGuire, best remembered for writing the semicult film *Bad Day at Black Rock.* In the mid-seventies, Don turned out an original comedy, *Paging Donna Darling,* later changed to *Would I Lie to You?* It was the story of a down-and-out actor working in a drag club, desperate for better and more meaningful work, who becomes a star after his agent lands him a role playing a woman character on a popular TV soap opera. All the seeds for *Tootsie* were there—as well as the line in Don's script that got one of the biggest laughs in the final film: "How do you feel about Cleveland?"

Don quickly got financial backing for the project from sometime producer Charles Evans, brother of onetime Paramount head Robert Evans (there are more relatives in Hollywood than at a Mormon Father's Day picnic), and commitments from two actors to play the leading roles: Buddy Hackett for the part of the actor's agent, and George Hamilton for the part of the actor. That this version, with this cast, mercifully never made it to the screen is enough to make one believe in George Burns.

The second writer to have a go at the script was Robert Kaufman. Bob's take on the premise was, according to Evans, funnier than McGuire's. It certainly was a good deal coarser.

After Kaufman, enter Hoffman. The indomitable Dustin. Never underestimate the power of a star. At a time when Hoffman was being implored to act in every third script being written anywhere in the world, he was determined to act in a drag comedy that had resisted being written in four attempts over a period of ten years. For some time, Hoffman and playwright Murray Schisgal had been looking for a property that would permit the actor to portray a female character, beginning with the idea of doing a story based on

Renee Richards, the female tennis player who started life as a male physician. My own feeling is that after *Kramer vs. Kramer,* in which Hoffman played a divorced father who also took on a mother's responsibilities, he wanted to delve even further into the feminine psyche; the chance to play a woman would also allow him to literally act out what would be an extension of his mother, who was very ill around this time. "Tootsie," Mrs. Hoffman's pet name for her son, became the new and permanent title of the film.

Murray Schisgal was the third and fourth writer to take on the script. Down the line, he became the seventh or eighth as well, but we'll cross that mishegas when we come to it.

After reading all four drafts, I met with LeMaire's boss, Frank Price, who was running Columbia Pictures at the time. This was shortly after Coca-Cola had purchased Columbia. On the bookcases behind Frank's desk, instead of the standard movie executive's display of Oscars, Golden Bears, Palmes d'Or, bound scripts, and photos of People Who Mattered, there were, spotlighted, cans of Coke—Classic and New, Diet and Caffeine Free, Tab and Sprite—a reminder that it didn't matter all that much whether a studio turned out good pictures or bad, the real money to be made came from the theater lobby. Price is always good company. A former working writer, he is one of those rare Hollywood types my friend Leonard Stern once referred to as an executive who knows what kind of work he's out of.

Price cut right to the chase. If I thought I could make *Tootsie* viable—that is to say, credible, comical, and commercial—Columbia would make the picture, and I would get a handsome fee for my work. If I didn't think I could do a successful rewrite, Columbia would pass on the project and I'd get a free Coke for all my trouble. Though I thought I could lick the script problems, I was not interested in writing just another boy-meets-girl-and-they're-both-the-same-person comedy. I had touched on this comic device in *A Funny Thing Happened on the Way to the Forum* on the stage and on TV put *M*A*S*H*'s Klinger into his first training bra. And in the universe of movie drag, Billy Wilder's *Some Like It Hot* can hardly be improved upon. To me, the challenge of *Tootsie* would be in developing the idea of how a man might view the plight of women after spending a period of time "being" one of them. (One of the first new lines I was to put into the rewrite I assigned to the character of Hoffman's agent, who remarks midway through the picture, "You know, you're a different man since you've become a woman.")

And so the work began. I met almost daily for nearly a year with Hoffman, talking endlessly about constructing a plotline and peopling it with characters to help it come to life. Hoffman is very stimulating. At times he can be *too* stimulating. His mind, when talking script, is like a Catherine wheel—it keeps going around and around, shooting off sparks in all directions. Idea 27 comes flying at you while you're still considering Idea 5. Largely, he was fun to be with. Right up until our last meeting, which wasn't much fun at all—but let's not skip to the ending just yet.

After I signed on, the director Columbia attached to the picture (movies happen only when key elements are snapped into place) was Hal Ashby. A former film editor, Ashby had directed the dazzling *Being There*, with Peter Sellers. It took only one meeting with Ashby for me to realize that we were not on the same wavelength, as typified by his tendency to laugh at a funny line several minutes after it was told, giving me the constant impression that he was not being there a good deal of the time himself.

Ashby was replaced by Sydney Pollack. A director with an impressive string of credits, Sydney was anxious about taking on the work because he had never done a comedy before. I assured him I would be as helpful as I could; that, as he insisted, I would be with him every inch of the way. Turned out I was thinking of more inches than he was.

Sydney and Dustin and I continued to hammer out a structure—at Sydney's house at the beach, at Dustin's house at the beach, and at my house, which is on dry land. At one point, Sydney flew through horrendous snow conditions to work with me in Vail, Colorado, where I was vacationing with my wife and kids. He and I continued working back in L.A., while Dustin was spending some time in New York. We were all over the place. Finally, Michael

Ovitz, head of Creative Artists Agency, who represented both the director and the star, arranged for star, director, and writer to finish our work by holing up somewhere in Connecticut, just the three of us. But I was the odd man out, not wanting to leave my family for a week. It was a refusal that would lodge itself in Hoffman's craw, an action on my part that eventually led to my exit. Working together once again in California (Dustin leaving his family in New York), we found the atmosphere chilled considerably, my once-positive relationship with the actor taking on what Lorenz Hart described as the faint aroma of performing seals. It wasn't long before Hoffman accused me of creating a "subtext of contempt for his ideas." It was even less time before I was asked to collaborate with other writers, an idea which I did treat with contempt.

My departure was the beginning of a writers' convention on *Tootsie*. It wasn't long before the names of many of them began appearing in the press. At one point, I called Sydney Pollack and asked what a certain writer was doing on the project, a writer I'd never heard of. He's not really writing, Sydney assured me, just stitching some scenes together. "Can you refer to him as a seamstress, then?" I asked. "All this coming and going of human word processors is definitely tarnishing the writing credit on this picture."

My concerns were the least of Pollack's and Hoffman's concerns. They were locked in mortal combat over the fate of the picture. Each had been promised final cut by the studio and each was trying to perform the final cut across the other's throat; each employed what they referred to as their own writers (a truly outrageous and insulting situation) to rewrite the script so that it conformed to their separate visions or versions of the film.

There are whole sections of *Tootsie* that *are* stitched together: a bit of my dialogue, then a bit of someone else's, then someone else's, then back to mine. I call it writing with a stapler. There is one series of scenes that are supposed to be taking place all on the same night. It is a night that would have to last a hundred hours. It bothered me then, it bothers me now.

The rewriting of *Tootsie* goes on to this day. The liner notes on the Criterion label's laser disc of the film describe how Sydney Pollack was hired to replace Hal Ashby as director and go on to say that I was hired after Pollack was, implying that all I contributed to the film happened post-Pollack.

Among the fixers of my fixes was Murray Schisgal, with whom I eventually shared screenplay credit (I shared story credit with Don McGuire). In Hollywood, when people are listed as cowriters of a film, it's a good bet that they never sat down and worked together, but that they merely sat down with one another's pages. In 1983, when the New York film critics honored the writers of *Tootsie* with an award, it was at the lectern, while being handed the critics' citation, that I met my "collaborator," Mr. Schisgal, for the first time.

Most of the scars have healed by now. And my experience with Hoffman taught me one lesson of immense value:

Never work with an Oscar winner who is shorter than the statue.

SCENE 10

OH, GOD!

David Susskind, producer, entrepreneur, talk show pioneer/host, former agent (and we can never have too many of those), cut a wide swath in TV, a moderate one in the theater, and almost no swath at all in films. Continually trying to improve his movie batting average, Susskind obtained the screenplay rights to a novel called *Oh, God!* Written by Avery Corman, the sweet and funny book had a history of being optioned for movie adaptation, resisting any sort of reworking, then moving on to the next bidder. If memory serves, even only at a reduced speed, at one time it was possible to option the book's screen rights for no money at all. David Susskind, shrewd trader that he was, secured them for five thousand dollars.

David and I had a long association turning out a string of TV revues for Art Carney, and so mine was the first phone number he rang, hoping that someone could succeed in bringing *Oh, God!* to life on the screen. We also agreed that in the event the picture got made, I would act as its director. After ordering a pair of puttees for my debut as an auteur, I contacted Woody Allen and Mel Brooks to see if they would be willing to play the leading roles in the projected film, Woody as the nebbish who receives an unexpected visit from the Almighty, the latter to be portrayed by Mel Brooks. Woody, in mid-career, a status that never changes, politely declined. Mel was not interested in playing God, obviously not willing to accept the demotion.

Somewhere along the way, Susskind fell overboard on the project and when my script reached the screen it was produced by Jerry Weintraub. Carl Reiner was the director, the perfect choice, I thought—the novel had always seemed to me a literary extension of Carl and Mel Brooks's "2,000-Year-Old Man" interviews. In the starring roles were John Denver and George Burns.

Burns was a delight (this is a recording), and Denver, acting in his first film, gave a surprisingly good performance. The picture cost peanuts—just over two million of them—and made Warner Bros. so many millions more they could have choked an elephant herd.

What was filmed was essentially a first draft—a blending of Avery Corman's work and my own. I wish time had allowed me to develop more of the idea's potential. As unfinished as I felt the script was, it nevertheless received a nomination for an Academy Award. I never for one millisecond thought it might or deserved to win.*

I hate to be a fowl-dropper, but the night of the awards I was six thousand miles away, having Peking duck in a restaurant called the Peking Duck, in the city of Peking in China. With Carl Reiner, of all people, with whom I shared a magical, pre-Coca-Cola-post-Gang-of-Four tour of that magical country. It was an amazing meal. We were served every part of the duck but its quack.

---

*Seated at the Oscar ceremonies the year that *Tootsie*'s screenplay was nominated for an award, my wife said, "Forget it—you're not going to win." Me: "How do you know?" Her: "They didn't seat you on the aisle."

You can only win an Oscar once. An hour later, I was having Peking duck all over again.

When Gelbart sent along these two excerpts from the movie *Oh, God!* he said, in the accompanying note: "Would you believe, as I was retyping these, I started rewriting? Sick, sick, sick."

No, perfectionist, perfectionist, etc.—even when God has all the best lines. —Ed.

Here is an excerpt from the screenplay for *Oh, God!* It is the scene in which God, as a little old man in a windbreaker and golf cap, appears in the courtroom where Jerry Landers, the young man he chose to act as his go-between to tell the world that he still exists, is on trial (a trial to determine his sanity).

THE JUDGE   May I ask who you are, sir?

GOD   Better swear me in; you'll never believe it.

(*God takes off his cap, as the clerk extends Bible. God puts his right hand on it and raises his left.*)

CLERK   Do you swear to tell the truth, the whole truth, and nothing but the truth?

GOD   (*nods*) So help me me.

THE JUDGE   (*frowning*) So help you you?

GOD   If it please the court—even if it doesn't please the court—I am God, Your Honor.

(*There is a noisy stir in the court.*)

GOD   Why is it so hard for you all to believe? Having chosen this form in which to appear, is my physical existence any more improbable than your own? What about all that hoo-hah with the Devil awhile ago, from that movie? Nobody had any trouble believing he took over and existed in that little girl. All she had to do was wet the rug and throw up some pea soup and everybody believed. The Devil you could believe but not God, huh? I work in my own way. I don't get inside little children. They got enough to do just being themselves. Also, I'm not about to go around to every person in the world and say, "Look, it's me; I want to talk to you." So I picked one man, one very good man. (*nods at Jerry*) I told him God lives. *I* live. He had trouble believing, too. In the beginning, I understood. I'm not sure how the whole miracle business started; the idea that anything connected with me has to be a miracle. Personally, I'm sorry it ever did. It makes the distance between us even greater.

Jerry, the hero of the piece, is tested by a panel of religious figures to prove that he has neither seen nor met the Supreme Being. Locked in a hotel room, Jerry is given a set of questions to answer, answers they feel he would have no way of coming up with without divine help.

When the room service waiter arrives with his dinner, Jerry is disappointed that the hotel waiter does not turn out to be his new-found friend, God.

When there is a knock at the door moments later, the smiling busboy in the hall *is* the Almighty.

GOD They forgot the ketchup.

(*A bottle of which He holds in His hand.*)

JERRY Come in!

(*God closes the door, puts the ketchup on the cart and lifts the cover on Jerry's dinner—a steak sandwich.*)

GOD Eleven dollars for a steak. Who would have thought? With me, cows were an afterthought. Just to give new mothers a rest, you know?

JERRY Boy, am I glad to see you.

GOD Eat, it'll get cold.

(*As Jerry complies, God goes to the bed and picks up the panel's questions, puts on a pair of bifocals. The room's TV set is still going quietly.*)

GOD (*re questions*) Ah hah. Pretty cute.

JERRY What is it?

GOD They made sure you couldn't answer. The questions are in the ancient tongue of Aramaic.

JERRY Is that what that is?

GOD   You've figured out so many ways to talk to each other down here that finally nobody can. Let me see what they want to know . . . (*reads*)

"What is the true origin of the Universe?" . . .

"What is the source of the planet Earth?" . . .

It's a history final, right?

(*He glances at the next question and begins to pace. Becoming aware of the TV set, He shakes His head in dissatisfaction.*)

GOD   So many repeats. (*turning the set off*) Get me a pencil and paper.

CUT TO:

INT. THE HOTEL ROOM—LATER

God and Jerry have been working for some time. God has his uniform jacket off and is in a shirt and suspenders. Jerry has several handwritten pages of answers at his elbow. God reads the questions aloud, then composes His answers. Jerry takes dictation.

GOD   "Did man fall from Grace in the Garden of Eden?" (*a beat*) I'll tell you something never came out. I made Adam seventeen. Eve was fifteen, sixteen, tops. I thought sixteen, seventeen was middle age, you know? Who knew people would live so long? Trees, I figured, had the best chance. Now, I realize they were kids, babies. Young people can't fall from my Grace. They're my best things. Put that down.

(*Jerry writes, as God looks at the next question.*)

GOD   "Number Seven. Is Jesus Christ the son of God?"

(*Jerry looks at Him eagerly.*)

GOD   Jesus was my son. Buddha was my son. Mohammed. Moses. You. The man who said there was no room at the inn was my son—and so is the one who charges eleven dollars for a steak in this one. (*looks at papers*) Let's mush on.

CUT TO:

THE HOTEL ROOM—LATER

God and Jerry continue to work.

GOD   *(reading)* "Will there be a Judgment Day for Man?" . . . Well, if they mean a Doomsday, end-of-the-world thing, I'm certainly not going to get into that. But if you want my personal opinion, I wouldn't look forward to it, because there would be a lot of yelling and screaming and I don't need that any more than you do. Got that?

JERRY   *(writing)* Got it.

GOD   "What is the true meaning of Man's existence?" Put down that man—and women persons—put down that their existence means exactly and precisely, not more, not one tiny bit less, just what *they* think it means and what I think doesn't count at all.

JERRY   That's deep.

GOD   Sometimes I get lucky.

JERRY   There's one last question.

GOD   As if there is such a thing. *(reads)* "Why have you chosen to appear at this time?" Write that I'm here to tell everyone that everything that they can see and smell and feel and hear, that they should delight in all this. That what is here are some of my very best ideas and I want everyone to try very hard to make sure it doesn't all go down the drain. Okay?

JERRY   Thank you, God. Thank you for these answers.

GOD   I hope I get an "A."

After many movies, Gelbart came, years later, to appraising two books, which, while favorable notices of the books themselves, are also revealing of Gelbart's own feelings. The first, with its account of experiences much like his own, with only the cast of characters changed, reveals two principles of the motion picture arts that transcend writers and scripts, directors, subjects and treatments, and such: (1) *The Face is all* and, in the words of the Watergate movie (but not the book), (2) *Follow the money*.

First, a piece written for *The New York Times Book Review*, March 2, 1997. —Ed.

MONSTER: DELIVERING THE MOMENT (OR) DELIVERING FOR THE MOMENT

"Schmucks with Underwoods" was movie mogul Jack L. Warner's favorite appellation for writers, John Gregory Dunne informs us in *Monster: Living Off the Big Screen*. Writers were the fools that the Warner Brothers (and nephews, cousins, and indigent in-laws) had to suffer until they handed in their scripts, which scripts would then be passed among any number of other fools to pound away at on *their* Underwoods, so that eventually, a studio executive reading through all the many versions of a screenplay was apt to find his lips raw and bleeding.

The monster in Mr. Dunne's title refers not only to studio bigwigs, however, but to that which stokes them and the industry over which they rule: Money. Money is the monster that must be fed in order to generate even and ever more money. It is the monster that makes studios play it safe, play it again (via remakes and sequels), and finally makes them play dead when questioned about why no one else gets his fair share of the monster's take.

After years of being molested—not in darkened theaters, but in brightly lighted executive suites—I have decided to swear off bitching* about how tough it is to be a screenwriter in Hollywood. I, for one, am no longer interested in collaborating in my own unhappiness, in helping those who get me to compromise myself and then yelling rape.

Make no mistake. John Gregory Dunne is not one of the crybabies. You will never spot Mr. Dunne standing in the deposit line with tears running down his face. *Monster* is an account of just one of the many campaigns in the movie theater of war that have

---

*At least for several pages of this book.

turned him and his writing partner and wife, Joan Didion, into battle-hardened veterans. (Mr. Dunne reminds us that before the team's version of *A Star Is Born* went before the cameras, a total of thirteen writers worked on the screenplay, including such eminent authors as Barbra Streisand and Jon Peters.)

In the spring of 1988, Ms. Didion and Mr. Dunne took on the task of writing a film script based on *Golden Girl,* a biography of the late network correspondent Jessica Savitch. In the spring of 1996, when the film, starring Robert Redford and Michelle Pfeiffer and bankrolled by the Walt Disney Company, was released, it was called *Up Close & Personal.*

Far more than the title had changed in the script's journey from word processor to cineplex. Jessica Savitch, in real life, died in an auto accident. Jessica Savitch, in the screenplay, would not. She would not die because the monster minders did not want her to die. Death was only one of Ms. Savitch's many problems. There were also her abortions, her drug abuse, her two marriages, the second to a gay gynecologist who, less than a year after they were married, hanged himself in their home; and her own suicide attempt, as well as her lesbian episodes. While her own life was all that a platoon of screenwriters, if not Ms. Savitch herself, could have hoped for, it was all a bit much for the Magic Kingdom crowd, even though they intended to distribute the film through their Touchstone division, which was created to handle such un-Disneyesque fare. (It was Touchstone that released the Cinderella-as-hooker film *Pretty Woman,* to protect Mickey from becoming known as the mouse that whored.) But all's well that's changed to end well. In the Dunnes' completed screenplay, Jessica Savitch is not Jessica Savitch at all. She has been transformed into a totally fictional being. Jessica Savitch, the middle-class Jewish girl from Kennett Square, PA, has become Tally Atwater, trailer trash from Stateline, NV. And it is Tally's husband, no longer a suicidal gynecologist but rather a fallen reporter who mentors her career as a journalist, who must die. *Golden Girl* has become *A Brenda Starr Is Born.*

In the eight years that *Up Close* intermittently absorbed their attention, the Dunnes separately wrote two novels (one each) and six nonfiction books. They also worked on seven other screenplays, wrote numerous magazine pieces, the time span allowing Joan to cover *two* different presidential campaigns. Meanwhile, John reported at length about Rodney King, then the subsequent riots, then turned out an hour-long CBS documentary on Los Angeles, a city with no apparent limits, neither geographically nor in matters of bizarre behavior, and which seems in competition with the movie business in turning out one overheated drama after another.

Costing $60 million to produce, *Up Close* took only seven months to enter the charmed circle of films whose domestic and worldwide box-office gross pass the $100 million mark. With video sales, cable, mainstream television, and all other ancillary markets computed into the revenues, a senior Disney executive declared that the picture made "a small profit."

The minefield the Dunnes had to cross was not small. It was the sort that members of the Writers Guild crawl through on their bellies on a daily basis, dealing with the never-ending notes and commentary that they find coming at them from everyone connected with the enterprise, whether by fax or by phone, to their faces or behind their backs.

At a time when almost as many people are taking screenwriting courses as there are actors reciting tonight's dinner specials, *Monster* offers a crash course in getting a script through the hazards of the present-day studio system. A sampling of the notes the Dunnes received as they submitted ever-different versions of the script:

"Keep it light. Keep the fun level up. Deliver the moment. Better but not good enough. Don't let it go dreary. Better line to the same point. Lose or improve." "Too hostile. Modulate. Redo. Lose." "Deliver the moment. Cut. Change. Heat up. New line." "Punch up. Bring down. Rework. Identify." "Make this scene more of an event. Clarify or change. Deliver the moment. More beats. Deliver the moment."

It was Scott Rudin, the movie's once and future ex-producer, who offered the writers the soundest possible advice about the kind of suggestions that can help improve a script right into the ground:

"You do what you want to do, ignore the rest, they can't even remember them. Forget their solutions, look for problems, and come up with your own solutions."

When the increasingly note-weary John Dunne asked Rudin what the picture was really all about, Mr. Rudin's reply hit the nail right on the head. "It's about two movie stars," he said.

Precisely.

In the beginning was the Word. However, that applied merely to all of Creation. The first line in the Hollywood Bible states: In the beginning, it was the Face. The face of the star. From Pickford to Pfeiffer, from Keaton to Cruise, it has been the stars, that select group of former mortals, who are responsible for drawing the masses into the movie houses. Their faces and physiques, and not for one moment any of the words they say. The stars are blessed, according to Robert Towne, as having "features that are ruthlessly efficient," as being able to convey a staggering amount of information or allure without ever opening their mouths.

Stars are the monster's best friend. Stars are the money. Content, cogency, cohesion are secondary to the monster, and so are the scripts that take forever to do and redo (writing costs on a feature now exceed entire motion picture budgets of only a few years ago), fashioned only to serve as the fuel for star-driven vehicles. Such scripts tend to be filled with any number of plot holes, individual scenes that work while the whole of the picture doesn't, all too often leaving audiences as much in the dark as the theaters they're sitting in. Increasingly, to court and to please the stars, the monster is turning out movies that have a beginning, a muddle, and an end.

Happily, throughout their ordeal, the Dunnes had a secret weapon. They had each other. What a comfort to have your wife and best friend, who happen to be one and the same, present to witness the inanities and indignities of "creative" meetings, to have someone to throw a look to, to suppress a smile with. When such a get-together is a true disaster, Mr. Dunne will turn to Ms. Didion, or vice versa, and say, "White Christmas"—the song played over the Armed Forces Radio Network in April 1975 as a signal to the few Americans left in Vietnam that the war was over, and that they were to bail out. For the Dunnes, it meant exactly the same thing: Let's cut our losses and split.

The writers alternately split and stuck with the project through twenty-seven different drafts of the screenplay; through two other writers; four new contracts with the studio; Mr. Dunne's valve surgery and a number of other cardiac episodes; the death of John Foreman, the Dunnes' original producer and close personal friend; other deaths, births, marriages, divorces, and "whole life cycles." *Up Close* finally reached the screen, and Mr. Dunne and Ms. Didion were free to go elsewhere to do a few more choruses of "White Christmas." Pros that they are, they will always hang in. Although some pros have been known to split—permanently. In his essay "A Qualified Farewell," Raymond Chandler explained why he was giving up trying to be a screenwriter: "I have a sense of exile from thought, a nostalgia of the quiet room and the balanced mind. I am a writer, and there comes a time when that which I write has to belong to me, has to be written alone and in silence, with no one looking over my shoulder, no one telling me a better way to write it. It doesn't have to be great writing, it doesn't have to be terribly good. It just has to be mine."

What was true in Chandler's time, and before, and is true with a vengeance even now, is that in Hollywood the play is not the thing at all. It is the rewrite of the rewrite of the play that is the thing. Which would, no doubt, have been news to Shakespeare. (You remember Shakespeare. He was that schmuck with a quill.)

In an introduction to a veteran screenwriter's book, Larry shows some of the same ambivalence about their shared trade, craft, and art. —Ed.

ERNEST LEHMAN: GETTING IT ON

I really didn't need to read his book. At my age, I don't need any extra envy.

Envy is only one of the many subjects explored in Lehman's *Screening Sickness,* a collection of thirty-four essays, many of which originally appeared in *American Film* magazine. The collection adds up to what Ernie knows about Hollywood. And what Ernie Lehman knows about Hollywood is everything. Having functioned as producer, director, and writer (I'm so brainwashed, even *I* gave the writer third billing), his writing is sometimes a cry from the heart; but, more often, it's a *zetz* from the spleen.

Lehman's own advice to dyspeptic writers on films: "If you can't say something nice, say it." And say it he does, about stars, agents (he writes about one member of that species who "broke a tooth eating his heart out"), and others. He takes shots at exhibitors, theater managers, ushers; even the audience isn't safe. He knows why Hollywood makes good pictures, why some people make bad pictures, and why other people can't get to make any pictures at all.

One of the latter appears in the essay "The Producer," a masterly study of the independent variety. (Lehman's definition of an independent producer is someone of whom you can say, "What's *he* got to be independent about?") It is a sad tale of a man totally deluded about his place in the business—which is precisely nowhere. It's been too many years since Courtney Einfeld's turned out a picture. (Lehman's names for his fictional characters are always on the money. Only his choice of "Ernest Lehman" seems forced to me.) The description of Einfeld's activities—all mundane, nearly all on the cuff, and most of it all in his head—and the two-year-old fantasy that he is preparing for his next hit makes it one of the best sections in the book. Sad as it is, it's funny as hell.

But then it's easy for anyone to get a picture made. "Getting It On" is a treatise on how a movie finds its way to the screen these days, as seen through Lehman's jaundiced, lopsided, completely cockeyed, and totally accurate view of this, the new Hollywood. Other towns start young and get old. Not Hollywood. Youth, good looks, slender bods. That's the new Hollywood. No one is allowed to have a pot at the end of the rainbow. In "Logan's Run," Lehman deals with Hollywood's preoccupation with staying young and how one fictitious producer (aren't they all, really?) handled the problem. This piece has an added bonus, an O. Henry ending. Lehman has a lot of different pitches. One of the joys in reading the book is never knowing which one he's going to throw next. Gloriously neurotic himself, he knows exactly what makes everyone else tic. He knows what kind of cars we drive and why, whom we play tennis with and why, what kind of parties we give and why, although he informs us that neither he nor his friends have ever found the fabled "Hollywood Party."

Lehman: "We keep tripping over each other at sedate, refined, respectable, fully clothed, thoroughly enjoyable dinner parties, always asking, 'Have you found it yet?' 'Nope, have you?' "

Other than that, Lehman knows it all. He knows studio heads and studio tales, the traffic patterns of incoming and outgoing executives. None are safe from his scornful wit, his disapproving looks by the baleful. And yet, like some great Jewish shark, he will just as easily turn on himself and ridicule his own entrails.

The title essay, "Screening Sickness," describes the effect that screenings have on the screenee, the stresses and strains caused by the screening of a film, the work of someone you know quite well, shown at the Academy, or at a sneak or on the Bel-Air circuit. What you once thought of as a dream way to see a movie can prove to be a nightmare. Lehman: "Relationships are not harmed in Hollywood by the critical remarks people make to each other about each other's films, but by the rude things they say when they feel the opposite in the supposed interest of preserving the relationship."

"Screening Sickness" is perhaps the most serious essay. But Lehman's sense of proportion never deserts him. It is no task for him to be serious without being Serious.

And when he wants to be silly, he's delightful. In "Advice to the Lovelorn," he describes how it is possible for a family of four to go to a movie today and have the experience cost them $633.60. Looking at the situation through the wrong end of the lens, Lehman sends the same family to the same movie and they wind up making a profit of $3,466.00. It's all worked out in precise, insane logic.

"Anthropology" is a glimpse into the future. A college class is studying the way we were, which is to say the way we are: competitive, envious, mean-spirited. It's not a flattering portrait of any of us, but that's not because Ernie Lehman is a sloppy painter—it's because he is such an accurate photographer. He writes about "having to survive the hostilities of detractors, the jealousy of friends." (My own definition of a friend is someone who has the decency not to send you a thank-you note after you've had a failure.) With the publication of this book, Lehman's detractors would find it easy enough to be hostile, if they choose not to be fair and objective, and his friends are sure to be miserable because the book is a total delight. Consider "Exterior," Lehman's mock review of a film by the great Swedish director Inevar Broodman, who decides to do a switch and create an out-and-out comedy. This is the flipped side of the Woody Allen *Interiors* situation, in which Woody dropped the laughs and went for out-and-out Bergman. It is a delicious piece that kills off, among others, Bergman, Allen, and Pauline Kael.

Or his description of working with Alfred Hitchcock, for whom Lehman wrote *North by Northwest* and *Family Plot* (while we're on the credits, Lehman wrote, among others, *The Sound of Music*, *West Side Story*, and *Sweet Smell of Success*), which is a perfect dissection of a collaboration. He articulates the unspoken rules, the etiquette that must be observed to keep the delicate balance required for two talents to maintain respect for each other, without allowing that respect to prevent the critical judgment of each other's contributions that is so necessary to the enterprise.

Like any other screenwriter worth his salt, Lehman knows the twin necessities of getting the work off the ground, as well as providing an exciting ending. He succeeds in both tasks: first, by starting the collection with an introduction by a Helman Sterne, who we are told is with the National Institute of Mental Dysfunction in Washington, D.C. Sterne seems an odd choice to introduce the book. He quickly lets us know that he considers Lehman a name-dropping malcontent, a brilliant mathematician who should never have become a writer. Sterne heaps such abuse on Lehman, it soon becomes apparent that Lehman is Sterne, an anagrammatic poison pen name. The author has elected to be as stern with himself as he is with everyone else in his book.

Surviving his own savage attack upon himself, Lehman goes on to give the book a rousing, exciting finish that is the equivalent of any cinema chase, clinch, or cavalry charge.

In his final essay, "Hooray for Hollywood," having run out of people to offend, he delivers a paean to all who toil in films. And what a delivery. At the top of page 239, Lehman begins a sentence that runs clear to the bottom of page 240. "Runs" is wrong. It sails, it flies. It is a tour de force filled with insight and style, with elegance and grace. And there is not a nasty bone in the whole of the remarkable two-page sentence, one continuous sentence filled with love and respect for the very same people who, until this point in the book, have only been sent up or put down:

> At the risk of being reviled (which is no risk at all, because you won't be able to *find* me, and what the heck do I know anyway), I will now tell you what I have long believed to be true, and have just as long been reluctant to acknowledge. The film community of California, hereinabove referred to as Hollywood, is a community of serious-minded, industrious, highly skilled specialists—artists, craftspersons, technicians, executives, supervisors—interested to the point of obsession almost exclusively in their work, proud of their accomplishments, miserable over their failures, consumed by the demands of their occupations, striving endlessly for elusive excellence, dreaming constantly of artistic

and commercial success, reluctantly taking bits and pieces of time off to play, but mainly eating work, sleeping work, talking work, thinking work, working work, forever getting up off an infinity of floors after numberless counts of ten, walking into unending storms of rights and lefts to the chin and to the heart as well, taking the jeers of the critics when they deserve it and the indifference of the public when they've earned it, coming back, coming back, coming back, always coming back, wanting another chance, maybe this time they'll get it right, refusing to face the possibility that they really don't know how, anything to keep getting the chance to try again, angrily brushing off ill health and onrushing time, cursing anything that gets in the way of their determination to keep on doing whatever it is that they've learned how to do and to do it well and have it noticed and admired and rewarded and applauded, and the amazing thing is that out of all this striving and struggle there comes a great boon to the world, comes pleasure, comes entertainment, comes laughter and tears and illumination and knowledge and identification and understanding and relief from care for all the people in the world who need it in their lives, which is everyone, just about everyone, and these hardworking members of the film community of California, who occasionally do something right, who now and then see a fragment of their dream come true, who see a marvelous movie magically come forth from their efforts, some of them do, once or twice in their lifetimes, the fortunate ones do, which is why there are a hundred films or so that no one alive will ever forget, out of the thousands that have been made, these foolish, touching, single-minded dreamers who spend the best and the worst years of their lives putting all this effort into trying to get something good up on a movie screen, will take all the ridicule and contempt and derision you can throw at them because they know that it comes with the territory, which is known as Hollywood, just as an Alaskan will take snow in winter if he wants to be an Alaskan, and nothing will stop the people of Hollywood, certainly not the snow in winter, certainly not you with your scorn and your sniping and your condescension from afar, you'll never stop them, nor you with your patronizing pronouncements from the Olympian heights of your subway trains, you'll never stop them, they'll just keep on coming back for more, and coming back and coming back, and not even death will stop them, because right behind them are all the others waiting for a chance to have a go, who'll take all the misery and pain and punishment you can inflict on them as long as they can continue to fight and struggle to get back up again and try to do something well, to get something right, even though they know that it's just about impossible to do, that a good picture is a miracle that almost never happens, but that's not going to stop them, *nothing* is going to stop them, but go ahead, keep trying, like you've been trying for years, and don't let defeat get you down, just as *they* don't let defeat get *them* down. But have some fun now and then, will you? Don't take the effort so seriously. Relax, laugh a little, enjoy yourselves.

It is the moment of truth: Ernie Lehman *loves* the movie business, and if all he ever carps about are its warts, it's only because his affection for it makes him want it all to be perfect.

Reading this final passage makes you giddy. It sweeps, it soars; a thought rolls on and on and builds until it hits a comma, the comma serves as a thermal, and the sentence rises again—and again, the accumulative effect is quite stunning.

Helman Sterne is a fool. Ernest Lehman is a writer. A writer's writer. Happily for the public, a reader's writer, too.

I believe I've just gone past envy, right into admiration.

When Gelbart's next original TV movie was being previewed recently for the trade, there was not much laughter, according to two reports in *The New York Times*. James Sterngold, writing from Los Angeles, said that there was a "brief moment" during the screening there when "there is suddenly hope that this bleak comedy about the tabloidization of America might ease back into mere satire. . . ." But, he adds, "Not a chance . . . Watching the movie's supremely cynical ending, about the packaging of tragedy as talk-show fodder, it is clear that Mr. Gelbart, long recognized as one of the country's finest comic screenwriters, is finally letting off steam as one of the country's angriest."

Larry seemed to agree. "The real surprise was that I let me do it. But I became aware that my internal editing department said that you cannot

produce a work that says that we're just diverted by all this. I guess I was just angry."

Buck Henry told Sterngold that "the American audience has been particularly resistant to . . . black political comedy, because it doesn't make for fun . . . What's more important, black comedy doesn't speak to the young audience. . . ."

Gelbart said: "I've lost a lot of life hiding behind comedy. I wanted to do something truer here."   —Ed.

SCENE 13

WEAPONS OF MASS DISTRACTION

JULIAN MESSENGER   *He who controls sports controls it all. Pay TV is a river of money; a raging torrent of dollars and Deutsche marks; of French francs and Swiss francs, of lira and pounds, and currency beyond counting. Only sports lets the couch people forget their dried-up marriages, their dead-end jobs, their dusty dreams that all the six-packs in the world cannot wash away. And while they're rooting for the winners they themselves can never be, you promote all your series, your movies, you name it, to bombard what's left of the poor buggers' senses.*

Bob Cooper and I concentrated on our menus in the dining room of the Peninsula Hotel in Beverly Hills. The head of production for Home Box Office under Michael Fuchs, Cooper ordered three things: a Caesar salad, an iced tea, and a screenplay he wanted me to write. The "tabloidization of America" was what Cooper visualized as its theme: an examination of this country's shameless appetite for gossip and scandal. My response was to ask for a Diet Coke, a hamburger, and some time to mull over the idea.

By the time I completed the screenplay, putting my spin on the subject—tabloidmeisters and other media moguls trapped and chewed up in their own machinery—Michael Fuchs had been asked/told to leave HBO and Bob Cooper had left to become the head of production at TriStar Pictures. (Ironically, that was a position offered to me when that Columbia division first appeared by the director Sydney Pollack, who was advising the fledgling company when he wasn't busy looking in the Yellow Pages for people to rewrite my work on the *Tootsie* screenplay. See Index under "Irony.")

Weapons of Mass Distraction, written for movies/TV, could never have been realized if I hadn't done a piece at the American Repertory Theatre in Cambridge in 1990 entitled *Power Failure*. The play was an examination of the personal damage we do to one another; of the emotional fallout we can cause. Cambridge offered, as with *Mastergate*, the less pressured environment of regional theater, this time with the challenging task of dealing with multiple characters involved in multiple situations, unknowingly creating one catastrophic confluence after another.

The heart of *Weapons*, a power struggle between two fictional media tycoons, Lionel Powers and Julian Messenger, written well in advance of the real-life drama of Rupert Murdoch and Ted Turner's public and ugly brawl, turned out, quite happily, to be at least one or two headlines ahead of its time.

The finished film did what I always hope to do to an audience, but not all that often do to myself. It caught me completely by surprise. It was far darker than was apparent to me in the writing process. I had underestimated just how deeply I would feel about the actions of the characters in the piece—particularly the media barons, that extremely small group of men who, more and more, determine what the public reads, sees, thinks, and feels. Also unexpected (and reluctantly accepted with a profound sense of gratitude) was the realization that I could write as darkly as I wanted, that I did not have to coat the pills I was dispensing by dipping them in layers of comic sugar—that I was able, at long, perhaps too long last, to display anger and disapproval, to dispense judgment and disappointment without feeling the need to do a double-take at the end of a diatribe in the hope that those I've just assassinated will also have had a good laugh about it.

Here are a few splenetic examples of dialogue from *Weapons of Mass Distraction.*

Lionel Powers and Julian Messenger, both lusting to own the Tuc-son Titans, a pro football team, meet in the middle of nowhere, a vir-tual moonscape, to escape their own media-gone-mad creations. They confront each other in the sort of privacy and security they af-ford no other public figures.

EXT. EL MIRAGE DRY LAKE—DAY

MESSENGER   If we might just have a short ego break, I have a suggestion I would like to put forward. At the risk of losing you as
an enemy, why don't we go partners on this one? I'll be happy to
settle for a half share in the team. Dealing me in will go a long
way in helping your lapdog Senator Barrish make your conflict
of interest problem disappear.

POWERS   And give you the foothold you're dying to get in sports.

MESSENGER   What is a foothold compared to your stranglehold,
Lionel? Truthfully, my interest lies beyond just sharing the Titans with you. I would also like to be included in your Sri Lanka
operation.

POWERS   Who says I'm planning one?

MESSENGER   Don't crap a crapper, Lionel.

POWERS   *(a beat, then)* Only if I can get a like interest in your
South African satellite.

MESSENGER   South Africa's not on the table. But I will go half
with you on my all-Vatican channel.

POWERS   Your efforts to become my equal are as offensive as they
are pathetic. We inhabit different worlds. You invade, where I in-
novate. Where I pioneer, you plunder.

MESSENGER   I'm certain that, as we speak, the third of the work-
force you decimated after buying out Southwest Interbell are all
lighting candles for you to win the Nobel Prize.

POWERS You know a little bloodshed is always required to save the greater number of jobs. Stop running for God, Julian. It only makes atheism all the more attractive to me. Withdraw your efforts to buy the Titans within twenty-four hours. Withdraw, or things are going to get ugly. *Truly* ugly.

MESSENGER *(unruffled)* That is why I pay people to attend law school, Lionel. *(as Powers starts to go)* Lionel. *(Powers pauses)* Before I was ten years old, I had walked halfway across Europe. First, on my father's back, when he was hardly strong enough to take a step on his own, and then in the shoes I took from his body. Those shoes—those shriveled ghosts of my father. And on and on—and on. Walking always toward the flame. The flame in my head—the one that lit the way out of that unspeakable damnation. Do what you will, Lionel. Let's see if it's worse than anything that Adolf Hitler put me through.

POWERS I can only try, Julian. I can only try.

Tough guy, Lionel Powers. But then, he gives us fair warning in this excerpt from an address he delivers at one of his stockholders' meetings.

POWERS It's no secret my father started out cleaning septic tanks. Ever eager for expansion, he quickly realized there was not one of his cesspool subscribers who did not subscribe to the local newspaper, as well. Understanding this synergy between the papers—news and toilet—he bought the first of over three dozen publications, filling them mainly with what he intuited as the public's prime and insatiable interest—that is to say, who was sticking it to whom.

To those who contend that a steady diet of the titillating and the inconsequential tends to render society incapable of coping with life's harsher realities, I say let *them* offer more uplifting fare. I have no doubt as to which choice society will make.

It's a moot point, in any case, as I have become one of the half-dozen chief gatherers, editors, and suppliers of intelligence to the world. I am, happily, most ecumenical. Whatever the topic,

164 * Laughing Matters

large or small, each of you is entitled to my own opinion. And I will fight to the death for your right to agree with it.

Open warfare begins with Powers firing the first salvo at Messenger by publishing a scandalous exposé about the youthful transgressions of Messenger's grandsons. Messenger's reply is recorded on videocassette and sent to all of Powers's seventeen residences.

MESSENGER   The first blood goes to you, Lionel. You have sucked the joy out of this family. It is not as though I, too, haven't skimmed the gutter in search of the vilest behavior. That is our stock in trade, yours and mine; providing the raw meat so endlessly craved and licked over by a public unashamed of its collective envy. But I, at least, have always obeyed the primary law of our particular jungle. *We never go after each other, Lionel.* You know that. Not *ever* on a personal level. Need I remind you that not one of us—ever—*ever*—outed Malcolm? Even after the last bagpipe had been blown. To say nothing of the last biker. To this day, we continue to treat him with kid gloves. Through an unspoken understanding, we allowed him to be buried in the manner of a king, instead of branding him the raving, road warrior queen that he was. We have—each of us—any number of skeletons just waiting to be rattled. Yours had better be very well hidden. Very well hidden, indeed, my friend.

I will now freeze this close-up for you, Lionel, should you find it suitable for framing—a pastime at which you so sickeningly excel.

The New York premiere screening produced sober reactions from many of its invited guests. "Media folk," said Frank Rich in the *Times*, "did not seem to enjoy it. Perhaps no one fixed the futility of the Vietnam war more firmly in the mass American imagination than Mr. Gelbart did, under the guise of writing about Korea in *M*A*S*H*. And perhaps no writer in any medium so fully anticipated Whitewater. His savage 1989 play . . . *Mastergate* foresaw the next, inevitable whatevergate." Were *Mastergate* to be revived on Broadway now, Rich wrote, "it might pass for the evening news."

He quoted Gelbart as being angrier about the media barons than about the tobacco executives he had spoofed in *Barbarians at the Gate.* "Tobacco executives are only dangerous to smokers (and those nearby). But we all smoke the news. We all inhale television. They're much more dangerous . . . I'm mad as hell, to quote the immortal Paddy," referring of course to the late Paddy Chayefsky, whose hero cried out about the trashing of TV news in the movie *Network* twenty years ago.

"Given that *Network,* a huge hit, did nothing to slow the cultural collapse it decried," Rich added, "who or what will counteract the mega-media powers dramatized by [Gelbart]? Our real life Congressional watchdogs are just as impotent as the whorish politicians Mr. Gelbart satirizes . . . A Congress fattened by campaign contributions and fearful of unflattering TV coverage looks the other way while the media giants gorge themselves on corporate welfare and disdain the public interest."

Perhaps Mr. Rich himself had taken up the challenge to face those weapons of mass distraction.   —Ed.

SCENE 14

THEY'RE OUT THERE, WAITING FOR YOU

Mr. Gelbart, asked to address film school graduates,* tells them—and us—what to expect. Among them—surprises, plus the facts of life.

He begins by expressing his pleasure at the invitation and especially the fact that it had been extended to a writer. He offered one of his favorite definitions of the role of the author by citing Thomas Mann, who said, in what must be one of the few examples of German understatement, "A writer is someone for whom writing is more difficult than it is for other people."   —Ed.

*At the University of Southern California, in 1991.

Not long ago, in an issue of *World Press Review,* a compilation of news stories from everywhere, the following item appeared:

"Reza Pahlavi, the twenty-three-year-old son of the late Shah of Iran, lives in luxury in Rabat, Morocco, waiting for a chance to go home and assume his father's role. The monarch-in-exile believes the Iranian people are waiting for liberation, and that many oppose the present regime. If he cannot regain the Peacock Throne, he says he would like to become a movie director."

An anxiety to begin such a career is more than matched by the great numbers of people who are just as anxious for you to get started. Have you any idea how many and how varied those people are?

To begin with, the major motion picture studios are waiting for you—waiting for you to create blockbusters, the kind that miraculously break all previous box office grosses while never threatening to show a profit.

ABC, CBS, NBC, PBS, and the IRS—they're all waiting for you, too, gleefully anticipating how much revenue you're going to generate for them.

The Japanese, busy reading *What Makes Samurai Run,* are also waiting for you. The folks at the Bavarian Motor Works, they can't wait for you to get started either. Wall Street is waiting for you—waiting for you to help drive up the price of entertainment company shares and of the value of those corporate sponsors who are also waiting—waiting for you to create the kind of TV programming that will sell more and more products that help viewers smell better, smell less, or maybe not ever smell at all.

Parking spaces are being prepared, fresh stencils are being cut, headwaiters are learning to pronounce your name, prison inmates are vying for the privilege of stamping out your personalized license plates—and your dental hygienist is busy on the second draft of the screenplay she's going to spring on you the next time she gets you into her chair.

Last, but hardly by any egotistical means least, I am waiting for you. As far as I'm concerned, you've graduated not one moment too soon.

Take a good hard look at our cinema. Try, if you can, to do the same with television. The state of the art is in a state of emergency. The nation's screens, of every size, are awash with films and programming that are more a reflection of dedicated deal making than they are of meaningful filmmaking. Commissions have replaced commitment. Packaging has replaced passion.

American mass entertainment, always to some extent based on the bottom line, is increasingly manufacturing "product" that is distinctly from the bottom of the barrel. We are currently plagued by the proliferation of motion pictures that are, in fact, feature-length trailers for their own next feature-length trailer—which are, in turn, etc., etc. Why this need to play it so creatively safe? To make movies by the numbers? A couple of reasons come to mind.

A good many of today's studio decision-makers began their executive careers in television, some of them as viewers while still attending day school. They were quick to learn that in the world of TV what mostly pays the rent, theirs *and* the networks', are long-running series. And what is a long-running series but a string of sequels? The same title, the same cast, the same basic plot, week after week, year in and year out. Hundreds and hundreds of episodes. By that yardstick, a movie marquee that boasted *Rocky* and *2001* would not necessarily indicate a double feature.

There were, of course, movie sequels in the past, but hardly in the numbers we see them today. They were, for the most part, "B" pictures, programmers. They had none of the bloated importance of today's sequels, any of which can often decide the financial fate of the company that has the nerve-racking distinction of releasing one of them.

Today's movie audiences, too, are largely television trained, most of them exposed to it almost at birth, learning to watch before they can crawl. And what constitutes their appreciation? What forms their standards? Simple plots, simple problems, and simple solutions, everything tied up neatly three minutes before the end of your time slot and the last commercial. Just as in real life.

All's well that ends well, and positively everything, increasingly, *has* to end well. Unhappy viewers are in no mood to go out and buy a car or a beer. Or do both at the same time. There is no call on their involvement or their emotions; only their happy buttons are pushed. And so the audience, conditioned as it is, demands none of these qualities when they're old enough to ask for enough money from their parents to buy a ticket to the movies. Indeed, many of them do not know they exist or that films can affect people in deeply personal terms. They are, without question, far more technology-oriented than audiences of the past, but past audiences were far more emotion-empowered.

I don't mourn the good old days. I implore you to bring us some wonderful, far better new ones.

That the ever-changing, never-changing cadre of motion picture and television decision-makers tend to clone past successes, that they actively discourage originality because of the high financial risks of dream making, is hardly news. Neither is their corruption of the creative community, all too many members of which are more than willing to take a number and wait for the opportunity to be corrupted. Somewhere along the line, however, we have to understand that we cannot go on collaborating with them—as talents—and as audience—and not take our share of the (dis)credit for it.

What we need today is no less than a revolution. We need to do violence to the cliché, create havoc with the tried, the tired, and the tested.

It seems criminal to ask youth to perpetuate the cinematic senility that has set in since Hollywood has chosen to transform itself into a software factory, one whose product is designed to make a relatively few wealthy, while impoverishing our culture to a devastating degree. Let's not settle for a simple wind of change or just a breath of fresh air; let us aim for a tempest of originality—a hurricane of audacity.

If, in the current fashion, a hurricane needs a name, how about "Rosebud," the one word in film vocabulary synonymous with innovation and experimentation? The one word that evokes the memory of a young newcomer's bold commitment to employ every corner and shadow of the screen, filling it with vibrant characters engaged in an utterly compelling story.

Hard to believe that in just fifty short years, we've gone from Orson Welles's filmic feast to such mediocre, standardized, trivialized fare. That we have witnessed such a devolution in the film world. That's what happens when moviemakers take the pulse of only other moviemakers and superimpose the results on an audience they know only as so many statistics.

Anyone for a conspiracy? A conspiracy not just to make movies, but to make a difference? A conspiracy to reintroduce emotion, *feelings* to the screen—some other emotion besides fear and hate? A conspiracy to deal honestly with problems that are deeply rooted in our society? As well as the true consequences of those problems? Or do we continue giving our American and foreign overlords nothing but happy endings, when so many people in real life are having such miserable beginnings and middles? Do we go along with this country's compassion fatigue?

Feel-good movies, more than anything, mostly make film distributors feel good. They do little to reflect or interpret the human condition—especially for those who exist in conditions that fall below that standard. If the conspiracy fails at everything else, hopefully it will succeed in restoring some element of humanity back to films.

There is, I believe, a group consciousness, some primal need to offer evidence of our existence, reach up and put our handprints on the wall of the cave. Beyond proof of our physical presence, there is an obligation to record our emotions, to remind one another that we *are* one another; that just as we share the same physical fate, so do we share what is in our hearts and minds.

Where is the humanity we once witnessed on the screen? In these tougher, rougher times, audiences have become so desensitized, it takes a cannibal, the popular Hannibal Lecter in *Silence of the Lambs,* to excite them; a monster, incidentally, who is not punished for his unspeakable crimes but is left alive at the end of the film—to perhaps return sometime in a sequel. Or two, or three, his appetite depending entirely upon our own for him at the box office.

And, finally, let's have a conspiracy of substance over style, of text over toys and technology.

Surprise us. Astonish us. Offend us, if you must. Put the movies, put TV, put the whole town, in turnaround.

If I take a dim view of this sometimes relentlessly sunny part of the world, it's only because I've been faithful to a definition of a personal philosophy, one voiced by the venerable French director Abel Gance. "I take life tragically," he said. "But never seriously."

SECOND INTERMISSION: WRITERS

One characteristic of the character named Gelbart is his generosity and his appreciation of the work of others, which may be one reason why, despite occasional exceptions, he is such a remarkable collaborator.

Generosity not being exactly epidemic in Hollywood, it may also explain why, too, despite a cutting-edge wit, he is so well liked. What follows are some notes on a few of the writers whose work and whose manner he enjoys, plus an essay on writing, and in particular the writing of comedy. Sounds as if Larry thinks that what was once the central idea, that of the human comedy, has sunk too often to inhumane comedy. —Ed.

DOC

Milton Berle tells of seeing *The Odd Couple* on Broadway, and laughing long and hard at the very first joke, which occurs almost before members of the audience have even had a chance to remove their coats.

He laughed just as hard at the next line, which arrived within milliseconds of the first one, and then as hard or even harder at the next, and then the next.

Feeling a tap on his shoulder, he turned to find himself face-to-face with the man sitting directly behind him. Clearly annoyed by

Milton's laughter, he asked, "Are we going to have this all night?"

I've never written for Milton Berle (although he is so, well, absorbent that, having written for so many comedians, I have in a sense also written for him), but if I had, I would have told him that the proper response to the irate theatergoer was "Yes, sir, that's correct. We are absolutely going to have this all night." He might have added that we are also going to have this all day at the show's two matinee performances. And not only at this particular theater in New York, but very likely in two or possibly three others in the city as well, where additional Neil Simon works were being simultaneously presented, to say nothing of the countless playhouses throughout the land and in countries abroad where theater audiences were rolling in whatever their word is for aisles at translations of Neil's works that were being performed in assorted accents and in more tongues than even the Carnegie Deli can boast.

Because of Simon's uncommon, almost supernatural ability to make us laugh—and cry—either alternatively or, if he chooses, at the same time—we, that is to say, the world, have not only had this all night, we have had this all generation.

Actually, for much more than a generation Neil has been committing his heart and his mind to paper, in order that actors might don the skins and screw on the heads that he has fashioned for them to relay to audiences the latest accounting of his hopes and his fears, and the revelations of those dreams that he has harbored—dreams that have collapsed, or, even more cruelly at times, that have double-crossed him by coming true.

I first met Neil—Doc, then, as I've said, and for me, Doc forever—in the early fifties, when I was trioed with him and his brother and mentor, Danny, on a pilot script for a proposed half-hour series for Jack Carter on CBS, called *Love That Guy*. The title was wishful thinking. Nobody did. Starting with CBS, which all but canceled the pilot during the shooting, while we were on a break to reload film in the camera.

The next time I encountered the Simon frères was when we passed each other in the revolving door on the then chaotic Red Buttons show, where, as the head writer, mine was the first to roll.

It was in 1955 that Doc and I found ourselves working together on *Caesar's Hour.* I *think* it was '55. Contrary to popular belief, it's not the legs that go first; it's remembering the word for legs. But there is no forgetting Doc in those early, internship days, days he captured with such accuracy and affection in his play modeled on the experience we shared working for Sid Caesar.

Once in the writers' office where the air was thick with laugh lines lobbed like grenades, each seeking to land in the script at hand, Doc asked if he could use a joke that he thought I had written. He was quite surprised when I told him it was a joke that *he* had written. He put it into the play, but he still believes that the credit belongs to me.

(Turnabout is fair play. I have often been complimented for writing the musical *Little Me,* which is one of his best works.)

Edmund Kean, or Edmund Gwenn, or maybe even Edmund Lowe, asked on his deathbed if dying was hard, supposedly gave the much-quoted answer, "Dying is easy. *Comedy* is hard." It's definitely the other way around for Doc. Comedy, for him, is as reflexive as breathing—and equally essential to his survival. He was fabulous in the *Caesar's Hour* writing room, giving as good as the rest and the best in that supercharged atmosphere heavy with street smarts, urban blight transformed into urban bright, fairly crackling with the electric energy generated by a half-dozen gifted, twisted minds, all high on their own comic speed. Even then, Doc was in himself the oddest of couples; an intro-extrovert, a quiet, self-styled observer of his own life and the lives of those around him who distilled (as he still does) his and our joys, our pain, our trials, and our glories, and celebrates them in nearly endless fireworks displays of comic creation.

And they are endless. When I think of his constant string of opening nights, I could kick myself for not buying stock in Western Union when he first began writing. One of my theories about Simon is that many years ago, when he has said he was in the army, he was actually off somewhere writing a play that ran to a couple of thousand pages, and each year he just saws off two acts of it.

My other theory is that Doc *is* a play and he just keeps writing his life down as fast as he can.

An example: When Simon was living on Central Park West some

years ago, a young man appeared at the front door to collect Doc's clothes for the cleaner. Doc gave him a suit, a blazer, and a pair of pants. He never saw the stuff again. The kid was just one of the five or six million scam artists who inhabit New York City. That kind of thing never happens to me. Never. God, or the Play Fairy, or whoever is in charge of this kind of thing, always directs the experience at Doc.

Whatever the means or the process, he is a tireless collector and curator of angst, an eye in the sturm and the drang who holds up a mirror to his own experiences at such an angle that we are all able to see our own faces in it alongside his.

If I envy Doc anything, it's his watch. His seems to have so many more hours on it than mine does. So many more minutes to listen to that little writer in the back of his mind, who he claims really does the writing for him while he's off doing other things. What a gracious, modest front man Simon is for that "little writer."

He has said that every time he writes a new play, it's a new life for him. I, for one, wish him as many lives as he can find a pencil for. I'm confident that in each and every one of them he will display the same sense of humanity, the same grace and generosity, that have gone such a long way toward my being able to forgive him for his altogether remarkable career.

From the *Random House Dictionary of the English Language:*
line (līn), *n., v.* . . .
    10. Usually, **lines.** the words of an actor's part in a drama, musical comedy, etc.
om•ni (om´nē), an element of Latin origin meaning "all."

How fitting then that Neil Simon, anagrammatically, is Omni Lines.

Who other than Doc seems to have written all the actors' parts in all the dramas, all the musical comedies, and, for all we know, all the et ceteras we know? If he chooses to keep giving us new works and not rest on his laurels, it can only be because he is afraid of heights.

HERB GARDNER

Long before *I'm Not Rappaport*, Herb Gardner's first Broadway hit was *A Thousand Clowns* ("Everybody out for volleyball!"), which opened in the sixties during the initial run of *A Funny Thing Happened on the Way to the Forum*. We knew each other only through our work. Called in as a play doctor by the producers of an ailing musical, *Hot Spot*, Gardner, not interested in committing to the whole job, said that he would rework the first act if they could get me to do the same with the second. Intrigued by Gardner's novel approach, I agreed to his plan. After initial meetings to discuss the ailing show's symptoms and possible cures, we ended our medical conference by going off to try to save the show from the rigor mortis that was rapidly setting in. We extracted a major condition from the show's producers and its director, Morton Da Costa: they would have to put in all of our changes, each and every one of them. We were the doctors and they were the parents of the patient. If we were to try to save their offspring, they must accept whatever surgery we felt might be necessary. They were more than happy to agree to our terms.

While Herb and I worked on our separate parts of the body, Da Costa was fired and his replacement turned out to be the director I'd worked with some years earlier on *The Notorious Landlady*, Richard Quine. Knowing Dick, I felt reasonably comfortable about the arrangement.

If I've learned one professional lesson in my life, it's that comfortable is foreplay for a disaster.

When Gardner and I gave him the numerous new pages we had written, Dick said that he liked a good deal of what we had done, but not all of it. We informed him that he was now working by the rules of the theater. Here it was not the director, but the writers who had final cut, and we had reinforced that principle with the producers. Dick's response was that the producers had said *he* would be the final judge of what changes went into the show. We said that either he used all of what we had written or we would withdraw every bit of it. He chose the latter, extreme option, but warned us that he wasn't responsible for what a good memory he had and that he couldn't guarantee that some of our changes—the ones he liked—wouldn't somehow find their way into the show.

I said I didn't think that would be a very good idea.

"What're you going to do, sue me?" he joshed.

"Not at all," Gardner said, without a trace of josh. "We'll take you out behind the theater and smash your head up and down on the pavement."

It was a wonderful scene. Better than any that ever appeared in the show—which, of course, contained not one word of what Gardner and I had written.

WOODY

When I first met Woody Allen, he came up to my knees. He still comes up to my knees. In every other respect, he is a giant. Not since Charlie Chaplin has anyone turned out such a body of movie work, functioning as a writer, actor, and director. It's not that Woody is adept at changing hats. It is simply that he is hydra-headed.

After *Caesar's Hour* went off the air in the late fifties, Sid Caesar signed with Chevrolet to deliver two one-hour television shows. When he asked me to work on them, my one condition was that I be allowed to write them alone with him and not in a room full of cigars attached to a platoon of writers. Gifted as the old team was, I had had enough of collaboration by committee.

So it was that Sid and I began to prepare the first of the two shows. It took a day or two before it got very lonely in the relatively smoke-free writing room. (Sid was never without seven or eight burning inches of Havana sticking out of his mouth.) But Neil Simon wasn't there, mumbling brilliant jokes that Carl Reiner picked up and then acted as an amplifier for. Mel Brooks wasn't around to not be around by being hours late and then to compensate for his tardiness with remarkable contributions.

That all changed when in walked Sid's stand-in, a stand-up comic, the late Milt Kamen. (Why, incidentally, are the dead always referred to as "the late"? I mean, it's not as though they're ever going to show up, is it?) At any rate, the as-yet not late Milt, a lovely man, seemed all the lovelier that day when he announced that he was bringing us some writing help, someone he introduced as "the young Larry Gelbart." Funny, I thought *I* was the young Larry Gelbart. In walked the writing help, in a most unlikely package. Woody looked to be all of six years old. His previous writing credit, I assumed, must have been learning the alphabet. We invited him to sit with us, as a matter of politeness, but I don't think Sid or I really expected him to make much of a contribution. Then as now, he is not very impressive physically, not that size in any way is a measure of anyone's wit. It was just that he seemed so fragile, so unformed, a tadpole in horn-rims. Then he started pitching jokes. Magically, he became instantly handsome, growing a foot taller with each fresh and funny punch line. This frog was a prince of comedy.

For the next two weeks of writing sessions with Sid and me, Woody did more than pull his own weight; he was capable of lifting us both. One day, for reasons that are somewhere on my long list of escaped recollections, Woody and I were chauffeured to Sid's house in King's Point, where we had been summoned to work. In mid-afternoon, Sid, in predictably unpredictable Caesarean fashion, announced that he was going to take a steam bath and suggested the three of us continue working in his sauna. I was game. I'd worked with comics on planes and trains, in cars and in bars, in dressing rooms, changing rooms, men's rooms; in trucks and yachts, and limos and liners; backstage in theaters, at the front in theaters of war; but the one way I'd never worked with a comic was in the raw. Woody wouldn't hear of it. When Sid and I entered the sauna, Woody stayed outside, refusing to get undressed, saying he couldn't be funny naked.

As I said, Woody was quite young. He had yet to realize that everyone is funny naked.

A year or two later, Woody and I, fully clothed, wrote a TV revue for the late, and again not in the tardy sense, David Susskind. Our writing sessions took place either in Woody's apartment in Manhattan or at a small farm I owned in upstate New York. I remember picking up Woody and his then wife, Harlene, at the train station, the first time they came to visit for a working weekend. Understand, this was rural America, the Midwest of the East, the real thing, costumes by Oshkosh. In his three-piece suit (at least), button-down shirt, and black tie, Woody got off the train looking like a rabbi in mid-elopement. Harlene, resembling his bride and widow all in one, wore a black dress, a veiled hat, and elbow-length gloves. I'm certain Woody brought their passports.

I quickly learned what a totally urban creature Woody is. He hated flies; feared them, really, not so much that one might bite him but rather possibly carry him off. He never went near, let alone into, the swimming pool. There were "things" in there, he said. To him, the sparkling blue water was a black lagoon. A hundred and twenty-five miles north of Manhattan, Woody gave the impression of someone lost in the Amazon. He is simply not an outdoor person. He was not too crazy about being in my farmhouse either, since those indoors were completely surrounded by so much of the dreaded outdoors.

~~~~

I was in the audience the night Woody debuted as a performer at a New York club called the Blue Note, which was the preeminent showcase for comedians in the fifties. After the performance, I joined him in his dressing room. The cabaret critic for the *Daily News* had been in there moments earlier to type his review of Woody's act, and had thrown the carbon paper into the wastebasket. Reading it, Woody was crushed. The critic had characterized him as an intellectual Menasha Skulnick, an actor/comedian of the period famous for his thick Yiddish accent, but certainly not for his intellect. Woody had worked so hard to come off as hip and sophisticated (which he was), and here he was being compared to a shticky, immigrant comic (which he definitely was not).

He did work a lot like Elaine May. And by design. Woody often said how much he admired her delivery. Her influence was evident in his timing and his inflections. For someone who always claimed that his mother reminded him of Groucho Marx, it must have been a relief to find a maternal figure who didn't have a mustache and smoke cigars.

Years after that night at the Blue Note, I saw him perform before several thousand people at a Democratic rally in Washington, D.C. The transformation was total. He'd become a performer who exuded confidence and authority, doing joke after joke about how little he had of either of those qualities. After a good deal of practice and acceptance, he was no longer a male Elaine, or a young me, or an anything anyone else. He was Woody Allen. And Woody, the writer, was supplying Woody, the comic, with absolutely stunning material, material that showcased his gift for defying and deflating that which disturbs him the most: life, sex, no sex, not enough sex, too much sex, and of course, that old standby, death. It is a gift that has allowed him to deal with those fears that have dogged him throughout his life, triumphing over them one laugh at a time.

I encountered him recently, walking on Fifth Avenue. We got in about six city blocks of reminiscences and, as we said good-bye, I stepped off the curb without bothering to watch for oncoming cars and felt him pull me back sharply.

"Careful," he said. "Let's not turn this meeting into an anecdote."

ON WRITING

How to begin a writing project? Put your ass down in your chair, and hope that your head gets the message.

〰〰

I don't know which it is writers welcome the most: praise or interruptions.

Writers, to a man, to a woman, welcome any reason, any excuse, not to write.

I have, on occasion, facing a deadline, found it necessary to shave four times on the same day. I will answer a letter that has been sitting on my desk for as long as five minutes. (It's usually from someone who wants to know how to get started as a writer. I can tell them how to start a career. It's the mornings that are a problem.) After I get that out of the way, I'll settle down—and take a call from a salesman who wants to sell me some toner for my copy machine. There comes that moment, though, when I've simply run out of creative ways not to be creative, and I'll finally start to write. But not before I take the time to sharpen my pencils to the point where they're able to perform brain surgery.

～～～

Expect that some days you're not going to get anything done; that you're just going to have to sit and wait for the creative tide to come in.

～～～

Some lines I create consciously. Others I discover I've written when I look up at the monitor and see that I've responded to some metaphysical sort of dictation. Some lines are shaped because of the wonders of the word processor. I will look at a thought in mid-sentence on the screen, a word will stand out; it will suggest certain comic possibilities, then some sort of internal thesaurus switches on and my mind kicks over other uses for that word. It's one of the great joys of this way of writing, as we all know. Words become clay, to be shaped and worked this way and that; they're playthings that you can turn back-to-front, or turn inside out to see if one contains a surprise no one but you has ever found before.

Of course, one thinks of lines away from the workplace and these are employed in the work later on, but usually lines occur to me in the normal process of writing. It was true when I worked with pencil and pad and it's even truer now when I look at the monitor as a form of cinema at which I am the only patron.

I put in everything from ten- to twelve-hour days to zero-hour ones. On the days I don't write I always seem to be able to invent some reason or other for getting to my desk and doing something, anything that has to do with words.

I'm at it even before the sun comes up. I seem to be getting up earlier and earlier. Maybe it's just a sneaky way of living longer. I like to, if I can, start my working day at around 6:00 A.M.

I find an electronic bulletin board is a good way to start the day, to start watching my fingers reveal what my mind is thinking. I have an office that is separate from the main house. Feels more like I'm going to work that way. There are a number of phone lines in my home office, but the way it's set up, none of them rings. All my calls go through the house proper and they tell me by intercom who's calling. When I'm being superdisciplined, I try not to return any calls until the end of the working day.

Hungry or not, I keep invading the refrigerator, one of the attractions and chief drawbacks of working at home.

〰〰

I think it's best to work on something that absolutely insists itself upon you.

When I get frustrated enough in any sort of writing situation, I just cool it, I do something else. I'll pull weeds in the garden, futz around with meaningless busyness; do anything but try to write, only all too often find myself as obsessive about weeding as I am about wording.

Before too long I become the beneficiary of all the thinking that's been going on without me.

Of course, I'm aware that this process takes place, but I keep pretending it's all very magical and metaphysical, just to please my subconscious.

〰〰

Part of the enjoyment of writing is looking up at the screen (or down at the paper) and seeing a line or a thought or an observation or a plot twist appear that has worked its way through my system and surprised me by its appearance.

〰〰

The best work is the work you don't ever want to finish.

〰〰

Without getting into the fine points of the distinction between a writer and a storyteller, a concept I've never really thought about, let me say that I am unalterably opposed to scenes that "cheat."

For me, it's impossible to go from *A* to *C*, without the information contained in *B,* as a writer and as a member of the audience.

Once a story springs a logic leak, I can never again invest any interest in what follows.

〰〰

I don't have to wait until I wake up in the middle of the night to realize I've "cheated" my way through something the day before. My system kicks in a whole lot faster than that. You know pretty quickly, too, when part of you is trying to put something over on the other half of the writing team, which is also you.

〰〰

Somebody once said, "What if the phone doesn't ring in this scene?" That is to say, what if the characters are *not* interrupted, what if they *have* to go on talking about whatever it is the phone call lets them avoid? I'm not for the phone not ringing. The bells toll for me.

〰〰

It's a mental sort of hunt and peck. Connecting the dots, the dots being the major turning points in the structure.

Characters have as many dimensions as you're able to give them. Just keep turning them in the light and you'll see their many sides.

〰〰

There's only one way I know to try to come back after a failure. And that's fast. It's the one sure way to revive your confidence in yourself. After enough years, you begin treating your failures in the same way as you do your successes. Either one is the natural consequence of your work, and so you just mush on, regardless of the outcome of your most recent experience.

〜〜

I find myself laughing less and less these days, I'm afraid. It goes with the mortality business. An awful lot of stuff seems less and less funny. Or perhaps one is less inclined to deny with laughter some of the grimmer facts of life.

I admit to being somewhat jaded. It's hard to be surprised by a punch line after all these years, having teethed on, either as a member of the audience or as a member of their staff, some of the funniest people in the world.

I don't laugh at a lot of the young comics. I laughed at a lot of what they are doing when it was done by the young comics of a generation or two ago.

〜〜

The first change I noticed in comedy was when sick jokes and race jokes came on the scene in the 1950s. Prior to that, I don't remember ridiculing racial groups, except in whispers, or quips about deformities and handicaps. I don't know whether the change meant we were merely becoming more honest about our prejudices or getting more comfortable with our callousness.

When rock and roll came in, there wasn't a lot of humor accompanying it. Then, along came drug humor, which was a very noticeable step away from mainstream comedy. I believe that, in a sense, laughter made drug taking acceptable, and corporate America, the landlords of TV and the movies, bear a heavy responsibility for providing the means of disseminating this destructive notion.

In TV's earlier days, there were a lot fewer television sets in the country, and the sets being expensive, they were owned chiefly by affluent people. Affluence is usually the result of education. That early audience understood, demanded a higher standard. Not nearly the number of children watched and controlled the sets as do now, so you could write much smarter material.

A lot of the television comedy in that era was the work of people from other fields—radio, motion pictures, would-be playwrights and novelists. They brought a lot to the medium. But, increasingly, the work came to be turned out and ordered by people whose only exposure has been to television; they are feeding on themselves.

So much of today's comedy seems aimed at the minds, to say nothing of the nether regions, of the predominantly young audience. Today's chief movie ticket–popcorn, extra butter–nachos–hot dog–large Diet Coke, not too much ice, please buyer represents a generation that has been weaned on TV comedy, one influenced by cookie-cutter material evoking either laughter from a machine that produces that sound on cue or actual laughter so mechanically sweetened it can cause mental decay. Today's audiences, some of them, their impoverished training providing such reduced standards, simply do not have the ability to be demanding or discerning.

A good many of the film studios, currently run by former agents who are now telling their former clients they are not worth what they used to demand for them, select ever more formulaic, innocuous material, including products that are the work of artists of drugged insensibilities, whose substances of choice are paid for out of their films' budgets, giving a whole new meaning to drug free.

〜〜〜

Laughter is a very personal act. It has to start with the individual, although it can end up a group experience. But first, it has to work for you; then you can work in a crowd.

We've all sat in a large gathering and seen everybody else falling on the floor, and we've wondered what was so funny. We've also had the reverse experience where we were the only ones in a crowd laughing.

Some people are better laughers than others. They seem to be wearing feathered underwear. They are always primed to laugh. You go to a Neil Simon play and people are laughing as they get out of the taxi. They're ready.

〜〜〜

You have to take an audience's word for what is funny. Comedy is not negotiable. They like it, they buy it. They don't, you offer them something else. You can't think of anything better? Look for some other kind of work.

〜〜〜

Everyone wants to collaborate with the writer. "They" want to tell us how to make our work better, brighter, sharper, funnier, sadder, longer, shorter, less subtle, more subtle, more socko, more boffo, sicko, psycho; improvements they're all qualified to make because of their various titles and because, unlike the writer, they're not too close to our work. (As though feeling or being close to your endeavors is some sort of sin. "Someone else is going to finish that ceiling for you, Mr. Michelangelo. The pope feels you've gotten too close to your work.")

Writers should direct. If they can. Or positively need to. Some of us just like to—positively need to—just write. We who do know the inevitable pain that's likely to follow once all the other hands get laid on, but that is just one of the costs of following your own path.

I once worked on a screenplay that Roman Polanski had written with Gérard Brach in London back in the sixties. Polanski, who was to direct it for MGM, greeted my new pages with appreciative laughter and great enthusiasm about the changes.

After I'd finished, he said he was no longer interested in the project, since I'd made the script much more me than him. In other words, he loved my work so much, he was no longer interested in working with me.

〜〜〜

I'm convinced that the screen's most successful comedies are the results of one person's individual vision. A lot of help is needed to get that vision up on the screen, but it's that one vision that needs to dominate. Only in Hollywood do so many people feel they need to rescue a script, even those that need no rescuing at all. It's like a bunch of lifeguards who try to save you from drowning even before you get into your swimming trunks.

Humor is such an elusive, subjective quality—I'm almost tempted to say *virtue*—let's settle for necessity. Commercial comedy demands of those who practice it one needed skill above all others: restraint—even delicacy. It's no accident that Charlie Chaplin could also dance ballet. Too hard an effort, and the weight of the delivery can crush the intention; too big a sell and comedy quickly turns to embarrassment. It's far too fragile to survive the committee process unless everyone connected with the project shares approximately the same sense of what is funny. Nothing compares to the sinking feeling you get when the director you find yourself working with tells you a joke and you discover in an instant that your ideas of humor, of timing and taste, are miles apart. In the theater, the writer is less likely to have to compromise on the choice of director and cast. In films, for various reasons—and I believe that money is all of them—the writer often is not in the company he chooses to keep.

On the subject of auteurs, I have always found it hard to believe that France, the country that gave the world the gifts of wine and open-mouth kissing (and usually in that order), that the very same France created and successfully exported the fantasy that the director of a motion picture is its author. Can this be the same France that enshrined Molière, and Sartre, and Jerry Lewis and Sylvester Stallone? Unfortunately, the American critical community and the media at large perpetuate this Gallic nonsense with almost every film review: that the director is the author, not simply the guiding light, the linchpin of the enterprise; and that the writer, that is to say, *the author,* is no such thing at all. It is an Orwellian perversion of the language—and an ongoing insult to those who "merely" write.

~~~~

If I feel I am right about something, in terms of a script, I don't have a choice but to fight for my position. I don't feel I'm right because I've been in the business longer than the person who is suggesting—or demanding—the changes. Or because I'm older, or wiser. *Telling* me to write something or write in a way in which I do not believe is asking me to write in a language that I've never heard, let alone ever tried to speak.

⌇⌇⌇

Sometimes I've handled total control well, sometimes not.

On balance, I think some opposition and even authority is healthy. Fighting for your ideas tests their strengths and your belief in them.

I think I'm a good critic of my own work. Certainly, I'm a severe one.

So's my wife. And my daughter, Cathy, and my son, Gary. They are tough, they are knowledgeable, honest, and articulate. The more I hate what they're saying about any of my work, the more I know they're right.

⌇⌇⌇

What annoys me most about what I think are bad films or TV shows are the reviews I read that told me I was going to see something wonderful. This is truer of film critics than of the TV variety. TV critics, their eyeballs propped open perpetually, *Clockwork Orange* fashion, seem to me far more likely to call a turkey a turkey. Perhaps hundreds of hours of exposure to garbage has eroded their capacity for politeness. But film critics are a special breed, and new ones are bred with alarming frequency. Failed actors who can't qualify as TV weathermen or women, people who are better at reading a review off cue cards than they are at writing one, become film critics. These are the people who tell us that *Barton Fink* or *Bob Roberts* may well be this generation's *Citizen Kane*. These are the critics who give so many thumbs-up to so many stars and so many helpful hands to so many dreadful films.

Of course, there have always been bad films and there have always been critics on the take. Do I detect a proliferation of both these vices?

⌇⌇⌇

However . . .

With no disrespect to my fellow and sister ten-thousand-and-something members of the Writers Guild of America, West, and I don't know how many East, we're not all good. There never has been a surfeit of quality or exceptional work in the world, that's what makes the things we treasure so valuable. They are reasonably rare. I don't know that there will ever be a deep enough talent pool that can provide some twenty thousand choice hours of prime time a year on network television and who knows how many more on cable; it's just not possible. What talent there is has to be very careful not to be corrupted by success, or the desire for success, the need to compromise, to get that second Mercedes. You have to do it fast, you have to do it with a set of standards that are artificially induced by the medium. It's *unnatural* to write a drama that needs four or five or six or eight act breaks, and yet your writing has to conform to the television proscenium. TV comedy writing has changed to some degree; there was a time when much of it was written by freelancers. If you were good, in one season you could do, say, two M*A*S*Hs and two *Marys* and two *All in the Familys*, and make your nut for the year. Your work would invariably be rewritten, because the people responsible for those shows would perforce make changes that brought your script in line with what was going on in the show in terms of character evolution, or actors' demands, or for any number of reasons that you, as an outsider, had no knowledge of. Today's shows are almost entirely staff-written; that explains partly why 72 percent of the Guild's members are unemployed. One of the things that diminishes quality is repetition. On M*A*S*H we were never pleased to do the same thing over and over again; we weren't worried about losing our audience. Many shows are. They are forced to worry by network pressure. Conformity also reduces quality. It's not a bright picture; nor is the one we see on the screen. For all the hand-wringing about violence on TV, the chief victim on TV is originality.

~~~

It's a bad idea to base the amount of script doctoring you do on the price you're being paid to do it. You should only change what you think needs changing, and those decisions should not be based on money, or ego, or whim.

After my experience on *Tootsie,* I made a pact with myself that I would never again rewrite the work of others. My work on that picture (and *Neighbors* just before it) amounted, to me, to writer molestation. I have broken that personal pact, with a few provisos: that I will treat the original work with respect, try to ensure that my presence does not reduce the original writer's financial participation, and be perfectly willing to accept no credit for the work.

Unfortunately, a hell of a lot of rewriting goes on because someone other than the writer needs to have his or her vision fulfilled.

~~~

Comedy is that surrogate reality that allows us to observe the behavior of clowns and inferiors, while we go on conducting our own lives in sensible, superior ways.

It is the indispensable device that allows us to reinterpret Shakespeare and take comfort in thinking "what fools *those* mortals be."

~~~

If anything I've ever written in any way reflects this dreamlike passage called life, I can only hope that the mirror I've held up to it is sufficiently cracked.

~~~

Every day that I am able to write is a day off from life.

~~~

I hope to continue writing until I am unalterably interrupted.

~~~

Each draft of any work is practice—practice that helps you chart and define, teaches you to understand the piece you're writing. Inspiration rarely comes with instructions.

~~~

Ernest Hemingway said that all first drafts were shit. Who would dream a writer of that stature didn't own a thesaurus?

~~~

Generally speaking, in Hollywood the first draft of a screenplay is what the writer meant. Every other draft reflects executive decisions about what the writer *really* meant.

~~~

I agree with Dorothy Parker. "Wit has truth in it—wisecracking is simply calisthenics with words." Unfortunately, I have spent too much of my life doing verbal aerobics.

~~~

Research is absolutely essential for me. The trick is to know when to finally stop doing it and actually go to work.

~~~

Outlines can bend and reshape themselves endlessly once you start off on your theoretical vision of the script, but I try not to embark on the long journey that a movie or play is without a road map.

~~~

There are those of us who have a problem being personal in our personal lives who are much more comfortable in work that deals with our lives that is meant to become public.

~~~

There is nothing like a brand-new project to give you a refresher course in humility.

LOCATION SHOT 2:
9021 OVER THE TOP

Our next location is within greater or lesser L.A. itself, the much-maligned, seldom-climbed hills of Beverly. We've all heard that the police consider walking in that area of closely cropped lawns and high-security walls a crime only slightly less heinous than breaking and entering. But we've learned much less about the tear-down-and-build-anew Taj-o-mania that Larry describes—and despite the fact that the Beverly Hills Hotel has opened once more since he wrote this piece for *Harper's Bazaar*, in August 1993, he refuses to retract a word.   —Ed.

In a place where the way you looked last year is unacceptable and the way you will look next year is unthinkable, Beverly Hills has undergone the ultimate in face-lifts. House after house has been bought, leveled to the ground (the ownership of which was the real object of the exercise), and then replaced by a series of out-of-scale, invariably rectangular, inelegantly elephantine mini-palaces. Fair enough. Business is business. Money talks. And for the last few years, in terms of Beverly Hills real estate, at least, it's been speaking Farsi.

The city's relatively new, huge contingent of Persians—people who were smart enough to get out of Iran before the Shah hit the fan (and who prefer not being called Iranians)—are said to be amused by what other BH folk think about the outsize houses they've erected or selected; never mind that the city's residential

area has been drastically changed by the addition of these cocka-
mamy alcazars.

Extremely home-oriented, Persian families tend to be bigger and
tighter than their neighbors and far less divorce-prone than others
in a community where even preschoolers know what *prenuptial*
means. For their active social lives, they prefer large—giant,
really—interiors with high ceilings and floor plans that create the
flow of light they require. Consequently, many of the newer struc-
tures in Beverly Hills seem not so much houses at all, but
grandiose containers for all the goodies within.

With luck, the trend to Tehranize the architecture of Beverly
Hills has hit a speed bump. Changes in the building codes mean
that new houses can no longer be built in the Brobdingnagian proportions we've all come to know and dread. The city's most invin-
cible yet invisible presence, however, is still in an upsizing mode.
The Sultan of Brunei is the richest man in this and probably any
other world; in fact, the SoB became wealthier by several million
dollars in just the time it took the rest of us to get through this sentence. His Sultanship—His Bruneisty?—His Moneyness?—seems
to acquire properties by inhaling them. His Royal Whatever is the
present owner of a place as fabled as its zip code, the Beverly Hills
Hotel. He purchased it from Marvin Davis, who bought it from
Ivan Boesky, a man so fond of trading on the inside, he finally
traded being on the outside for the privilege.

If anyone wondered why such a powerful potentate would want
to bother with getting someone's eggs Benedict just right or changing their dirty sheets, the mystery was cleared up when, shortly
after the sultan took over the hotel, the word spread that he had
asked the city for permission to turn the hotel into a single-family
residence.

That's right: a residence for a single family. Just the sultan, his
wife, their children, and the immediate kingdom. He is reported to
have made the same proposal to the Plaza Hotel in New York at one
time. By some miracle, the Beverly Hills City Council did not say
that His Sultancy, having plunked down a quarter of a billion dollars, could have any kind of two-hundred-room house he wanted.

So, mercifully, happily, the Beverly Hills Hotel remains open to the public. Except for one thing: it's closed. The new owner, it seems, has decided to lavish the same sort of funds and attention on redoing the landmark establishment as he did on his Dorchester Hotel in London. And so the power has been cut off at all breakfasts at the Beverly Hills as the hotel undergoes a two-year, two-hundred-million-dollar renovation that, it is hoped, will restore glamour and perhaps even some business to the pink pile whose own history is so intertwined with the city that shares its name.

~~~~

Built in 1910 by the Rodeo Land and Water Company, the first and future centerpiece of Beverly Hills was situated at the corner of Nothing and Nowhere. Standing in the middle of a vast bean field, rising from the dirt as though someone had struck hotel, the place was intended to promote the fledgling subdivision of Beverly Hills, to attract guests and tourists who might, in turn, be so captivated by the then incredibly blue (and now all too often brown) sky that they would be tempted to purchase property and settle down in the virgin land (both still being plentiful in those lovely, bygone days).

The place was an instant hit, succeeding on two levels: as a watering hole for the wealthy and the royal and as a shill for the city that owes its existence, in part, to the great popularity of the hotel. Now the people who live in the area surrounding the place are preparing themselves for two years of dust, dirt, and dump trucks, while neighbors for blocks around are either turning off their hearing aids or preparing for the eventuality of needing them, once the walls of the venerable inn are assaulted by the sultan's mighty wrecking balls.

Meanwhile, just a precious stone's throw away up the road—Tower Road, to be precise—the collective blood pressure of inhabitants such as Jack Lemmon, Jay Leno, and MCA president Sid Sheinberg has been raised sufficiently to have formed a group called Citizens for the Preservation of Beverly Hills in order to fight off some manor mania that's a little too close to home. One wishes them success, but it might prove to be a case of locking the barn door after a ballroom's been built inside. The cause for all this alarm is a gentleman named Robert Manoukian.

Mr. Manoukian is a London resident who purchased three houses on Tower Road at a cost of nine million dollars. You're yawning. Big deal these days. Well, what Mr. Manoukian proposed to do with his acquisition was first demolish the three houses (once they'd been emptied of the former owners, of course) and then use his nine-million-dollar empty lot to erect a 41,000-square-foot, two-story, ten-bedroom residence that would include a gymnasium, grand ballroom, cinema, library, wine storage area, china vault, and elevators. His plans also called for the building of a six-bedroom security gatehouse, an 8,000-square-foot, five-bedroom guest villa, and parking for ninety-three cars (a few of them presumably not his own). The estate's buildings were to have a total of 59,000 square feet of floor space.

Mr. Manoukian, it turns out, is also strongly family-oriented. That much living space (to say nothing of the fifty-two toilets), he maintains, is essential for his seventeen-member family during the one or two months of the year they plan to spend in Beverly Hills.

Responding to his critics, Mr. Manoukian has agreed to cut back on the size of the house and to limit his entertaining to half a dozen parties a year with no more than four hundred guests at any one time. It is doubtful that any of them will be members of the Citizens for the Preservation of Beverly Hills.

There are those who speculate that Mr. Manoukian, who has advised the Sultan of Brunei on various business deals in the past, including the purchase of the BH Hotel, may be fronting for the sultan in the matter of Tower Road. Perhaps the sultan still feels himself down and out in Beverly Hills since he was not allowed to convert his hotel into a palace away from his palace.

This kind of extravagance is not at all new to Beverly Hills. In the early days, when the IRS was a pup, captains of industry and field marshals of movies satisfied their every fantasy in building their estates, treating themselves to galleries and chapels, walk-in silver and fur vaults, commercial-size laundries, bowling alleys, and rooms large enough to make a Persian purr. And on their vast, park-size grounds, the Harold Lloyds, the Doug and Marys, the Hearsts and the Warners installed their own golf courses, zoos, stables, bridle paths, vineyards, formal gardens, private fire departments, woods, and railroads. They made their wettest dreams come true by creating man-made lakes, waterfalls, and fountains, canals for canoeing, ponds, pools of Olympic proportions, indoors and out, pools with sandy beaches, and, naturally, an assortment of reflecting pools—what could make an actor happier?

There were few neighbors to concern oneself with in those days. Your own miniature country wasn't smack-dab alongside someone else's half-acre lot. The titans of those early times didn't have to worry about the neighborhood. They *were* the neighborhood.

~~~~

A great many more people get to dream the Beverly Hills dream now. What's becoming increasingly difficult is for those dreams to make any sort of aesthetic sense when you see them standing or, much more likely, towering over the houses on either side of them.

Dorothy Parker, who said just about everything bright there ever was to say about anything, said that Beverly Hills was a combination of the best house in every hometown in America.

It just might be that finally, finally, too many best—and biggest—houses will turn Beverly Hills into the kind of town that makes you want to run away from home.

ACT THREE

THEATER

GAR

BILLIE   *Harry . . . Do me a favor.*
HARRY   *What is it?*
BILLIE   *Drop dead!*

It was exactly fifty years ago that I made my maiden visit to New York at the tender, more like raw, age of eighteen. Growing up in Chicago and Los Angeles, I had been exposed to stage presentations mainly of the variety variety—big bands, dance acts, comics, vaudeville, basically. I don't remember ever seeing a professional performance of a play as a youngster. So, eager to make up for lost time, I'm not sure I even bothered to unpack before heading for Shubert Alley to see my first Broadway production. Because the show I chose was a huge hit, I was lucky to get a standing-room ticket. Watching from the back of the house, I saw a piece of magic that dazzled me so, I was grateful for the two intermissions that provided intervals to recover my breath.

The play, destined to become an American classic, was Garson Kanin's *Born Yesterday.* Long before the final curtain, I knew I had been exposed to a standard of playwriting that would inform whatever work I turned out for the next half century.

A fable set in a Washington, D.C., hotel suite, the play involves a crooked junkyard magnate (Paul Douglas) who wants his dumb-blonde girlfriend (Judy Holliday) to help in a scheme to bribe politicians and expand his empire. But when she falls for the tutor he hires to make her more presentable, she starts asking all the "wrong" questions.

My taste in entertainment—more like an insatiable hunger—had been developed over an endless string of Saturday afternoons, mesmerized by one silver screen after another. After I had seen Holliday and Douglas performing as the leads in Kanin's play, and later watched countless other movies, the movies suddenly felt like so many trailers for the real thing, for the *living* thing—the theater. One picture may indeed be worth a thousand words, but, by my emotional arithmetic, one play can be worth a thousand pictures. Those were not images of humans I was watching up there on that stage that first time in New York. Those were not perfect, trapped portrayals that would be repeated to the end of time with the same inevitable precision. I could hear these actors breathing; see them applying an intensity and a dedication in the service of courting my approval as they recited their lines.

And what lines. An entire evening airborne: two and a half hours carried along on the fresh, breezy quality of dialogue in a greater quantity than you'd find in half a dozen double features—even those that might have been the work of Garson Kanin, the screenwriter. *Born Yesterday* was crammed with romance, politics, patriotism, and social commentary, all of it so entertainingly and seamlessly intertwined, I got the sense that Mr. Kanin, the playwright, sat down one day and, not bothering to take so much as a single break for coffee or a cigarette, wrote the whole of the piece, all three acts, from beginning to end, pausing only, if ever, to consider a matter of punctuation here or there. It was, and remains for me, a work of perfection, filled with sharply defined characters engaged in a conflict of wits and will, a piece filled with lofty, civic ideals—a master's lesson in how to deliver it all with the kind of humor that does not for one instant trivialize the play's noble intentions. The play is a stunning example that proves it is not necessary to offer the audience a lollipop to get their minds off the injection you've just jabbed them with, but rather better to learn to hone those lollipops until they achieve a hypodermic-like sharpness.

In time, many years later, I was to meet Garson Kanin. It was a struggle to keep myself from gushing. I did manage to refrain from saying that if I had never attended another play in my life after seeing *Born Yesterday*, it wouldn't have mattered.

Fast forward to December of 1989. A musical for which I had written the book, *City of Angels,* was in its final week of previews before the official Broadway opening. Never able to see one of my own works sitting in the audience, preferring to pray in private, I was watching the performance standing in the back of the house. The laughs came in all the right places and they were all good-sized—not one that you had to throw back into the water. The applause was generous, the curtain calls were prolonged and robust. It was a night of answered prayers.

As the audience rose to leave, talking about the show and not about the shortest way to get to the garage for their cars (always a good sign), I spotted a familiar face in the traffic coming up the aisle. It was the gifted actress Marian Seldes. On her arm was her still very gifted husband, Garson Kanin. God, *he* had seen *my* show. What did he think? Or was that, what did God think? Did he have any idea how important his opinion was to me? Of course, he had an idea. He hadn't been Garson Kanin all these years without knowing how smart Garson Kanin was.

"The show is marvelous," said Marian. "I had a wonderful time."

One down and a thousand to go.

Kanin waited a moment, letting an entire eternity pass, then he took a step that brought him close to me, within striking distance.

Wait a minute, I reminded myself. He may not have liked my work, but surely he's not going to hit me.

And then, finally:

"I have some advice for you," he said. "If you wouldn't mind."

If I wouldn't mind? Did Moses say, "Leave me alone, Lord. What makes you think I'd be interested in any commandments?"

"Please. Anything, Gar. Anything at all."

"I haven't got that much to say," he replied. "Just one thing really. Only one."

He took a step closer. And then this, whispered in my ear, from the man who wrote *Born Yesterday:*

"Don't change a word of it."

That was more than eight years ago.

The glow has never diminished.

It was a long passage to *City of Angels* from Gelbart's first experience with a musical. Interestingly, that early episode began with a little number (which remained little) called *My L.A.* It must occur to anyone who has ever typed the words *Los Angeles* that an easy typo lurks which is also gorgeously appropriate. And it sometimes takes all one can do to resist leaving it, or putting it down, as Los Angles. —Ed.

SCENE 2

WHOSE L.A.?

My L.A. was a musical revue for the stage, based on a daily column in the *Los Angeles Times* by a columnist named Matt Weinstock. The show was considered by many a bold venture for a city so globally movie-struck back in the forties, and with little or no interest in live theater. The man who put it all together was a German immigrant, one of the many in L.A.'s refugee gridlock, an actor-turned-producer named Wilhelm von Trenk-Trebitsch. Willy Trenk was quick to tell everyone that back in Berlin, it was he who had created the role of Mack the Knife in the original production of *The Threepenny Opera*. After fleeing Europe, Willy found work in Hollywood playing countless headwaiters and heartless SS men. (Ironic that future generations, viewing World War II movies, will see mainly Jewish actors, people who fled the Nazis, portraying their Aryan tormentors onscreen.)

To adapt Weinstock for the stage, Trenk hired a trio of radio writers to come up with the sketches (ten- or twelve-minute comic playlets). Larry Marks was one. My *Duffy's Tavern* mentor, Bill Manhoff, was another, and the third was me.

Inspired by material from Weinstock's columns, we were to collaborate on *My L.A.* for four years, endlessly writing and, at Willy's insistence and prodding in the manner of a Gestapo cheerleader, rewriting enough material to paper the freeway. However frustrated we were, writing for the stage was a giant step up from the routine commercial work the three of us continued to do, an opportunity to perhaps one day escape from the grind and anonymity of turning out radio comedy that disappeared into the ether the moment it was spoken.

Two men with an endless list of hit songs, Sammy Fain, composer, and Paul Francis Webster, lyricist, were engaged to write the score. Another refugee, Harry Horner, a master of set design, created an onstage Los Angeles that captured all of the glamour and quirkiness of a city that had boundless quantities of each. Our choreographer was Trudi Shoop, a co-refugee, *natürlich*.

It was a very potent lineup. We couldn't miss.

Uh-huh.

The show ran four nights. Given what a disaster the final offering turned out to be, it's a miracle we didn't close during the intermission. *My L.A.* was a very expensive omelet, losing a hundred thousand dollars a night, to be precise, since the show was mounted at a cost of $400,000, a good deal of money at the time. (A *Funny Thing Happened on the Way to the Forum* was produced on Broadway a dozen years later for a mere $275,000. And just to comment on the cat's cradle aspect of this business, for which there is mercifully no other business like it, did I mention that the theater that housed *My L.A.* was called the Forum?)

Given our modest advance, working on the show as long as we did, Bill and Larry and I made roughly three dollars a week over the four-year period—and that was *not* a good deal of money, even in those days.

Willy Trenk was, all along, a tireless promoter for the show. He ate, drank, and lived *My L.A.* He was able to do all three handsomely by raising tons of money for the production and paying himself lavishly for his efforts. While the production ran such a ridiculously short time, Willy lived anywhere from midway to high on the hog on his hapless investors' money. What really helped sink the enterprise was Willy's insistence on being the show's director, as well as its chief producer and executive sponger. We should have fought him on the issue, but how did we know he didn't have our families locked up in the next room? Willy's sense of humor was hopelessly *mittel*-European, his idea of funny being doctors getting sick or undertakers dying. He might have been able to direct performers singing witty lyrics and acting in comedy sketches in a revue called *My Dusseldorf,* but the touch he brought to the material in *My L.A.* had all the lightness of a German jazz band.

Willy disappeared almost immediately after the show did the same. Although he left the business altogether, becoming a refugee refugee, I still catch a glimpse of him now and then on TV in the umpteenth rerun of a period movie; see him as a headwaiter in a B-minus picture showing a pair of faded stars to their ringside table, or as a jackbooted Nazi officer tormenting some poor soul in the same way he tormented the pathetically few patrons in *My L.A.*

And yet, the Anne Frank in me, finding some good in everyone, is grateful to Willy for giving me the opportunity that he did. His show, in terms of the theater, was my baptism by drowning. Four years of work, four hundred thousand dollars, four performances. I couldn't wait to do my next one.

I should have waited.

SCENE 3

HELL, THE CONQUERING HERO

SGT. MURDOCK *Lovely sermon, Minister. I really enjoyed it.*
THE MINISTER *You attend church often, Sergeant?*
SGT. MURDOCK *Oh, yeah. It's a great place to kill an hour.*

The multifaceted Bob Fosse was the director and choreographer. The score was by the gifted team of Moose Charlap and Norman Gimbel. The producer was the estimable Robert Whitehead: and I was bringing whatever I had that was estimable to the book, a musical comedy adaptation of Preston Sturges's film *Hail the Conquering Hero.*

Retitled *The Conquering Hero,* it was another four-night run.

The challenges of creating a successful musical, tantamount to housebreaking a dinosaur, are as vast as they are varied. The writer, the lyricist, the composer, the cast, the set and costume designers, lighting and sound people all want their particular part of the enterprise to shine. The trick is to make the group, composed of solo talents, into a cohesive, productive ensemble. A lot of egos have to be checked at the door, all the differing objectives have to meld. Bob Fosse's ego would have required a *double* door. His objective was to do *everybody's* work—so much so that he was fired while the show was in pre-Broadway tryouts in Washington, D.C., after unsuccessfully auditioning for the authors and the producer to replace the show's leading man. A director stepping in as the star? It was unheard of. With Fosse and his lawyers engaging Whitehead in litigation, *The Conquering Hero* became the only musical I know that ever opened on Broadway listing no director or choreographer. It arrived on the scene as though someone had left the show in a basket under the marquee. An orphan nobody wanted.

My theater box score now read: two productions, eight performances. Should I quit while I was behind? I was too busy to entertain the thought. All the time I was involved in *Hero*, I was working on another musical, one that was to open in 1962 . . . and continues to run to this day.

SCENE 4

A FUNNY THING . . .

PROLOGUS (entering, center stage; to the audience) *Playgoers, I bid you welcome. The theater is a temple and we are here to worship the gods of comedy and tragedy. Tonight, I am pleased to announce a comedy. We shall employ every device in our desire to divert you.*

A Roman Comedy was its working title. We were far too busy trying to get the piece right to take time out to think about what some lucky show poster would read if we ever actually completed it to our satisfaction. There were to be ten different drafts written over a five-year period before we arrived at the last, merciful version of the book and score, one that represented the most successful execution of our vision. It was not so much that we kept getting it wrong all the time. It was more a matter of never getting it right, all at the same time. In the process we wrote and revised it endlessly. Revised it, rethought it, restructured it. You name it, we redid it.

If *Duffy's Tavern* was college for me, then working on *Forum* was postgraduate work. It was incredibly instructive in teaching, most important, patience. A good deal of what I had learned in radio and television—"Get it out, finish it! Come on, damn it! Where are the pages? We go on the air tomorrow!"—had to be unlearned. Time had to be discovered; time to look for solutions that did not have a deadline attached. Giving ourselves all the time in the world to complete our work on the musical, it seemed as though we took all the time in the world before we permitted ourselves to write that sweetest of all words in the playwright's vocabulary, *Curtain*. Only then did we dare christen it, if one can apply that verb to a pagan comedy.

Why the particular title we hit on? Wanting to suggest that the play was a comedy without actually using the word, we chose the phrase "A funny thing happened on the way to . . ."—the stock opening line comics have used for ages. *Forum* was chosen to complete the title, hoping audiences would immediately associate the word with Rome.

Irwin Shaw once said that writers, in order to withstand criticism from without and compromise from within, have to be vain about their work. Until *Forum*, I confess there was little I had done that warranted any sort of vanity. Over thirty years after its first performance, having written enough words in the interim to paper the globe dozens of times, it remains for me the best piece of work I've been lucky enough to see my name on.

The initial idea for the show came from Burt Shevelove, who had done an embryonic version of a Roman comedy in his university days and had long felt that a professional, full-blown Broadway production had a good chance of success.

Although Burt and I had worked together in television during the fifties, starting with Red Buttons, Burt acting as Red's director, we had never before functioned as a writing team. Working in separate capacities, we learned that our tastes in comedy were identical; that we both laughed at the same things and, happily, always at the same moment.

With Stephen Sondheim as the third member of the team, *Forum* was to be the first Broadway show for which Sondheim wrote both words and music; previously he had "merely" supplied the lyrics for *West Side Story* and *Gypsy.* We began the task of digging around in the twenty-six surviving plays of the third-century B.C. Roman playwright Titus Maccius Plautus. We began to take extracts from his works, a many-chambered catacomb, filled with nothing but funny bones, cribbing a character here, a relationship there, creating connective dramatic and musical tissue to bond our work to his by fashioning a cat's cradle of a plot. If one could take *Forum* apart, unscrew the back of it, so to speak, it would be very much like looking at the inner workings of a computer or a telephone's jumble of multicolored wires.

Our theory was that over the years, the providers of what Broadway called musical comedy had managed to improve the quality of the first at the expense of the latter. Musicals had come to rely on performers who could sell a melody and a set of lyrics but who thought a punch line was a queue of people waiting to ladle drinks out of a bowl. Fewer and fewer leading roles demanded comic skills. The Rodgerses and the Hammersteins, the Lerners and the Loewes—brilliant masters of music and artists of great refinement—had created a vulgarity vacuum on Broadway. One that we were happy, indeed eager to fill, by celebrating the panderers, philanderers, fumblers, and bumblers enumerated in Steve's soon-to-be-legendary opening number, "Comedy Tonight."

Our goal was to construct a show based on Plautus, who, borrowing liberally from the Greeks, had expanded the devices of theatrical comedy, teaching amphitheater audiences up and down the original Caesar's Circuit to laugh for the first time at character and situation instead of those old staples they found so amusing, bloodshed and tragedy. Certainly, there was comedy in everyday life before Plautus set pen to parchment, but it was he who created countless comic conventions and made use of humorous wordplay within the discipline of well-made plays.

The master at his quickest, most perceptive, timeless best, in a stage exchange over two thousand years old:

> Two citizens meet and greet each other on the street.
> FIRST CITIZEN   How is your wife?
> SECOND CITIZEN   *(sighs)* Immortal!

With an astute appreciation of the demographics of his day, to say nothing of his audiences' secret desires, the poet-playwright wrote a string of comedies that mirrored their relationships and experiences, arming them with stand-up-like opening monologues, plus puns, malapropisms, tongue twisters, the double entendre, insults, disguise, slapstick, mistaken identity, mime, wit, and witlessness. Turning his back on the VIPs of Olympus, he depicted the affairs of earthbound mortals and their less than lofty and, more than likely, far messier lives. To populate this new genre, Plautus gave audiences on the Great Appian White Way a then fresh catalog of characters who have enriched every form of popular entertainment for over twenty centuries. From the works of the Bard to the boards of burlesque; from Jonson and Molière to Moe and Larry and Curly, Plautus's people abound—particularly his ageless creation, who was to serve as the leading character in *Forum,* the ever-resourceful, crafty slave, a nimble liar able to wiggle out of any tight spot with one tongue tied behind his back.

Other Plautine characters we employed were his self-infatuated braggart warrior, a man who should have been born twins in order to give himself all the self-love of which he was capable; the henpecked husband, ever ready to make amends for sins he has no real awareness of ever having committed; the moonstruck young man who longs for the heart of a virginal lass, the lass with a body and mind as unused as the day she was born; the dirty old man who chases after all manner of maidens, with only the dimmest memory of what's to be done should he actually catch one; doddering old geezers barely able to see or to hear, but with an infinite capacity to make fools of themselves. (We learned from Plautus that nothing succeeds more with theatergoers than giving them a preview of what senile idiots everyone else around them will one day become.)

When a slave in *Forum* slips into a diaphanous gown, plops a blond wig on his head and pretends that he is a nubile young thing in order to deceive an unwitting male, modern audiences get to witness a piece of theatrical shtick in well over its two-thousandth hit year. Whatever sophistication two millennia have provided us, people still relish comedy based on broad female impersonation. The efforts of *M*A*S*H*'s Private Klinger to get out of the service by cross-dressing, the success of *Tootsie, Mrs. Doubtfire* (or as I think of it: *Tootsie vs. Kramer*), and *The Birdcage* all attest to that fact.

The second year of our labor brought forth the first director to express an interest in joining the project. Jerome Robbins, who had worked with Sondheim on *West Side Story* and *Gypsy,* was intrigued by Steve's description of our comedy set in ancient Rome (and we were not building ours in a day, either). There followed a series of endless sessions with Robbins, sessions during which he mostly listened—but Jerome Robbins listening with the idea of collaborating with you on a musical play is a thousandfold more valuable than almost anyone else talking with you about it. Encouraged and energized by his eventual commitment to direct *Forum,* we hammered away at it, finishing a draft that we felt was good enough to attract a comedian, one with Broadway star power, to take on the lead role of Pseudolus.

Who better, as our first choice, than Phil Silvers, the man whose TV character, Sergeant Bilko, could trace his comic roots all the way back to the wily slaves of Plautus's plays? The obviousness of our selection made it feel no less inspired. We sent the book, the libretto, for the show over to Phil's apartment, telling him we would play the score for him later, after he said yes to what was so clearly a perfect marriage between our material and his comic gifts. A lifetime later, I can still remember where I was sitting when

Phil's call came, the one in which he substituted his no for our yes. He simply didn't have a clue as to the tone and style of what we had written. I don't think Phil Silvers got a lot of scripts that asked him to work in a toga and to play a character whose name he found unpronounceable. It was clear from his comments that he felt we were trying something arty, precious, some sort of minor-league, very confusing Shakespeare.

"What would I do if we got in trouble with this show out of town?" he asked. Meaning what could he do, what could he use from his bag of tricks in a show unlike any he had ever done—or seen—before? I assured him he could use more of himself, more of his professional experience in our piece than he could ever imagine; that, despite the show's classic setting, it was grounded in the very traditions of vaudeville and burlesque that had so shaped and sharpened his skills.

He just couldn't envision the final outcome, or what it would take to arrive at it. Ours was a difficult concept. Even when it's realized and playing on a stage, audiences, looking at their programs before the show begins and reading the cast list—Pseudolus, Hysterium, Senex, Lycus, Domina, and Miles Gloriosus, to name a few—and discovering the action takes place in Rome before the birth of Christ, wear the skeptical faces of those who are not sure they bought a ticket to a show they really want to see.

And so the search for a Pseudolus began. The search for a director, as well. Robbins, after three years of working with us, decided he was no longer interested in the project. No explanation, no apologies, just abandonment, sent in the form of a message conveyed to us through a third party. It was a shot between the eyes.

We began to meet with the leading Broadway directors of the period. Having been dropped by a name, I won't bother to do the same. Many were interested, none would commit. It's possible that Burt and Steve and I had done our work too well. So many leading directors are used to "saving" material by insisting on extensive, quite often unnecessary reworkings of a work, on staging it in a manner that they feel minimizes what they consider its flaws. After a year in the wilderness, we found our director—a man so perfect for us, his presence on the project shook my faith in atheism.

George Abbott, who would live to be 106, was in his adolescence, a mere 75 years old, when he agreed to become the director of *Forum*. *Legendary* takes on a whole new meaning when discussing Abbott's accomplishments in the American theater as playwright, actor, director, and producer. He was no stranger to Roman comedies either, having written and staged *The Boys from Syracuse*, a collaborative effort with Rodgers and Hart. He was a stranger, happily, to any displays of ego—his own or anyone else's. His virtues, to me, were endless. Lincolnesque in stature, he was Washington's match in honesty.

Credit for bringing him into the fold goes to the show's producer, Hal Prince. The show's third, more precisely, producer. Second was David Merrick, who stepped out of the picture when Jerome Robbins made his own participation contingent upon our disassociating ourselves from Merrick. Robbins (along with half the population of North America) had had a difficult time with David Merrick somewhere along the way. In retrospect, the ease with which Robbins dropped people should have alerted us to our own future fate. Merrick let us go, saying we owed him a hit one day, a debt that will never be repaid. (But I did let him tear my heart out on *Rough Cut*, so I guess we're some kind of even.)

Hal Prince, a good friend of the young (and older) Sondheim, had optioned the show along with his partner, Bobby Griffith. Some years earlier, in their first Broadway venture, Griffith and Prince produced *The Pajama Game* and asked my wife, Pat, to play the female lead. After reading the book of that show, so that I might offer her my opinion, I told her I didn't think the show would make it. Although she turned the part down, she did get to replace the leading lady in the second year of the show's run. (Parenthetically, *The Pajama Game* was directed by George Abbott, and its choreographer was Bob Fosse. Despite the hundreds I've met and worked with, they all soon seemed like the same three or four people.)

Bobby Griffith died almost immediately after agreeing to produce *Forum*—I like to think there was no connection between the events—and Hal Prince set up an audition with Abbott for the authors to familiarize him with the work.

Steve played the score at the piano in Abbott's office, and I read the book, acting out every part. It was an arduous, painstaking effort—two men performing a show meant to convey the comic antics of a stage full of people for the benefit of one man listening attentively, never once cracking a smile. It was like performing for the Lincoln Memorial—and the old statue just wasn't amused. At the end, after almost two and a half hours of nonstop exhaustive selling, Abbott looked at his watch, said, "God, I didn't think this was going to last so long. I've got to get to the dentist." And out he went, sidestepping the shattered hopes scattered all over the floor.

"He'll tell me later. I'll call you," Hal said. "I think he liked it."

Six o'clock.

Ring.

"Didn't I tell you? Abbott's crazy about it. He wants to get started right away."

Abbott's craziness, his welcome wish, was our command—and for me, as it turned out, a personal treat. Rarely addressed as "George," he was universally known in the theater world as "Mr. Abbott." Meaning no disrespect, I asked, early in our collaboration, if I might call him "George."

"Of course," he said.

When I asked why everyone called him "Mr. Abbott," his reply was "Damned if I know."

The man's no-nonsense approach was invaluable in guiding a show whose chief aim was to infect audiences with nonsense itself.

It was time to turn our attention back to finding our lead. It had been a long time since Milton Berle had performed in a Broadway show. Signing him would have been a coup. Once again, Steve and I performed the show in Abbott's office, this time for a sellout crowd of two: Berle and his wife, Ruth. Ordinarily a terrific audience for quality material and one who appreciated a good laugh, Ruth was not able to give us a single one that afternoon. Having just submitted herself to plastic surgery, she had twenty stitches in each of her eyelids. But Milton could laugh. And he did. Long and hard. And clearly, Ruth was having a good time, too, even though her eyelids were not.

And so we had our Pseudolus. While the various lawyers did what they do to make things both possible and impossible, as lawyers are wont to do, Abbott summoned the authors. After much consideration, he felt that the book was far too complicated, that the multiplicity of plot twists and character relationships would prove impossible for an audience to follow. He wanted us to drastically simplify the show. We disagreed. *He* had followed it (or had he?), Berle had followed it (but admittedly Silvers had not). We asked him to have faith. Abbott was all for having faith. He was all for having authority, too. When he agreed to direct the show, he made it clear that the production could have only one boss. Without that understanding, something as wild and daunting as a Broadway musical simply cannot be tamed. We agreed to make the changes he asked for, but with a condition: if the show turned out to be too thin in terms of plot during our out-of-town tour, we could restore whatever complications we felt by mutual consent the show could support.

This being acceptable to Abbott, we went about making our cuts and trims, pruning what we thought might prove to be excessive. We then sent the revised version of the show to Berle.

He was appalled.

"This isn't what I said yes to."

We explained why we had done what we had done.

He wasn't willing to gamble on Abbott's promise to restore the cuts if that proved to be the wisest choice.

"You've ruined your work. You've killed it. I can't be in the show."

And so, another Pseudolus sank in the east.

Our eventual star, suggested by Hal Prince, was Zero Mostel. (However much it might strain credulity, one of Plautus's plays was entitled *Mostellaria*.)

Opening night in New Haven, the first of our pre-Broadway performances, went like a dream: the kind of dream that is so slow and boring it would put you to sleep, were you not already in that condition. The show was dull. Far too dull. And far too something else, as well. Far too simple. Our fears, Berle's assumptions, were all proved correct. We began immediately to put material back into the book, thickening the plot, restoring the complications. Eventually, we put in more than we had taken out. Audiences relished them. Complications were part of the joy for them, as indeed they had been for us in writing them.

Some time later, when Berle came to see a performance of *Forum* in New York, he said, *"That's* the show I wanted to do. *That's* funny."

But before New York, we had to finish New Haven and then we had to finish Washington, D.C., whose drama critic, Richard Coe, almost finished us with his deadly review.

Although the show had been vastly improved, its one great flaw was that we did not prepare audiences quickly enough for the kind of raucous time they had in store for them. Steve's opening song, "Love Is in the Air," a very light, sweet, soft-shoe number, gave no clue as to the manic nature of what was to follow, and in the period of uncertainty and mental gear changing, we were using up a good deal of the audience's patience and interest.

This obstacle, too, was overcome in our last days in Washington, just one week before we were to go to New York, when it was decided to bring Jerome Robbins in to stage a new opening and to help with other aspects of the musical staging we felt could be improved. Robbins was a dicey choice. Not only had I sent him a mildly worded telegram when he quit the project earlier ("Your cowardly withdrawal is consistent with your well-earned reputation for immorality"), but years earlier he had "named names" before the House Un-American Activities Committee, in the custom of the day as a way of being able to rescue his own career. While he had not named Zero Mostel, who had spent years on the blacklist, Robbins did not spare an actress named Madeline Gilford. As others called before the committee had named her, too, her career was effectively over. Madeline's husband, Jack Gilford, was playing the second lead in *Forum*.

In an act of common sense as rare in the theater as it is in the world at large, both Jack and Zero declared that they would boycott no one on the basis of their politics.

From such unfunny stuff was "Comedy Tonight" born. It was

that song, which Steve Sondheim wrote in no more than a night or two in Washington, and which Jerry Robbins (I feel I can call him "Jerry," now that I've named him) staged with such invention, such speed, and such appropriateness, that provided us at last with the one ingredient that had been missing to make the show as durable as it proved to be.

Zero won an Antoinette Perry Award, a Tony, for his Pseudolus.

In the 1979 revival of the show, Phil Silvers won one for his.

In the 1997 revival, continuing the tradition, Nathan Lane received a Tony for *his* Pseudolus.*

Whoopi Goldberg, who assumed the role of Pseudolus after Lane spent a year in the part, was not eligible for the award, but what other performer has ever made the choice of a role a standing ovation in itself?

Gazing back from the vantage point of my rapidly approaching senility, I remember very little of the pain and almost none of the pressure involved in bringing *Forum* to life. What I recall most, what replays itself when my mind is in rewind, is standing in the back of the house, watching a performance of the show early in its original run. Sitting on the aisle, about six rows in front of the stage, was a man who was clearly having a good time, laughing to his (and my) heart's content. At one point, finding he couldn't laugh any more, completely surrendering to the joy he felt, the fellow threw his raincoat up into the air. High above his head. What a compliment, I thought. How exciting to be able to tickle someone to that degree.

That was over thirty years ago.

I still see that coat in the air.

*One more for the Small World Department: Lane's dressing room in the St. James Theatre on West Forty-fourth Street is the same one used by my wife when she appeared in that theater in *The Pajama Game*.

SCENE 5

SLY FOX

(Feigning illness, the better to bilk his gullible friends, master con man Foxwell J. Sly is asked by his servant, Simon Able, how in truth he really feels)

SLY No one's better! No one's more fit! I've got enough health to start another man! Catch me sick with a new day dawning; the bay glistening like diamonds, the hills as green as cash and the sun the color gold. Ah, bright, shimmering, glimmering gold. Warming gold—the centerpiece of the sky! Gold, hiding under and teasing under the ground. To find it, to fondle it, the best reason for living. To lie next to it in the earth, the only advantage of dying. Gold, gold, God with an "l," gold.

But here in this chest is where it belongs. Not in the sky above or the earth below but here, at the foot of my bed, is all that I have gained by wit—using my own and what others lack of it—providing the double joy of enriching me while depriving someone else. And as it all rests quietly, side by side, coin by coin, you watch the show that wealth can buy.

People fall out of the trees, crawl out of the woodwork, they squeeze through the woodwork to court you. Women appear in your linen, merchants lend all the money you ask, and men doff their hats even before you come round the corner.

They need only smell it—and you mustn't let them have more than a whiff of it, these leeches—and they fall into your hands, soused on greed. That is the first lesson you must learn about the underbelly of human nature, my boy. Never think too little of people. There is always a little less to be thought.

The project started with a phone call from Arthur Penn, in New York, to me, in Palm Springs. Though Arthur and I were old friends, we'd never worked together. "Have you ever read Ben Jonson's *Volpone?*" "Of course," I lied. "Have you ever seen it performed?" "Yes." My lengthening nose was pushing the receiver away from my mouth. "I think it would make a wonderful television show," he said. "A special." Arthur was trying to raise funds for the Actors Studio in New York, an organization very close to him. He had convinced CBS to go along with the idea of involving actors like Al Pacino and Gene Hackman, big names, who got a lot of money but would take only a fraction of their asking price and put the difference into the Actors Studio. Arthur envisioned an adaptation of *Volpone,* set in post–Gold Rush San Francisco, and wanted to call it *Sly Fox.* I love it when people call up with whole ideas like that that make me seem so smart to people who think I think up all the ideas that other people call me up with. The only catch is that CBS didn't want to fund the writing of the adaptation. You can imagine them not wanting to spend money for any version of *Volpone;* I mean Ben Jonson—to them he was a cowboy actor.

Arthur's next call was to Lew. (Lew was then merely *Sir* Lew Grade. His Lordship had not come in yet.) Lew quickly agreed to commission a script and I did a draft or two, or three, for *Sly Fox—* over a lifetime I've produced more drafts than the north wind—to present the piece as a TV production. When we agreed that we had the best of all the versions, Arthur announced that he was going to put a pickup cast together to do a table reading at the Actors Studio in New York City.

The reading took place on an extremely cold February night, but the wintry weather didn't daunt me one bit. I was in L.A. About eighty people sat around in chairs as Art Carney played the title role of Foxwell J. Sly and Lee Strasberg played the near senile Crouch. Arthur called me early the next day and said, "It's just as I suspected. The play is indecently funny." I have no trouble accepting compliments, but still, I'm always surprised when I find one lodged in my ego. "What would you think?" he added. I knew what was coming. "How would you feel about forgetting it as a television show? I think it's got a wider, longer life ahead of it as a stage play." And so I went about the business of redoing the work with the freedom one knows the stage has to offer: the freedom of language, the freedom of bolder ideas.

A few more drafts down the line, Arthur sent the play to George C. Scott, hoping he would consent to star in it. As a backup, Arthur also sent it to Walter Matthau. Both actors said yes. But Matthau didn't want to go to New York; besides having just had heart surgery, he said he was no longer interested in wearing galoshes again. When the cast sat down to read the play in the Minskoff Building in New York, it was George C. Scott; Trish Van Devere, his wife; Jack Gilford; Gretchen Wyler; Hector Elizondo; and Bob Dishy who did the honors. From the minute the reading started, my heart sank, ever lower and lower. My work was, in a word, terrible. It was, in two words, really terrible. I couldn't imagine why everybody, the cast, Lew Grade, and the show's other producers, the Shubert Organization, thought that it had even the slightest chance of succeeding. I said to myself, "If they think *this* is good, let me show them what *I* think is good." From that moment on, until our opening night in New York some eight weeks later, I never stopped making changes. Act I, page 21, is the only page that is pristine; the rest just kept being reworked, reworked until the paper bled.

Arthur was a terrific critic. We would stand at the back of the theater every night of the out-of-town tryouts. "Wouldn't he [Sly] think that that was the cause of that, and therefore do this?" The "this" being something altogether other than what I had written. He was invariably right, his major contribution helping to create a new ending, and one more suitable for our times. People could still be shocked three hundred years ago at some of the things Ben Jonson said in the original. After Watergate and the string of assassinations in this country, contemporary audiences have no difficulty expecting the worst in everybody.

To be perfectly honest, although I don't know how I can be imperfectly honest, I finished *Sly Fox* without ever reading the source material, Ben Jonson's *Volpone*. What I used as my guide was an adaptation by Stefan Zweig. In 1924 Zweig, an Austrian playwright, did a German version of the play, which was produced in

America—in an English translation—in 1928 by the Theatre Guild in New York. Zweig streamlined the original, made it a much more modern work, and that was what served as my template. Jonson's play is very arcane and, at times, very difficult to fathom. Had I read it, I would not have known how to approach the piece at all. Stefan Zweig's name never appears anywhere in connection with my adaptation, but that was not a choice I had a voice in. Zweig committed suicide in Brazil a number of years ago, and we had to deal with his nonagenarian attorney in London to obtain the rights. The Zweig estate received some money from the production of the play, but his lawyer's chief stipulation was that Zweig's name never appear anywhere. I think he thought we were going to do some sort of posthumous damage to his client's reputation. The man had never heard of George C. Scott, he had never heard of Arthur Penn. My guess was that he suspected it was a bunch of amateurs who had decided to put his client's work on.

Zweig's ending was different from Jonson's, and mine was different from Zweig's. I say "mine," but the idea for the ending came from Arthur. That is to say, the ending we did in New York was Arthur's. The idea for the ending we did in the Los Angeles production two years later came from George C. Scott. That is one of the most particularly satisfying aspects of the theater for a writer— its plasticity. The work is simply not recorded for all time at any particular time; it is always a living organism. What astounded me about Scott was that during the rehearsal and tryout periods, he never once asked to see the changes, never physically took the new material in hand. He would ask me to read him the revised pages I was turning out constantly. And as quickly as I read him the new stuff, he knew it. He memorized it as he heard it, whether it was three new words or a whole new scene. This, in the out-of-town period, was where actors were memorizing new material by day but still doing some of the old by night. None of that fazed Scott. I have never known an actor who could do what he did in that respect.

If you're lucky enough in this business, before they take you away in a rubber stretch limo, you might just be blessed to work with actors for whom it is unnecessary to ever have to write a stage direction; actors who look at your words and hear what you wrote, who feel your tempo, who sense your rhythms, who hear your drummer. George Scott is one of those actors. In *Sly Fox* and then, later, in *Movie Movie* (in which I was doubly blessed, since he played two parts), he was for me, flawless. When he spoke, other people heard dialogue—I heard music.

The more I worked on the script, more specifically the more I worked with Scott, it became not only a matter of Scott inhabiting the character I was writing. Scott was, in fact, beginning to inhabit me.

I was giving his character some of Scott's own characteristics: his energy, his power, his sense of danger, a form of cross-habitation going on. He made *Sly Fox* one of my best set of professional memories. It was one of those jobs you hate to finish. If there is show business after death, I hope I get that job again.

This book began, or rather my pursuit of Gelbart for a book began, when I wanted to publish the text of a theater piece he had written. Unable to persuade my then publisher to let me do *Mastergate,* a show I felt would play as well on the page as on the stage—indeed, the author wisely subtitled the piece, warning that it was a "play on words"—I dragged colleagues to the performance. While some felt it was wordy, I thought so, too, and also that the words were wonderful—wonderfully inane, wonderfully dangerous in their lack of precision, even in their meaninglessness, words that were everywhere around us, in the air, words from the witnesses, the witless, the Congress, and the press.

It was difficult to tell who was funnier or more menacing—the patriots, jocks doing end runs around the Constitution; the pols interrogating them; or the press, busily missing the point and misreporting, having missed the story when it was being played out, long before there was any need for hearings.

I knew then that there was a need for Gelbart, who could first of all *hear* in high fidelity and then set down his own playback in pages of, as Frank Rich wrote, "priceless" dialogue.   —Ed.

SCENE 6

MASTERGATE

A few years ago one of the larger wheels that makes Broadway go round asked if he could have the first look at a play I had just finished. The producer—anonymous here to save him any embarrassment (name available upon request)—was interested in optioning it for production. His reaction to the piece was dizzy-making. Funny, fantastic, the best thing I'd ever done; "brilliant" was small change.

"I just have one question about it," he said at the end of his lavish, gushing praise. "Can it be about something else?"

~~~~

The play upon which all that brilliance had been wasted, *Mastergate,* was an account of a fictitious congressional committee hearing trying to get to the bottom of some typical governmental malfeasance.

I understood Mr. Wheel's uneasiness. He had no interest in trying to raise money to put on a show that had anything at all to do with Washington. He is a member of a big club. There seems little or no passion these days for writing, producing, or seeing anything on the stage, in either comedic or dramatic form, that deals with ideas having to do with the nation's capital. It's been a long time since Broadway has offered a *Born Yesterday* or an *Of Thee I Sing.*

Collectors of irony, consider the following: of the three major sources of entertainment in America today—television, motion pictures, and the theater—only the latter grants the artist virtually total freedom from censorship or corporate interference in the expression of frankly political content. Only the theater is immune to the conglomerate's considerations; only the theater remains impervious to global, commercial demands. And the theater has chosen to play it safe, turning itself into a desert nearly devoid of writing that deals with those who populate the world of politics.

The reason holds no mystery. The behavior of our elected officials and their appointees—and disappointees—behavior ranging from the larcenous to the ludicrous to the libidinous, and all of it hurtling at us at such a relentless rate, makes the playwright's chief asset these days the ability to take shorthand. Such ongoing goings-on, such a multiplicity of duplicity, beggars the imagination; inspiration goes homeless. The never-ending confirmations and resignations of special prosecutors are anything but special any longer. Ever-new unethical issues face ethics committees, their members so busy they rarely get home to see their wives and thumb-sucking kids, parked before the TV, mesmerized by toe-sucking presidential advisers. Small wonder the public, getting a tellyful of their leaders' peccadilloes at home for free, are not likely to rush to the theater for the dubious pleasure of paying to spend a few more hours with them.

Running parallel with the scandals du jour is the proliferation of pundits, the McLaughlin mavens, the Novak know-it-alls, discussing and dissecting, chewing over events whose participants become all but interchangeable to a numbed citizenry awash in feelings of been there, done that, been done in by them.

〜〜〜

After a successful, limited run at the American Repertory Theatre, Cambridge—aided by a wise young director, Michael Engler, who helped me find the play I had almost completely camouflaged and sabotaged by writing perhaps a hundred thousand more words than it needed—*Mastergate* did eventually have a New York production. Subtitled *A Play on Words,* its aim was not to point out political corruption—tantamount to trying to get a patent on the wetness in water—but rather to dramatize, not through satire but through ridicule, the breakdown in communications in public life. Speeches have become speech. The more we're told, the less we know.

The members of the *Mastergate* committee and the witnesses who swear to get at the truth (with actors doubling throughout the

performance, so that, as is often the case, they are both the accused *and* the accusers) then go about abusing the language in any
way they can to dissemble and obfuscate, to deny and to distract.

To my amazement, some of the audience made no distinction between the tortured, often surreal questions and answers that surface during the "hearing" and truly proper, clear English.

Between Cambridge and New York, we tried to get the play
scheduled at the Kennedy Center in Washington. The offer was
turned down by the powers of the moment.

"Too political," they said.

Imagine Washington taking an interest in anything political.

A few passages from the play:

MERRY CHASE   This is Merry Chase, Total Network News, speaking to you from the Sherman Adams Room in the John Mitchell
Building in Washington, D.C., on this, the first morning of our
gavel-to-gavel-to-gavel coverage of the long-awaited start of the
opening session of the House Select Committee to Investigate
Alleged Covert Arms Assistance to Alleged Other Americans.
Given that these promise to be lengthy hearings, the Joint Committee can probably use all the excessiveness at its command
since—let's go over to the Chairman, who is about to—here is
Senator Bowman.

BOWMAN   Can we have it quiet, please? I'd like to get started on
time, if we can, inasmuch as we're late already. Thank you.
Thank you very much. Even though a few of the Members of the
Committee have not been able to get away from a roll-call vote
on the floor of the House, I'm advised that since enough of us
are not all there, we can go ahead with these hearings here. I
would like, if I may, to begin by presenting a preamble I've prepared for the purpose of broadly narrowing down the scope of
what these hearings hope to accomplish. (*reads*) "If we, as a nation, have learned anything from Water and Iran-Contragates, it
is that those who forget the past are certain to be subpoenaed.
Hence, the formation of this Permanent Select Joint Committee, which I share the coprivilege of occupying the chair of with
my distinguished colleague, one of my oldest and longest

friends, the Honorable Oral Proctor, of the House of Representatives; and which was charged some ten months ago by the
President of the United States with conducting an exhausting
inquiry into the most recent example of debilitating governmental self-abuse, which has become known throughout the media
as 'Mastergate.' This panel, which intends to give every appearance of being bipartisan, will be ever mindful of the President's
instructions to dig as far down as we can, no matter how high up
that might take us. Let me emphaticize one thing at the outset.
This is not a witch hunt. It is not a trial. We are not looking for
hides to skin, nor goats to scape. We're just trying to get all the
facts together in one room at the same time in the hope that
they'll somehow recognize one another. Our chief goal, of
course, is to answer the question: 'What did the President know,
and does he have any idea that he knew it?' "

*(The first witness called for questioning is Mr. Stewart Butler, for-
mer employee of the Justice Department.)*

HUNTER   Mr. Butler, as you know, I am Chief General Counsel for
the Combined Select Permanent Committees, and in that role
you and I have spent many hours in earlier, preliminary hearings,
in which you were interrogated by Staff Members of the Members of this Committee, and later sub-questioned by Sub-staff
Members of this Permanent Committee's Temporary Sub-
Committee.

BUTLER   I believe I know that, yes, sir.

HUNTER   None of my questions, therefore, should come as any
great surprise.

BUTLER   No, sir.

HUNTER   Nor any of your answers.

BUTLER   We can only hope.

HUNTER   Mr. Butler, you were, during the period in time in question, employed by the Department of Justice?

BUTLER   *(after an approving nod from his lawyer)* Yes, sir.

HUNTER   And what was your title, sir, during the series of past
events, the accumulative effect of which leads up to the present
time?

BUTLER   I was, in respect to that question, acting as Assistant to the Acting Assistant Deputy Attorney General.

HUNTER   In respect to that capacity, I would ask you to please direct your remarks to the meeting that took place in the Assistant Attorney General's office on February twenty-fifth of last year.

BUTLER   The year preceding this one chronologically?

HUNTER   The subject of the meeting was Mr. Victor Gamble, was it not?

BUTLER   In that it was, it was, yes, sir.

HUNTER   I would like you, if you would, to walk us through that talk, Mr. Butler; zooming in in particular on Victor Gamble himself, sir. He is an international financier, is he not? With financial interests on an international scale?

BUTLER   That is the spectrum of his range, yes, sir. Not surprising, since, while Mr. Gamble was originally born an American, he only spends depreciable amounts of time in this country, preferring to operate out of Liechtenstein through an offshore Libyan corporation, which is based in the Bahamas, while, for purposes of domicility, he resides in Switzerland in a consecutive series of unnumbered houses.

HUNTER   He is, for all intensive purposes, a tax fugitive?

BUTLER   That is my conviction, sir, based on several of his own.

HUNTER   Can you tell the Committees how much money Victor Gamble owes the United States government presently at this time? It's pretty well up in nosebleed country, is it not?

BUTLER   Yes, sir.

HUNTER   Two hundred million dollars, is it not, in back taxes?

BUTLER   Plus interest on those and other similar arrears he's behind on, plus fines, penalties, and court costs on his previous convictions for fraud, evasion, attempted bribery of federal officials, and several counts of perjury.

HUNTER   And Mr. Gamble has, more or less, put himself beyond the reach of the law of the land?

BUTLER   He has not been in the United States since the Chamber of Commerce voted him "Man of the Year."

(*The committee's next witness, Mr. Abel Lamb—"in government service for eight years and testifying for nine"—is allowed to read an opening statement before Mr. Hunter interrogates him about a second meeting on the 25th.)*

LAMB   I wish, first of all, to extend my extreme gratitude to the Committee for the privilege of being subpoenaed, so that I might clarify my version of the events under investigation. I secondly thank the Committee for granting me limited immunity, in that that gives me the leeway to tell everything I know without having to tell *everything* I know. It has been most difficult remaining silent during all I've said up to now, but in lieu of the fact that certain prior actions have been labeled as possibly criminal behavior in high places, I have felt it my duty to remain steadfastly evasive and selectively honest so as to protect the national interest and, above all, to safeguard presidential security. Looking back in hindsight, there are many things I would have done differently in the past, but I did whatever it's possible for me to say that I did because I felt I was doing my best acting in the interests of our Government. I also ask the Committee to remember that, ethics and morality aside, I felt I had a higher obligation to do as I was ordered to do. I'm aware that that's not an alibi, but I hope you'll agree that it *is* an excuse. Thank you, Mr. Chairman.

BOWMAN   Thank you, Mr. Lamb.

PICKER   *(Lamb's lawyer).* Mr. Lamb also has a closing statement he'd like to make, sir.

BOWMAN   Let's see if we can't just squeeze a few questions in between statements, shall we? Mr. Hunter?

HUNTER   Mr. Lamb, this second meeting on the twenty-fifth, can you tell us how many people were present?

LAMB   If you include me, there were two, sir.

HUNTER   There was one other person.

LAMB   Beside the one me, yes, sir.

HUNTER   You and someone else.

LAMB   I got the figure by crunching the two numbers, sir.

HUNTER   And in the person of whom would that other person have been?

LAMB   We're speaking of names?

HUNTER   With any luck at all.

LAMB   The other person was Mr. Slaughter, sir.

HUNTER   Mr. Wylie Slaughter? You must have been somewhat surprised to receive an invitation from the Director of the CIA, were you not?

LAMB   Somewhat and then some, sir.

HUNTER   Had you ever imagined that Mr. Slaughter was even aware of your existence?

LAMB   Only to the extent that Mr. Slaughter is aware of everyone in Washington's existence.

HUNTER   And yet, here he was inviting you, a considerably low-echelon player—

LAMB   The lowest, yes, sir.

HUNTER   Inviting you to meet with him.

LAMB   No, sir.

HUNTER   You just said that he did.

LAMB   He did, sir. But not to a meeting.

HUNTER   To a discussion, then.

LAMB   A nondiscussion, to be perfectly accurate, sir.

HUNTER   A nondiscussion.

LAMB   Yes, sir.

HUNTER   Can you explain the distinction?

LAMB   Sir, a nondiscussion is one in which the participants agree that though they are, in reality, having a discussion, for the purpose of future and probable deniability, they will maintain that no discussion, in point of fact, ever took place. Such an agreement must, of course, be nondiscussed beforehand.

HUNTER   I see. Mr. Lamb, can you tell us in what manner you received Mr. Slaughter's invitation to this discussion, non- or otherwise, that took place? Did it come through routine Government channels?

LAMB   Somewhat other, sir.

HUNTER   What sort of other would that have been?

LAMB   I got it from a waiter. In a restaurant, at the end of a meal.

HUNTER   Was it on official stationery of any kind?

LAMB   Not actually, no.

HUNTER   Actually on what then was it?

LAMB   It was in a fortune cookie.

HUNTER   Inside a fortune cookie, Mr. Lamb?

LAMB   Folded in half.

HUNTER   It was just assumed that you would open it?

LAMB   The waiter leaned down and said, "The fortune cookies are especially good tonight, sir."

HUNTER   That must have struck you as somewhat unusual. A message of that importance, inside a fortune cookie.

LAMB   And being in an Italian restaurant at the time.

(Senator Knight—played by the same actor who played Mr. Lamb—questions Secretary of State Bishop.)

KNIGHT   Mr. Secretary, some six months to half a year ago, you were questioned by the Subcommittee of this Committee. Do you recall your appearance at that particular time?

BISHOP   I believe I looked pretty much as I do now.

KNIGHT   Do you remember our discussing the Mastergate situation at that particular frame in time?

BISHOP   Senator, we discussed a great many subjects, as I may or may not recall. If you could possibly reload your question, sir?

KNIGHT   You testified then that you were categorically opposed to the entire Mastergate idea. And yet, subsequently and prior, and all the times in between, you did all that you could to make the plan succeed. Wouldn't you say that that was sending out a somewhat scrambled signal, sir?

BISHOP   Not at all. Since everyone knew I was against the plan, I assumed everyone would know that I was against whatever it was I was doing.

KNIGHT   Forgive me, sir, but how could you hope to convince anyone that you were opposed to something you were so busy supporting?

BISHOP   By resigning as often as I could—without actually damaging my effectiveness on the job.

KNIGHT   The job of implementing policies you had no particular faith in?

BISHOP   The Secretary of State doesn't spend his time just attending state funerals and going to poison gas conferences. It's not all fun and games, you know.

KNIGHT   It didn't trouble you, all the carrying on that was going on?

BISHOP   Senator, at the very onslaught to all this, I issued a strict appeal that I was to remain completely uninformed as much as possible about this whole operation, so that I could maintain a perfectly honest front about what was going on behind my back.

KNIGHT   And just how did you put your ignorance into action?

BISHOP   I was content to let Mr. Slaughter make whatever arrangements were being made with the person with whom he was making them with.

KNIGHT   And with whom would that person have been in the person of?

BISHOP   Vice President Burden. Before you jump to any conclusions, I hasten to add that the Vice President personally assured me that even though he approved of these arrangements, he can prove he knew nothing about them, since he was in the room at the time they were made.

KNIGHT   If the Vice President was present, how does that square with the fact that the Vice President has said repeatedly that he never knew of the plan?

BISHOP   I take that to mean that he knew of it until such time as it became impossible for him to know that he did.

KNIGHT   Would you say that the Vice President was there in the capacity of acting for the President?

BISHOP   The President needs no help with his acting, sir.

KNIGHT   Would it be your opinion that the President knew that the Vice President knew?

BISHOP   Knew what?

KNIGHT   Everything that he didn't know.

BISHOP   No one else in this government was in a position not to know as much as the President didn't.

BOWMAN   The Committee has no further use for you, Mr. Secretary.

BISHOP   I can't leave, Mr. Chairman, without staying to say that, yes, mistakes were made, I'll give you that. But it's hearings such as these which make it so hard for us to reach out to the business world to recruit those with the managerial experience necessary to make this Government work. You can't take these people out of their corporate positions and suddenly make them become answerable for their actions. It is hearings such as these which make it inevitable for private citizens to become public embarrassments. *(beat)* Yes, mistakes were made. Some dreadful ones. But they were honest mistakes. Honestly made. Honestly dreadful. I think this Committee ought to realize that if we're going to punish those who made them, we're only making it harder and harder to attract the people who will make the mistakes of the future. Thank you, Mr. Chairman.

(Major Manley Battle's appearance before the Committee stops the presses. The very model of a military hero, the major's many decorations spill over to adorn his lawyer's suit as well.)

BUNTING   Major Battle.

BATTLE   Senator.

BUNTING   Let us get right to the heart of the meat, shall we?

BATTLE   Ready on the firing line, sir.

BUNTING   I ask you to turn your attention—a position, I might add, at which you stand magnificently—to the production schedule at the Master Studios in Hollywood shortly after the time of the Government's engobblement of it in lieu of payment from Mr. Victor Gamble's failure to make good on charges of fraud, grand larceny, and a myriad of various other sundries. In particular, to a proposed picture show entitled, *Tet!, the Movie,* dealing with the Viet Cong offensive in which our B-1 bombers proved helpless against the North's godless ten-speed bikes because the Congress had not shown enough gumption to allow surgically selective strikes against the enemy's most residential districts.

BATTLE   I am familiar with the Tet offensive, Senator, having commanded several assaults on that occasion, including one against my own men.

BUNTING   Tell us, then, if you would, what you can, if you please, what you know on the subject of *Tet!*

BATTLE   *Tet!, the Movie,* or Tet the for real, sir?

BUNTING   *Tet!, the Movie,* Major.

BATTLE   Yes, sir. It was originally conceived as a high-budgeted action film, with a good deal of high-powered action, torture, and bloodshed, to be ready in time for a Christmas release.

BUNTING   And what exactly was the budget at the time of the movie's conceivement?

BATTLE   Eighty million dollars. Which is considered a lot of money in Hollywood, sir.

BUNTING   I'm sure it is.

BATTLE   I, as I have said I was, was aware of *Tet!, the Movie* not only from my own first hand-to-hand experience in Vietnam, but also from having read *Tet!,* the book, in manuscript form at the CIA, long before the Agency had decided who the author of it was going to be. The story dealt with a young American soldier who achieves his manhood by setting fire to a village school-house, filled with Viet Cong posing as five-year-olds. The original plan was to shoot the picture in the Philippines where, for a nominal monetary consideration, as much napalm and Agent Orange as necessary would be allowed to be dropped on the Philippine countryside and its habitants, such was the level of cooperation between Washington and the then-residents of the presidential palace in Manila, or Neiman-Marcos, as it was called in-house. However, at the direction of Mr. Slaughter, it was decided to move the location of the movie, to shoot it in the Republic of San Elvador. The choice of that country being dictated by its unmistakable proximityship to its immediate neighbor to the far left: the country of Ambigua.

BUNTING   I'm sure that this Committee, as well as the country for which we stand, would be most appreciative for you to share some of your invaluable daylight with us on that sad, proud, benighted land.

BATTLE   Yes, sir. The Republic of Ambigua—or La Republica de Ambigua—was yet another in a string of betrayed revolutions wherein a legitimate set of high ideals became cruelly twisted and cynically Sovietized. The United States has had a long period of the most intimate relations with the Ambiguan government, the last eighteen of Ambigua's presidents being West Point graduates. That is, until a military coup occurred and the reins of power changed hands when the former President of Ambigua, General Delinqua, and the country's Prime Minister, Mrs. Delinqua, were in New York City on an emergency shopping trip, at which point the Government was taken over by a Dr. Overtega, a former podiatrist, and his band of foot soldiers.

BUNTING   And, all the while, this country, the most powerful nation in the land, stood by, just sucking on its blanket?

BATTLE   Only semi-so, sir. There was a constant stab at efforts to appeal to Overtega to fold his country back into democracy. We tried everything from private persuasion to public assassination. What we finally scoped in on as our best hope was a group of idealistic Ambigualitos, still loyal to the Delinquan government, hiding in the hills in St.-Tropez, and willing to make any sacrifice to overthrow the overthrow, to once more make the People's Republic the Republic of the People.

BUNTING   This was the group known as the "Los Otros"?

BATTLE   Yes, sir. The "Los Otros." "The Others." A ragtag band of guerrilla fighters, badly in need of humanitarian aid . . . such as howitzers, rifles, grenades, mortars, and gunships.

BUNTING   And what sort of humanitarian aid?

BATTLE   Uh—medicine. Some blankets. Plus the necessary rocket launchers, tanks, and napalm to protect those blankets.

BUNTING   And yet, the very same Congress which had approved this aid, suddenly refused to vote more assistance to these very same Los Otros, correct me, Major, unless I'm wrong.

BATTLE   As correct as Congress was disgraceful, sir!

BUNTING   Disgraceful is a very strong word, Major!

BATTLE   I believe this particular shoe happens to fit like a glove, sir!

BUNTING   I know that you've been burned in this affair, Major Battle, but sitting here, under the shadow of this magnificent painting of the signing of the Declaration of Independence—a fine example of the kind of art that a whole family can watch together—I consider it both a shame and my honor to apologize on behalf of those countless men, women, and especially children who've been left without a prayer in our school system, who need heroes like you to grow up to. Hang in there, sir. There are millions of us in your platoon! Proud and honored to serve America's only four-star major!

SELLERS Thank you, Senator Bunting, for your most objective presentation of your own point of view.

BOWMAN The Chair recognizes Senator Sellers.

SELLERS Thank you, Mr. Chairman. While we're still in a tributary vein, I would like to add my chorus of approval for the major's many years of oft-repeated dedication to the defense of this country, which I, as a fellow serviceman, have also devoted countless weekends to.

BATTLE Every little bit helps, sir.

SELLERS America is a land worth fighting for, is it not, Major?

BATTLE I've got a head full of shrapnel to prove it, sir.

SELLERS This is the only nation anywhere in the world where members of the armed forces are free to publicly vocalize their criticism of the actions of the legislature, is it not?

BATTLE Does the Pope ride an encyclical?

SELLERS With that in mind, can you, if you can, implify your amplification that the Congress's decision to cut off funding to the Los Otroses was—"disgraceful"? I believe that was your epitaph, was it not?

BATTLE I consider the word a direct hit. Without further monetary-stroke-military aid, scores of Ambiguan freedom fighters who had gone way out on their life and limbs for us were literally cut off at the knees without a paddle.

SELLERS Ah, but not quite, as it turned out, inasmuch as Mr. Slaughter managed to "save" the day, did he not, wouldn't you say—in fact, have you already, repeatedly not, revealing the substance of what was a covert operation on countless talk shows?

BATTLE Publicity is a small price to pay for secrecy, sir. As for Mr. Slaughter: having assessed San Elvador's extreme adjacentness alongside Ambigua, he saw its immediate possibility as a base for providing shipments to the Los Otros.

SELLERS   Thereby permitting the United States to continue supplying the resistance with arms and humanitarian aid?

BATTLE   As the pipeline had considerably narrowed, we were only able to supply aid that was increasingly inhumanitarian.

SELLERS   And so you and the Director of the CIA simply took it upon yourselves to do an end run around the legislative branch of the United States government.

BATTLE   That's not exactly the way I would put it, sir.

SELLERS   And how exactly would you put it, Major?

BATTLE   I would say that that's when "Operation Masterplan" kicked in.

SELLERS   You prefer euphemisms, do you?

BATTLE   I prefer calling a spade by its code word, sir.

SELLERS   In whatever words you like, Major, suppose you clue us in on just how "Operation Masterplan" worked.

BATTLE   That would take us back to *Tet!*, sir.

SELLERS   The movie, the book, the war, or the album?

BATTLE   *Tet!, the Movie,* sir. The shooting script called for a number of battle scenes between U.S. and Viet Cong forces. Master Studios had purchased a good deal of military hardware from several other defunct countries and movie companies, plus a great many additional weapons from certain Middle Eastern powers anxious to dump them because they came with so many instructions. These battle sequences were scheduled to be filmed in San Elvador's capital city of El Sanvador in the north, which borders directly on Ambigua in the south. The plan was to ship somewhat more additional military supplies to the movie than had been indicated in the script, and then to reroute them to the Los Otros encampments.

SELLERS   And just how much more than somewhat are we talking about?

BATTLE   Eight hundred million dollars' worth.

SELLERS   Eight hundred million dollars of unauthorized expenditure? This tenfold leap from the film's budget of eighty to eight hundred million dollars, Major, this didn't raise an eyebrow or two at the studio? If not among the Government employees there, then certainly amongst the professional picture people?

BATTLE   The amount was finessed by cross-collaterizing the difference over the cost of several other movies being made by the studio at the same time.

SELLERS   No one in Hollywood was any the wiser?

BATTLE   As a rule of thumb, no, sir.

SELLERS   Not even when later, added costs to the making of the motion picture would finally escalate to one billion dollars?

BATTLE   One billion three, with the catering.

SELLERS   Major, you took an oath as an officer to obey your Commander-in-Chief, did you not?

BATTLE   I was standing right there when I did it, sir.

SELLERS   Would you feel it your duty if your Commander-in-Chief, the President of the United States, ordered you to break the law?

BATTLE   I do not believe my President would order me to do such a thing, not knowingly.

SELLERS   I want you to think hard, Major.

BATTLE   Starting when, sir?

SELLERS   Did the President know of the Masterplan plan?

BATTLE   I was told he didn't know.

SELLERS   By whom?

BATTLE   By the same people who told *him* he didn't know.

SELLERS   And they would be who, would you know?

BATTLE   Key members of his staff. Those players who keep track of what he knows, what he knew, and what he later won't.

SELLERS   The President, then, to the best of your knowledge, had absolutely none of his own.

BATTLE   He may have had knowledge of it, without knowing he did.

SELLERS   The President can't be expected to know everything he knows, is that what you're saying?

BATTLE   It's hard enough for him to remember all that he doesn't.

SELLERS   Tell me, Major: if *you* were the President, do you think *you* might possibly have liked to have known?

BUNTING   With all due respect to my learned friend aside, Major Battle doesn't happen to be one of the men who *is* the President at this time.

SELLERS   I beg to differ, sir. I happen to think that Major Battle was the President more than we'll ever know. As well as Secretary of State, of Defense, and God-only-knows-whichever-Secretary-of-what-else-and-whatever! Many a world leader has played with toy soldiers. What we have in Major Battle, I believe, is a soldier who played with toy leaders. Don't you think this country deserves better, sir?

BATTLE   I happen to think that this country deserves the very best, sir, although, in all honesty, it can't always be counted on to know exactly what that is for itself. I take pride in being in the company of that tiny fistful of men who steal into the night which others sleep so soundly through, to leave my wife and children every possible chance I get, to ride point on missions contrived to keep democracy in the win column against this country's enemies—without *and* within—half an eye over both shoulders, hoping to save this nation before our so-called "Congress"—(*makes the quote sign with his fingers*)—passes a law against that, too! I'm history, Mr. Chairman. And I certainly can't make any of it sitting around here!

(*Vice President Burden makes a surprise appearance before the Committee and delivers a ringing defense of his administration's actions in the Mastergate affair.*)

BURDEN   Mr. Chairman. Other members of the rest of the Committee. There's something I think's been pretty well lost sight of in these hearings. There's something a whole lot here way besides blame that's the cause of what happened. And it's not called blame at all. It's called "seizin' the initiative," that's what it is. We didn't ask the British, "Please, sir, can we become a nation?" No, sir. If we hadn't of broken every law in the books back in 1770-whenever—if we hadn't done the Revolution thing and stayed English, each one of us would of had to have driven to Capitol Hill here today on the left side of the road—and our President would of been a Queen!

(*An even more unexpected witness to confront the Committee is Mr. Wylie Slaughter, the former head of the CIA—most unexpected since Mr. Slaughter passed away several months before the hearings began.*)

SLAUGHTER   I am Wylie Grimm Slaughter. September 24th, 1904–April 3rd, 1989. Having anticipated this hearing, I took great pains to produce what you see before you—a holographic image that creates the illusion that I am present in this room, whereas, you all know that I've passed away for reasons you've read in newspaper accounts, accounts prepared under my specific misdirection. I will, of course, answer no questions here today. This is no time for me to learn new tricks. Swearing me in, were it even remotely possible, would serve as little purpose now as it ever did in the past. I am not here to plead ignorance or to pass the buck. I am here to take responsibility for it all; to *bask* in your blame! At this moment in time—*your* time—Operation Masterplan will have self-destructed to the gleeful satisfaction of the media, those self-anointed guardians of the nation's interest. Let me state this one last time that I have never been opposed to the belief that the press has the right to print or broadcast everything it knows. I simply maintain that they don't have to know *everything*. If putting the freedom of this nation ahead of freedom for the press is a crime, then I am guilty! If putting the US ahead of the UP is treason, then wake the firing squad! For me, any means whatsoever is permissible to stave off the mortal danger that was posed when the first Red Dawn darkened the sky shining down on Karl Marx, as he dipped his pen in human suffering to write his infamous *Mein Kamphital*! Marxistism is not, however, our only foe. The biggest threat exists here at home from those who spout the Constitution and the Bill of Rights, as though they owned them, for the purpose of aiding and abetting the malcontents who are sworn to destroy those very instruments! Firemen fighting for the rights of arsonists! These misguided dupes, as cancerous as any Communist cell, have permanated every level of society! But, rest assured, this country will be saved in spite of its principles! Mastergate was not the last operation I set in motion. Not by a long shot. Keep reading your morning headlines. Watch your nightly news. It's only a matter of time before you're "scandalized" by the stars of the next, inevitable Whatever-Gate: another crowd of photo-opportunistic nobodies who grab the limelight before either being sent on to jail or up to higher office! (*beat*) This hearing is just one more episode in a series that will never end. (*taking a remote TV channel changer from his pocket*) You will convene no further, Mr. Chairman. Until next time, this Committee—(*aiming at the audience*) And you! You're *all* adjourned!! (*He clicks the remote and darkness envelops us all.*)

SCENE 7

CITY OF ANGELS

STONE (voiceover) (on seeing Alaura Kingsley enter his Private Eye office.) *She had the kind of face a man could build a dream on . . . a body that made the Venus de Milo look all thumbs . . . and only the floor kept her legs from going on forever.*

One day in 1987, writing something entirely forgettable, I was interrupted by a call from Cy Coleman. I was anything but annoyed. I agree completely with the late Dr. Robert Oppenheimer, who said, "We live for the interruptions." A composer of note, indeed of multiple notes, Cy had been talking with me for years about one day collaborating on a show, but the talk had remained just talk. In the back of my mind I knew that if I thought about it long enough, Cy would come up with something. And indeed he had. What about a musical based on the private eye movies of the forties?

It was a perfect idea. Those are exactly the kind of movies that have been replaying themselves in the video section of my mind for years. The sort of musical scores featured in those films—the wailing trumpet, the mournful sax—would allow Cy the opportunity to do the jazz score for a musical he'd long wanted to do. True jazz, not tamed for Broadway or watered down, jazz that still had the sound of gin in it. The world of the theater being largely populated by people seeking sanctuary from security, our choice of collaborator was David Zippel, a Harvard Law School graduate. Instead of going into practice, David is a lawyer turned lyricist, an open-and-shut case of someone choosing rhyme over reason.

My secret, unseen writing partner was the city of Los Angeles, which has served as the background for so much of my real life, the one in which I starred, the city that produced the backdrop for so many of my fantasies.

The dismal experience of *My L.A.* years before and its shelf life of only four performances had two positive effects. The bug to write for the theater had been implanted so deeply it could only be removed by major surgery (the sort of surgery usually performed by theater critics—and always without anesthesia). It demonstrated for me, since all of the material dealt with life in Los Angeles, how theatrically marvelous that marvelously theatrical city is, given the golden, orangey look of the Nathanael West Coast, the flamboyant flora, the exotic folk, each tinged by some degree of sunstroke, qualities that made the town that made the movies seem very much a movie itself. I'd always hoped that somewhere down the freeway, I'd get another chance to use the city as a setting for a show, a show that would mercifully live for at least five performances.

DISSOLVE to December 11, 1989. Exterior. Broadway. Night. Camera pans the expectant, black-tie crowd arriving for the opening of a new musical comedy. Surprise: The music is by Cy Coleman, the lyrics by David Zippel. The show is called *City of Angels,* and it is set in the L.A. of the forties, the L.A. of those relatively innocent prewar, presmog days. And not only have the authors dealt with the showlike aspects of the place, we've also written a movie that we've placed *in* the show.

For *City of Angels,* in telling the story of a novelist, Stine, offers the audience scenes not only from his life, but from his work as well—that work being an adaptation of one of his books into a screenplay built around Stine's franchise, his hero, an ex-cop named Stone. Those scenes add up to an onstage mini–private eye scenario—a shred of Chandler, a dash of Hammett, so to speak. The result is a show that works on twin levels of those hardy perennials, reality and fantasy. The final result, however, is a show on four levels. The third is achieved when Stine's imaginary character,

Stone, steps out of the pages of the screenplay to confront Stine in the real world, to insist that his creator maintain the same moral values he ascribes to his fictional alter ego.

The fourth level, or the screenplay–within–the–stage play, is created by having our cast members appear in more than one role. As an example, in the screenplay's story line, Stone's secretary, Oolie, is played by the same actress who plays Donna, secretary to Stine's employer, the Hollywood producer Buddy Fidler. Got that?

In other instances we first meet someone in the screenplay, such as the femme fatale, Alaura Kingsley, and later discover the real-life model for that character when the same actress appears as Buddy Fidler's wife. We reverse the process by introducing Fidler himself, oozing fake charm, in Stine's life before revealing him in Stine's screenplay, depicted as an equally odious movie mogul, Irwin S. Irving, a man with absolutely no charm at all—real or fake.

It is the show's way of demonstrating how artists reward and/or punish the people in their private lives by the manner in which the artists portray them in their public works.

It is only when Stine, the writer, deals with the fictionalized version of those who populate his life that he has any control over them. But these role models are in no way guided by a few pecks at the keys of Stine's Smith Corona. They have hearts and minds of their own. Stine may be able to think the same of the worldly Donna as he does of the far simpler (and fictional) Oolie, but Donna, he comes to learn to his great unhappiness, is very much Donna's Donna, not Stine's idea of her. She is not his creation, she's her own.

To avoid confusion, the show, when performed, was helpfully, innovatively color-coded: the real-life passages were staged in vivid colors, the fictional ones in various shades of black and white. And black and white only—sets, costumes, props—everything except the actors' skin tones.

This same sort of doubling took place during the preparation of the show's book and score. Cy and David and I began by spending an intensive ten-day period plotting the show, outlining the scenes, defining the characters, deciding which of them would double as whom, determining what songs would be needed, and why, when, where, and by whom they would be sung. Ours was an especially tricky and complicated concept to execute. We had no recipe to cook by, no blueprint for what had never been built before. The incubation period is always a special one for authors since they are experiencing what an audience eventually will: the surprise, the discovery of what the show is about as it slowly reveals itself.

What we loved most of all was the title we had settled on for the work: *Death Is for Suckers.* One, it had the tough, hard-boiled sound we wanted, it had the cadence. It said "private eye" immediately: there would be no guessing what the evening was going to be about. Two, it was funny. Or, at least, we thought so. People laughed when we mentioned the title. Mostly, they did. We were crazy about it. Enter our director, Michael Blakemore. Tall, bookish, completely untheatrical in looks or mannerisms, Michael could pass for an Oxford don, but he is as show-wise as anyone I've met in a lifetime of meeting directors.

The word *brilliant* is thrown around so casually in the entertainment business, I won't embarrass Michael by saying that he is brilliant, too. He is something a lot more valuable and a good deal rarer than that. In addition to his formidable gifts, Michael is extremely intelligent. You think every director is? I have worked with a film director who changed the number of a psalm in one of my scripts because he thought his psalm number was funnier than mine. Another I worked with retyped my script completely, telling me he needed to feel as though he had written it. And in TV, I have worked with all too many video savants. Blakemore is a member of that vanishing breed of director—one who is there to serve the play rather than the other way around. In his direction of Michael Frayn's *Noises Off,* he displayed his masterly way of handling fast-paced, complex, physical as well as verbal humor. These qualities made him perfect for *Death Is for Suckers.*

There was only one hitch, he informed us, only one condition he demanded before taking the job: unless we agreed to change the title, to throw *Death Is for Suckers* into the shredder, he was not interested. He was so put off by it, he said he almost didn't read the script when it was first submitted to him.

Michael felt that *Death Is for Suckers* would send audiences the message that they were going to see a parody of a private eye novel, whereas the one in our show is a perfectly executed, respectful version of a forties film noir. For the sake of getting a laugh at the title, he believed, we were damaging the integrity of the show. Thus *Death Is for Suckers* became *City of Angels*.

Our reward was getting a director who was to guide the project with a sense of objectivity and generosity that enhanced all that he touched. While he contributed to every aspect of the production, from the book to the look of the show, not a single suggestion Michael made, not one of his rare demands was based on ego. Whatever glory he sought was for the production, not for himself. He put his hand to everything without leaving a single fingerprint.

Another hero in this most collaborative of collaborations was Robin Wagner, whose sets, from the black-and-white mean streets of L.A. to the champagne beige bedrooms of Bel-Air, were totally in sync with the dramatic and musical requirements of the show.

On a personal note, it was a treat for me to be able to write a forties movie from the vantage point of the eighties. Being able to dramatize the minefield a screenwriter has to run in Hollywood was, for me, one from the heart, one that's been dented by more than a few real life Buddy Fidlers.

Herewith, a few Fidlerisms:

• To Stine, the writer: "Sweetheart, I'm your biggest fan. I've read a synopsis of every book you've ever written."
• "Nothing was ever hurt by being improved."
• "Nothing any good was ever hurt by cutting. Circumcisions to one side, of course. It's all in how one does it. I could take ten seconds out of *The Minute Waltz,* and nobody'd ever know."
• "I know your book started with a flashback. If I wanted to just shoot the book, I'd take pictures of the pages and save a fortune on actors. Anyway, flashbacks are kicked. They're tired. Flashbacks are a thing of the past."
• "You can tell a writer every time. Words, words, words, that's all they know." Instead of so many words, producer Fidler pleads with Stine, with irrefutable logic: "Give me pictures. Paint me scenes.

Movies are shadows. They're light. They're dark. They're faces ten feet high. You'll get it, you'll see. Sweetheart, nobody gets a hole-in-one their first time at bat. There's people who make a fortune writing movies, and they don't know how. I mean, no offense aside, everybody and his brother writes books, but a screenplay . . ."

Going with the flow, knowing Fidler won't recognize the sneer in his voice, Stine replies, "That's a ball game of a different color, right?"

There is no attempt at humor when Stine discovers that Fidler has rewritten an important passage in his screenplay and that even Donna, with whom he has been having an affair, has meddled with his words, saying she only did it hoping to protect the integrity of Stine's work.

After I take enough painkillers one day, I am going to have Stine's response tattooed on my brow to display at Creative Meetings.

"Help? You'd need a divining rod to find the word *grateful* in me. Jesus, where the hell is everybody when they first deliver the typing paper? Where are all the 'helpers' when those boxes full of silence come in? Blank. Both sides. No clue, no instructions enclosed on how to take just twenty-six letters and endlessly rearrange them so that you can turn them into a mirror of a part of our lives. Try it sometime. Try doing what I do before *I* do it."

Damn! I could type that speech over and over all day long.

LOCATION SHOT 3:
PALM SPRUNG

**Writing episodes in and about Los Angeles and then Beverly Hills brings
the author, inevitably, to the place Angelenos of a certain economic stra-
tum call, informally, "The Desert." On many weekends, you can see
streams of them escaping the rare outburst of poor weather or the more
common phenomena of poor pictures, as they head east for spots that the
unknowing, back in the real East or in the mysterious Middle West, think
of as one place called Palm Springs.**

**Fleeing L.A., a place that has long since been typed as a collection of
suburbs claiming to be a city, built on a desert hidden from sight, they
rush away from the mountains and the sea to an area that has become famous as a haven for golfing ex-presidents and other wealthy entertainers,
for various kinds of self-abusers and addicts, and for a tribe of underpriv-
ileged Native American millionaires.**

**The "Springs" is more than one place, as Gelbart points out, and it is
built unabashedly on genuine desert, which looks the part—except for an
abundance of various sods, AstroTurf, toupees, implants, and imported
palms. —Ed.**

The seven cities that make up what most people call the Springs—
Palm Springs, Palm Desert, Desert Hot Springs, Cathedral City,
Rancho Mirage, Indian Wells, and La Quinta—are a medley of mu-
nicipal mirages that boast 85 golf courses, more than 10,000 swimming pools, 17 plastic surgeons (at the last nose count), and 328

days of guaranteed sunshine a year, capable of causing a megatan no plastic surgeon worth his smelling salt would recommend for the average peeled, lifted, tucked, implanted, and/or liposucked Palm Springer.

The area certainly has its share of people of every conceivable sex whose faces have gone into the shop more times than their Mercedes, for while you're allowed to drive no more than 55 to get to the Springs, God forbid you should look like that number once you arrive. Hence, the place abounds in establishments offering the possibility of facial renewal, a Palm Springs euphemism for a youth fix.

Palm Springs, however, needs a good deal more than a mere town-tuck. Currently hit with a deadly dollar-drought, the town suffers from a trio of troubles: a depressed economy, a huge deficit due to tax losses, and a retail vacancy rate that is an absolute disaster. Not even Sonny Bono, Palm Springs' former (mercifully) mayor, with all of his vast executive experience, was able to put things right before he passed away and was elected to Congress.

For more than half a century, Palm Springs enjoyed a great run as a home away from home for the stars and a home away from the funeral home for the aged. In my memory bank, filed under "Haunting," is a recent visit to a Springs retirement center where I watched an assembly of seriously senior senior citizens singing "Jingle Bells"—in mid-July. Obviously, a few of them were not going to be around to join in on Christmas, including the ones who had been facially renewed. Like a number of these old dears, I'm afraid, the Springs seems finally to have sprung.

It all began, or rather stopped, back in the seventies, when the Palm Springs city fathers decided on a no-growth policy. Pleased with the look and scale of the town, they saw no need for any further expansion of the growth that had been going on for a millennium. Native Americans, in fact, had encamped around the region's natural hot springs for more than a thousand years before the birth of the town. Some primitive irrigation ditches discovered in the region are thought to be pre-Columbian—which in Californian means before Harry Cohn started his studio. Palm Springs' first residents, the Agua Caliente band of the Cahuilla Indians, were around long before the Spaniards hit California and, in their missionary zeal, started putting Native Americans' eyes out as an aid to helping them find religion. Happily, the Agua Calientes were spared this rather direct form of converting people to blind faith. They also survived the later arrival of the Mormons, whose men-folk were far too busy constantly posing for wedding pictures to have much time to do them any harm.

The turn of the century saw the building of the area's first hotels and resorts, whose proprietors began selling the desert climate as beneficial to people with tuberculosis. It worked. Patients came panting and wheezing from miles around, and Palm Springs was soon able to boast hotels with TB in every room.

The town really hit its stride during the Depression, when the Springs became, for the Hollywood set, the Happy Humping Grounds, the place to take it off and get it on. And it was at the fabled Racquet Club that most of the beautiful people did all those beautiful things to one another.

The club was founded in 1933 by two popular movie actors of the period, Ralph Bellamy and Charles Farrell, thought to be loco by the Palm Springs locals when they bought up fifty-three acres of desert nothingness for the then grand sum of $3,500 and set about turning the land into a sandbox for the stars. They began erecting two tennis courts, the first of an endless series of erections the club went on to inspire. From Arbuckle to Zanuck, the movie elite flocked to the spot. Miles away from Hedda and Louella, this was the perfect hideaway, the place to be seen when you didn't want to be seen. It was at the Racquet Club that leading ladies who were so inclined could find new leading men to do love scenes with, where certain leading men who were so inclined could also find new leading men to do love scenes with, and where the most popular diversion was watching starlets bobbing in the pool for producers.

But things being things, it was all bound to change. Today the movie crowd can be as naughty as they like anywhere they damn well please, their only fear the possibility that it might not make the papers.

Whatever star power is left in the Springs, its wattage has been turned down considerably. If tourists can't actually get a look at the man himself, they can at least travel along Frank Sinatra *Drive*, for it's rare these days to get a peek at a star on the streets of the Springs.

Today they *are* streets. You can take Bing Crosby Drive until it hits Gene Autry Trail, then take a right at Barbara Stanwyck until you get to Greer Garson, or hang a louie on Danny Kaye, Groucho Marx, or Jack Benny Road (a nice civic gesture, since years ago Benny had trouble getting a hotel room in the Springs because he had the poor taste to be Jewish).

Despite all its past glory, today Palm Springs attracts tourists who arrive with five dollars in their jeans and leave without Abraham Lincoln ever once having to squint at the sun. Most of the new and inviting shopping centers, the latest in condos and hotels and golf facilities, have been built miles away in Palm Desert, which is where all the money for expansion went when Palm Springs committed city-cide, going from nongrowth right into slow death.

But there's always hope. Thanks to federal grants, some 32,000 acres of prime Palm Springs–area real estate belong to the 263 Native Americans still living around there, the U.S. government having generously made them a gift of land that was all theirs to begin with. The city's planners have trouble attracting builders of malls and golf courses because the Indians lease their land instead of selling it, and almost all of it has been leased to others until the year 2025.

It's those very same Native Americans, though, who could turn out to be the town's saviors. In a neat twist on the western cliché, it won't be the cavalry but the Indians who are going to ride to the rescue of the town.

~~~~~

During the golden, palmier Springs days, the place held an extra attraction for those who went there seeking sex and a suntan—the lucky ones sometimes managing to get a little of both simultaneously. Just over the city limits, in Cathedral City, the third lure existed: a few illegal gambling casinos that flourished over the years but were eventually shut down. Gambling is, in fact, permissible, but only on one condition: that it take place on Indian land. God only knows why, and it hardly makes up for Wounded Knee, but that's the way it is.

This being the case, Caesars World is just one of the many philanthropic organizations to express an interest in building big, shiny casinos for their new best friends, the Palm Springs Indians.

It is expected that within the next five years, when all the wheels and slots have been installed, when all the high rollers and bottom feeders hit the town, Palm Springs will be back on the map again, with the same hustle and bustle, the same glamour and elegance that gambling has brought to Atlantic City.

I don't know about anyone else, but I can wait.

Life, like a dramatic piece, should not only be conducted with regularity, but methinks it should finish handsomely. Being now in the last act, I begin to cast about for something fit to end with.

—Benjamin Franklin

EPILOGUE

At the end, Larry delivers himself of a confession about his profession—this, too, could be love, despite everything—and then an editorial. His penultimate words are about the rivalries between reality and fantasy, the recycling and regurgitation of "news" into a grisly form of entertainment, and assumptions about the audience.

But don't miss his untraditional take on the traditional "A Note About the Type" as an encore.   —Ed.

SO SORRY, NO VICTIMS HERE—
EXCEPT MAYBE . . .

The last thing this country needs is another victim, but I'm afraid the poor sods will have to move over and make room for one more. Nothing sordid, not a scintilla of titillation. I carry no childhood scars; I was an amused rather than an abused child. My welts, all relatively new, have been acquired in my professional, not my personal life.

I love to write. I would write in the shower, if someone came out with a laptop on a rope. But what to write about in these times? What is there in my imagination (as novelists have said) that can compete with the theatrics of reality? Would I dare contrive a story wherein Kobe, Japan, is all but wiped out by an earthquake exactly one year to the day after the jolt that devastated Los Angeles? Could I dream up a scenario that depicted the ongoing destruction of the jungles of Brazil, one that showed people using the Amazon forest for kindling, just to make room for cattle to graze, torching and decimating one of the wonders of the planet so that we can have an uninterrupted supply of Big Macs? Could I conceive of a Japanese religious cult that accumulated enough toxic material to kill a hundred million people, after getting high on sips of their leader's bathwater? How is it possible to top that kind of drama, drama that so finely mixes tragedy and absurdity?

One of the first to comment on the phenomenon, the near impossibility of any muse to compete with the news, was the sportswriter Red Smith. In 1951, in one of the most memorable sports moments of all time, the then New York Giants and the also then Brooklyn Dodgers, after a tense, nail-biting season, were slugging it out in the final playoff game that would determine the winner of the National League pennant. At the bottom of the ninth inning, Bobby Thomson clinched the pennant for the Giants by hitting the improbable, miraculous home run that inspired Red Smith to write: "The art of fiction is dead. Reality has strangled invention. Only the utterly impossible, the inexpressibly fantastic, can ever be plausible again."

Fast-forward forty years. I'm commissioned to update a 1937 movie classic, *Nothing Sacred,* the story of a small-town girl who pretends to be terminally ill and becomes a national celebrity when a big-town newspaper publicizes her plight. During the period in which I worked on the script, real-life events packed with unimaginable drama began to unfold at a remarkable rate, events that demonstrated that the mixture of modern-day technology with the public's insatiable appetite for gossip and scandal made notoriety possible in the blink of a TV camera's eye.

It became increasingly clear that there was no way to update the script successfully. Lying about your health is chump change in today's hype-happy society. Commit a murder, say, or better, two or three or four. Rape someone, beat someone. Or be beaten. Be part of any ugliness that offends people so much they can't get enough of it, and you, too, can be a star. You, too, can have your fifteen minutes of infamy.

Consider just some of the incidents that unfolded during the period in which I was trying to write the script: the beating of Rodney King, repeated on television so often it began to take on the aspects of a test pattern. That drill in sadism triggered the Rodney King trial, and—Hollywood being Hollywood—the sequel to the Rodney King trial, with a catastrophic riot serving as an intermission.

The riot gave us the Reginald Denny beating, complete with the hapless truck driver's own oft-repeated tape and his own televised trial, which culminated with Mr. Denny hugging the mothers of the men who had shattered his skull into so many Scrabble pieces.

In that same period, we were also treated to the spectacle of Judge Clarence Thomas's Supreme Court confirmation hearings, with Professor Anita Hill giving Coca-Cola millions of dollars' worth of free publicity by going public about matters pubic.

Then there was the Jimmy Swaggart scandal, in which we learned of the steamy evangelist's passionate belief in the second or even multiple comings. That was followed by the Jim and Tammy Bakker follies, and, for a while there, all we could hear was the sound of commandments breaking and smashing all around us.

From the sporting world, Mike Tyson went to jail for hitting below the belt. In his hotel room.

Meanwhile, elsewhere in the civilized world, we learned of the unspeakable acts of Jeffrey Dahmer and John Wayne Gacy. The latter, who was convicted of murdering more than thirty young men, demonstrating the current trend in high tech and low tack, established an 800 number from his cell on death row for those who wanted to hear his taped plea of innocence, thereby becoming the nation's first serial killer for serial callers.

The country also had its necessary, periodic Kennedy fix, becoming mesmerized by the Willie Smith rape trial, during which we learned that Master Smith had a penchant for young women with blue dots for faces. Then there were the revelations about the results of Magic Johnson's ravenous sexual behavior, revelations that ended an awful lot of hoop dreams, including his own. Add to these the charges against Michael Jackson, and those against the

Menendez brothers, who, having put their parents in their boxes, ended up on our own.

We also had the John and Lorena Bobbitt story, which taught us the infinite possibilities of recycling. And the poignant saga of Joey Buttafuoco and Amy Fisher—probably the only couple in the history of heat to make love *under* a car.

We had the demonic David Koresh and the Branch Davidian holdout and, finally, flameout.

We had the then just-beginning, but probably never-ending, Whitewater affair.

We were witnesses to Tonya Harding's effort to break Nancy Kerrigan's spirit, starting with her kneecaps.

And, of course, there was the start of the O. J. Simpson trial(s), which, for a while, we all seemed to have been sentenced to watch for life.

All this, in addition to the nonstop lineup of misfits, weirdos, and psychopaths spilling their guts and their secrets, daily and nightly, on the old Oprah, or the new Geraldo, or Montel, or Ricki, or Maury, or Jerry, or Jenny, or Leeza, or any of the other sleazeathons that tell us far more than any one of us ever wanted to know about the freaks next door: the flashers and the bashers, the batterers and the batterees, the adulterous adolescent bridegrooms, their teenage mates in maternity grunge, the drag queens and the porn kings, the pimps and the simps, the topless, the mindless, the cuckolds, the Kluxers, the neo-Nazis—the Niagara of nauseating nutsies we invite onto our living room screens, that we wouldn't let get past our front doors.

Let us not forget programs such as *A Current Affair* and *Hard Copy* and *Inside Edition*, or publications that range from the *National Enquirer* to far more traditional, establishment newspapers, steadily lowering their real or imagined standards by dishing out ever more dirt on ever more people, including those all too willing to dish it out about themselves. To say nothing of the television networks, which have, in their pursuit of ratings and revenue, dropped nearly all pretense of quality reporting and now bring us such timely events as ABC's devotion of a full hour to the Charles

Manson story, twenty-five years after his grotesque acts, acts committed when we still had a gram of shock left in us.

With all the promises of a communications superhighway, all we seem to get are more and more keyholes to peek in. Surely there ought to be a way the public could be weaned, given some relief from their own insatiable appetite for the trivial and the terrible. The short-term guilty pleasure we get from wallowing in prurience and sensationalism has the harmful, long-term effect of desensitizing us, making us immune to outrage, so heavily are the airwaves charged with outrageous acts. A good start might be for the media to cut down on the number of minutes or inches of space they devote to the seamier events of the day. Perhaps that kind of reportage could be confined to cable, to a single human-misery channel. We ourselves might somehow try to curb our appetite for human tragedy and foolishness. Maybe if someone discovered that bad news is fattening? Or that chaos causes cholesterol?

Our lives would not necessarily be all that much improved even if we could manage a new approach. This world stubbornly, doggedly refuses to be a better place. For proof, see Bosnia or Chechnya. See Somalia. See Palestine or Rwanda. Or just see Washington, D.C.—especially if you enjoy watching three-piece-suit mud wrestling. By watching and reading as much mind- and soul-numbing material as we're exposed to, we only validate the cynical attitude of the providers of that material.

Perhaps, all things being cyclical, this fixation with those among us who would not only kill for our attention but actually *do* kill for our attention will possibly diminish. And on that heavenly day, those of us who have to write because it's the only way we know we're still alive will be able to put our imaginations back into gear. Once again, we'll be able to engage the hearts of others and perhaps some of the brighter corners of human curiosity.

〰〰

Much of our TV fare treats us as though we were as small as our screens. So many films now *start* with the chase and *then* build to the excitement.

On Thanksgiving, my wife and I played hosts to our kids. Our kids and their kids. As darkness fell, and the briquettes started to cool, my granddaughter Nina, who is four, asked me to tell her a story. Now, over the years, with five children and five grandchildren, I can tell you I could have made Mother Goose a ton of money in residuals. A lifetime of rewriting always prompts me to try putting a different spin on the stories they love to hear over and over. So I started to tell her about a house in the woods that belonged to a Papa Bear, a Mama Bear, and a Baby Pig.

She did a four-year-old's take.

"You know that story, don't you?" I asked. "The one where they go off for a while and Snow White steals their house."

She took an even longer look at me, and then she said: "Grandpa, you're making me nervous."

〰

I live to make all producers, bankers, directors, actors, and my writing peers nervous. Words make me tick. In my case words are, in fact, a tic. The manipulation and management of them is an endless, involuntary, sometimes exhausting process. At times, a single word; sometimes two; other times, a whole group of them, traveling together as a thought; one way or another, they are forever appearing on the monitor of my mind.

The meaning of life is beyond me. The best I can do is deal with it one word at a time.

〰

Funny how, when the time comes and you know a work is finished—although for me everything, including life, is a work in progress—when we make our way out of the maddening mazes in which we seem endlessly to entrap ourselves, the day comes when we have no choice but to say good-bye to all of that terribly hard work that has become such a source of joy.

Odd that I should have that same feeling as I write this; once more reluctant to let go of the work, to give it up, to let it belong to the audience. But in my ongoing, internal theater, I hear the orchestra tuning up, I see the comics in the wings rehearsing their leers, the courtesans practicing their pouts.

Anyone for a comedy tonight?

—Larry Gelbart

A NOTE ABOUT THE TYPE

I don't want to brag, but when it comes to being a computer dummy, I don't have to take my dunce cap off to anyone. You know the type.

Loath as I am to admit this, for a long time I was a total idiot, a macromoron on the subject of computers. Had someone asked me years ago what IBM stood for, I would probably have replied that it was some sort of medical term used by proctologists. A baud rate, I suspected, was a price list in a brothel, the microchip an object used by tiny gamblers.

I came by my ignorance honestly. When starting to write professionally in 1944, I took the word *writing* literally. My tools were pencils and paper. I enjoyed the feeling, the almost mesmerizing ritual of watching my hand act as an extension of my head, delighted in the sensation of watching the soft, dark lead move across the bright yellow pad, as it took dictation from a voice I never heard. I worked this way until well into 1988, eschewing the typewriter (which is much harder to do than eschewing a pencil), when my son Gary, an early devotee of the computer, began trying to talk me into buying one.

Turning me on to computers, dragging me into the twentieth century, was the second great favor he did me. The first was to start earning his own living. The third, and greatest favor by far, was when he introduced me to Beth Slick.

At this point, I should warn you that this is about to become a love letter, for when Ms. Slick agreed to become my computer tutor/mavis (feminine for *maven*), my professional life changed completely.

To my wife's horror, my productivity increased tenfold. The quantity, if not necessarily the quality of the work, improved. The sooner I was able to see a word, the sooner I was able to play with it.

I was tempted to throw my hands away. My *head* had become an extension of my head.

~~~

Which leads me into the subject of who else there might be to thank for whatever luck I've had and for this book. I am—yes—reminded of a story.

One day, in New York, I caught a taxi just outside Sardi's.

Staring at me in his rearview mirror, the driver said: "You're a writer, right?"

I asked him how he guessed.

"The glasses," he said. "The glasses and the manila envelope. You get to know."

I told him I'd come to New York to work in TV.

"I wish ya a lot of luck," he said. "I'd like to see a success come out of this cab."

~~~~~

Fair enough. He saw the glasses and the envelope and he recognized the type.

I've had a fair share of praise and no wonder: I fish for compliments—and then I'm uncomfortable when I pull them into the boat. But I'm grateful for the sage advice of the director Robert Parrish, who said: "Strive to do good and blush to have it known." What I wish to have known are the names of certain persons who have done me good.

There have been, inevitably, a few less than happy relationships over the last half century, but as time works its awful wonders on my mind and body, I find myself knocking a lot more wood than I do other people. In the blink of a childhood, living out a scenario I would have once rejected as implausible, I went from being a teenager doing his homework while listening to the radio to a teenager asking his boyhood idols for a raise.

If over the years the comedy has darkened, if it's gone from one-liners for Hope to one-acters for hopelessness, it was perhaps due to the dread of forever remaining an unbearable being of lightness. Of feeling a growing need to sneak around behind my brain and see what was really going on back there. And while I was at it, checking under the spleen.

For all my years as a professional writer, I remain very much an amateur person.

Among those who matter most to me in helping turn me into a pro, I'm grateful to those I have written about in the preceding pages, and especially:

To my wife, Pat—for moving into my heart and my soul over forty years ago—and joyfully redecorating them nonstop ever since.

Grateful, too, to my mother and father, remembering that even when I was a child, they suspended all common sense by treating me as though I were a talented grown-up.

And my thanks to my kids and grandkids. I have, to my amazement, reached seventy, but all of them have the uncommon sense to treat me as a gifted child.

This book was set in Fairfield, the first typeface from the hand of distinguished American artist and engraver Rudolph Ruzicka (1883–1978). In its structure Fairfield displays the sober and sane qualities of the master craftsman whose talent has long been dedicated to clarity. It is this trait that accounts for the trim grace and vigor, the spirited design and sensitive balance, of this original typeface.

Rudolph Ruzicka was born in Bohemia and came to America in 1894. He set up his own shop, devoted to wood engraving and printing, in New York in 1913 after a varied career working as a wood engraver, in photoengraving and banknote printing plants, and as an art director and freelance artist. He designed and illustrated many books, and was the creator of a considerable list of individual prints—wood engravings, line engravings on copper, and aquatints.